Sister Verda,
Be Blessed and

MW00676258

Sister Sadie

Blessed, Healed and Delivered

Blessed, Healed and Delivered

A Daily Guide and Journal

Drs. George O. & Sadie McCalep

Orman Press
Lithonia Georgia

Blessed, Healed and Delivered

A Daily Guide and Journal

By

Drs. George O. & Sadie McCalep

Orman Press
Lithonia Georgia

Dedication

First we dedicate this book to the owner and originator, God Almighty, Jesus Christ our Lord and Savior, and to the Holy Spirit who moaned, groaned, and ministered to us in those cold, lonely, chilly days and nights, as well as the sunny warm days.

Secondly, we dedicate this book to our sons Michael Orman, George Orman III and Timothy Orman who have shared our Blessings, Healings and Deliverances. They are our wonderful sons who have grown up to be tall, strong, black and handsome men of God.

Thirdly, we dedicate this book to our adopted daughter and son Zipporah and Stanley King; daughter-in-laws, Susan Hope, Tracie Ann, and April and to our grandchildren, Christopher Orman, Neil, Bryan, Luke Orman and our princess Victoria Diana.

Fourth and final in this writing, we dedicate this book to our entire Greenforest Community Baptist Church family and other Christians and friends (in at least 42 states and a few foreign countries) who have prayed, fasted, showed patience, and demonstrated other methods of loving us through the ordeal of LIVING WITH CANCER.

Acknowledgements

We would like to acknowledge Mrs. Muriel Thompson for her transcribing, editing and original formatting; Mrs. Sarah Reid for her typing and reformatting the manuscript; Mrs. Debra Coleman for her assistance in so many ways; Mr. Tony Garvin for the artistic design of the jacket cover; Judge Desiree Sutton Peagler for her editing the final script; and Mr. Derrick Summerville for the final design and formatting.

PRAYER IS A KEY

He shall pray unto God, and he will be favourable unto him: and he shall see his face with
joy: for he will render unto man his righteousness. -Job 33:26

Jubilee Day is the day that the rebelling states freed the slaves in 1863. It was said that those who did not eat the traditional meal on Jubilee Day would have bad luck and go back into slavery.

Black-eyed peas were not the source of freedom for the slaves: God was. God heard the prayers and blood cry of every slave who called upon Him just as He hears our prayers now. How can it be that the God of all creation hears the prayers of each and every one of us individually? God is omnipresent: He can be in all places at the same time. God is omnipotent: He is all powerful. God is omniscient: He is all knowing. Most of all, God is sovereign. He can do whatever He wants to when He wants to and how He wants to do it. PRAYER is the "p" all Christians need to communicate with God daily.

MY SPIRITUAL JOURNEY

Do I believe God hears my prayers? If not, why not? If so, what are some of my testimonies assuring me that He does?

1) my deliverance from addictions
2) The gift of my son's life in
a home invasion
3) seeing me through the death of
my mother + father

1

PRAISE IS A WEAPON
Bless the LORD, O my soul: and all that is within me, bless his holy name!
-Psalm 103:1

E ver noticed cheerleaders at a football game? No matter how the team is doing, they keep praising the team. If the team wins the game, then the sacrificial praise of the cheerleaders becomes happy praise. That's exactly how Christians should behave during a storm. We should praise God before and during a storm. When the storm is over, we should praise God even more.

David declares in Psalm 65:1 that praise waits for God. Many see this verse and believe we are to wait for God to answer our prayers and then praise Him. David knew that if he continued to praise God before his prayers were answered, then God would turn his sacrificial praise into joyful praise. God answers prayers in His time. Praising God before and during a storm turns our common praise into Hallelujah praise after the storm. PRAISE is the "p" all Christians need while waiting on God to answer our prayers.

MY SPIRITUAL JOURNEY
Do I have an unanswered prayer? Am I praising God for His answer now or waiting for His answer before my praise?

Praising + Thanking Him now for all these blessing he has bestowed upon me & my family.

2

RATE YOUR PERFORMANCE

Praise awaits you, O God, in Zion; to you our vows will be fulfilled. -Psalm 65:1

How many of us have made promises that we failed to keep? How many times have we said that we would do something and didn't do it? God holds believers accountable for the things we say we are going to do. Our word should be our honor.

According to Psalm 65:1, David made a promise to God to wait in praise; therefore, he had to praise. He had to keep his commitment to God. A performer is a doer. A Christian performer is a doer of the word. We must keep our commitment not only to God but also to others. PERFORMANCE is the "p" all Christians need to keep our promises and diligently do what we say we will do.

MY SPIRITUAL JOURNEY

What promises have I made to God and man but failed to keep?

_____

_____

_____

_____

_____

_____

_____

_____

_____

_____

_____

PREVAIL AND PURGE

Iniquities prevail against me: as for our transgressions, thou shalt purge them away.
-Psalm 65:3

Psalm 65 is a song written by King David, based on his many experiences with God. He had good reason to write it. King David was a man who loved and sought after God, but like us, he, too, sometimes fell into sin's traps. Examples of his failures are when he used deceit so that he could have Uriah's wife, Bathsheba, and when he took a census of all the kingdom of Israel so that he could feel glorious. David, unlike many of us, prevailed back to his commitment and love for God, and each time, God purged sin from him. When sin prevails its ugly head against us, we must return to our commitment to God so that He will purge sin from us. PREVAIL is the "p" all Christians need for triumph. PURGE is the "p" all Christians need so that God will cleanse away all our impurities.

MY SPIRITUAL JOURNEY

Have there been times when I was tempted to sin and had to prevail back?

yes

_____

_____

_____

_____

PROCRASTINATION

The Lord hath brought forth our righteousness: Come, and let us declare in Zion the work of the Lord our God. -Jeremiah 51:10

An evangelist walked up to a man on the streets one day and shared by offering Christ to him. The man rejected his invitation of salvation and said, "maybe tomorrow." The man walked away from the evangelist, went into the street, and was hit and killed by a speeding car.

One of the worst things we can carry throughout life is the attitude of "I will do it tomorrow." Another day is not promised to us. Millions of blessings have gone down the drain because of procrastination. Procrastination is a sign of a lack of passion for something. Procrastinators believe in doing it later. They don't prepare for a test until the day of the test. Perhaps they are hoping an announcement will come stating that the test has been canceled. Unfortunately, the procrastinator sits down to take the test and prays that God will bring the answers to their remembrance when they never studied. Christians who love God don't procrastinate in doing His will.

MY SPIRITUAL JOURNEY

What is God asking me to do that I am putting off until tomorrow?

_____

_____

_____

LEAVE THE PAST BEHIND

But this one thing I do, forgetting those things which are behind, and reaching forth unto those things which are before. -Philippians 3:13b

---

The Israelites had a problem with hanging on to the past. Every time God presented a new challenge before them, they saw it as a problem and not as a challenge. They complained to Moses and wished he had left them in Egypt. Many people move to Atlanta but long for the city from which they came. One person goes back to Chicago for a doctor's visit while another person goes back to New York to get her hair done. We can't march into the future hanging on to our past.

Christians sometimes visit churches expecting them to be the same as their old church. They expect the choir to sing their former choir songs. They want the worship service to flow the same as their old church and ministries to function the same as old ministries. We must stop holding on to the past if we want to receive the blessings of the future.

MY SPIRITUAL JOURNEY

Is my past holding on to me or am I holding on to it?

I was holding on to my past

PAIN

Be merciful to me LORD, for I am faint; O LORD, heal me, for my bones are in agony.
-Psalm 65:1-3 (NIV)

Everyone deals with pain. Pain can be physical as well as mental. Physical pain can derive from a cut finger to a cancerous tumor. Mental pain can derive from the suffering of others or the death of love ones. Pain can paralyze us if we don't learn to deal with it.

King David knew pain, but he also knew how to handle it. When David's son became deathly ill, he fasted, prayed and mourned, hoping God would heal him. When his son died, he got up off the ground and went to worship God (2 Samuel 12:15-20). When we come to fully understand that God is in control, we can better accept pain by asking our heavenly Father to take control.

MY SPIRITUAL JOURNEY

Is there pain in my life that's crippling my walk with God?

yes

January 8
DO NOT FORSAKE THE ASSEMBLY

Not forsaking the assembling of ourselves together, as the manner of some is; but exhorting one another: and so much the more, as ye see the day approaching.
-Hebrews 10:25

Now and then reported in the news is an elderly person slowly traveling down the highway going in the opposite direction of traffic. But one doesn't have to be old to be traveling in the wrong direction. There are Christians traveling in the wrong direction but think they are going in the right direction. Christians traveling at a slow or fast speed, not looking at spiritual road signs along the way, will eventually be led to destruction.

These are Christians who think that because they are not attending worship on Sunday, they are on a right path of peace with God. Staying away from the Church helps them to avoid church conflict and elevates them to criticize the sins of those in the Church. They believe it somehow makes them better Christians if they remain at home. This way seems right to them but is not right because the word of God declares that we are not to forsake the assembling of ourselves together (Hebrews 10:25).

MY SPIRITUAL JOURNEY
Am I guilty of traveling down the slow path that leads to destruction?

_____

_____

_____

_____

8

Fret not thyself because of evildoers, neither be thou envious against the workers of iniquity
-Psalm 37:1

Christians traveling at full speed, only looking at some of the spiritual road signs along the way, will eventually lead to backsliding. Looking ahead and seeing the prosperity of the unbeliever and not seeing the plans God has to prosper us, will lead us to believe that the way of the unbeliever is better than God's way. It will eventually lead us to accept the "do it yourself attitude," which means "If you want something, you have to get it yourself."

Remember, Psalm 37:1 tells us not to fret because of evil doers, nor be envious of workers of iniquity. Why envy the possessions of others when God has made us His heirs? As heirs, He will supply all our needs. The grass is not as green on the other side as Satan would have you to believe. Advice: Slow down and evaluate both ways before crossing over (using the word of God as your traffic light).

MY SPIRITUAL JOURNEY

Am I bothered by the material possessions of others?

NO
_____

_____

_____

_____

_____

MEDITATE ON GOD'S WORD

But his delight is in the law of the LORD; and in his law doth he meditate day and night.
-Psalm 1:2

Many wives can attest to the fact that husbands are known to ignore road maps when traveling. The wife tries to get her husband to stop and look at the map purchased for the trip, but he insists on ignoring it. He keeps driving until they are lost. The same is true with many Christians whose lives are busy with all sorts of things. They have the road map, the Bible, but refuse to stop, read, and adhere to it.

Christians traveling at full speed and not reading the spiritual road map along the way will eventually get lost. Our spirit man is neglected when we clutter our lives with stuff and fail to fill it with prayer, praise, and the word of God. Psalms 1 tells us that the one who is blessed is the one who constantly meditates on God's word.

MY SPIRITUAL JOURNEY
What's on my full speed agenda?

To Praise God & Give Him all The Glory

THE RIGHTEOUS WAY

For the LORD knoweth the way of the righteous: but the way of the ungodly shall perish.
-Psalm 1:6

Have you ever realized that you were late for work or some event? You travel and go hurriedly down the road, but the person driving in front of you is driving the speed limit? How annoying! Why aren't they hurrying? Perhaps they have learned it is safer to travel at a moderate speed to get where they are going. This also makes it easier to read all the road signs, rather than hurrying and missing some of them.

Christians traveling at a moderate speed, reading their spiritual road map, and looking at all of the spiritual road signs along the way are victorious. When we look at spiritual road signs, we see signs that say "help", "reach out", "feed and clothe the homeless", "visit the sick and the bereaved", and "look out for the elderly people as well as those who are handicapped." When we follow these signs, Proverbs 21:21 says that, "he that followeth after righteousness and mercy findeth life, righteousness, and honor."

MY SPIRITUAL JOURNEY

What does it mean for me to travel at moderate speed with God?

Slow down & let God have his way.

GOD'S TRAVELING ORDERS

In all your ways acknowledge him, and he shall direct thy paths.-Proverbs 3:6

According to Joshua 6:3-5, God told Joshua to form a praise team and march around the walls of Jericho once a day for six days. On the seventh day, He instructed Joshua to march around the walls of Jericho seven times and then to shout "The Lord has given us the city." Out of his love for God, Joshua and the Israelites were obedient. To us, this type of battle makes no sense at all.

God is Spirit, not man. His ways are not the same as ours. There will be times when God will tell us to do things that may not be rational to us. That's why Proverbs 3:5 instructs us to trust God with all our heart and not our understanding. It is with our heart that we understand and trust God, not our intellect. Furthermore, Proverbs 3:6 urges us to put God first in all we do, and only then will He direct and crown our efforts with success. God's traveling orders may not agree with our understanding.

MY SPIRITUAL JOURNEY

Does God direct my travel?

Sometimes but I'm getting better because I have started

trying

LET GO OF THE HOLDING PATTERN

And they straightway left their nets, and followed him.
-Matthew 4:20

O nce on a returning flight home, the pilot announced that we were in a holding pattern. We couldn't land until we heard from the air traffic controller's tower that it was safe to do so. Like a flight holding pattern, there is also a Christian holding pattern. It is in those seasons when we almost reach the peak in our spiritual journey, but something else comes along and distracts us before we get there. God is calling us to the ministries our hearts have been yearning for, but we are letting life's circumstances keep us from getting there.

When God calls for us, we need to be obedient. If He is calling us, He will take care of whatever distractions are going on in our lives. Don't be moved by distractions, but be moved by God. God in His heavenly tower is saying "turn loose, let go, and come on up to the next level."

MY SPIRITUAL JOURNEY

Do I feel God calling me to the next level? Will I adhere to His call or remain in my comfort zone?

yes I will adhere to his call

WALK AFTER THE SPIRIT

That the righteousness of the law might be fulfilled in us, who walk not after the flesh, but after the Spirit -Romans 8:4

In Jonah 1:1-3, God gave Jonah traveling directions to a city called Nineveh, but he chose another route. Many of us are similar to Jonah in that we have rebellious egos controlled by the flesh. Flesh never wants to go in the direction of the Spirit. Jonah's flesh told him not to go to Nineveh and warn the people of their sins because they didn't deserve God's forgiveness.

Romans 8:4 tells us that those who walk after the flesh, honor the things of the flesh. Jonah was obedient to his flesh instead of God. Jonah did eventually obey God, but it was not until he removed his PRIDE problem. Pride is a sin, and the presence of sin in our lives pushes us in the wrong direction. However, there is a blessing for those traveling in obedience to God.

MY SPIRITUAL JOURNEY

Is there sin in my life that's keeping me from obeying God?

Yes

14

CONDITIONING WITH DISCIPLINE

Let us cleanse ourselves from all filthiness of the flesh and spirit, perfecting holiness in the fear of God. -2 Corinthians 7:1

Whenever a person's physique gets out of condition, he or she has to go through disciplined training in order to regain fitness. Just as the physical body tends to lose its shape, the Christian, too, can sometimes become unfit and need to undergo disciplined training for spiritual fitness.

There is a season when a believer must get rid of sin. Christians should no longer watch sin, and they certainly should no longer participate in sin. (Anyone in a relationship that they know is not pleasing to God, such as fornication, adultery, homosexuality, etc., should repent and get out of it.) We must lay aside the sin that besets us. We must learn to discipline ourselves if we desire to be closer to God. Conditioning with discipline requires consistently spending time with God, in His word and in prayer.

MY SPIRITUAL JOURNEY

What sin is in my life that I am willing to get rid of?

Smoking, Kussing or Profanity

A CHRISTIAN COUCH POTATO

...let us lay aside every weight, and the sin which doth so easily beset us, and let us run with patience the race that is set before us. -Hebrews 12:1

A couch potato can be defined as one who spends his or her time on a sofa, usually in front of a television set. A couch potato is "most likely not to succeed" because he or she has become lazy in well doing.

Refusal to exercise the mind spiritually will lead to becoming a Christian couch potato. What is a Christian couch potato? A Christian couch potato can be defined as one who doesn't exercise the mind by studying the Word of God nor exercise the heart in tithing and giving. A Christian couch potato does not evangelize or utilize spiritual gifts and is undisciplined in prayer. Furthermore, it could be a Christian who was once sold out in service for God but has now become discouraged by the cruel words of others. It could also be a Christian who has become burned out by trying to serve in more places than God has directed him. To prevent becoming a spiritual couch potato, we have to stay in constant fellowship with God.

MY SPIRITUAL JOURNEY

Can I identify with being a spiritual couch potato in some areas of my life?

Yes by not getting involved in ministries

CHRISTIAN JUNK FOOD JUNKIES

*Wherefore, lay apart all filthiness and superfluity of haughtiness,
and receive with meekness the engrafted word, which is able to save your souls. -James 1:21*

A junk food junkie is someone obsessed with eating unhealthy snacks like potato chips, buttered popcorn, cakes, cookies, and drinking sodas. Junk food junkies look forward to being on the couch.

There are Christians who can be considered as spiritual junk food junkies. These are those who refuse to exercise the mind spiritually. Christian junk food junkies feed on bad news rather than good news, and HBO rather than TBN. They feed on secular music rather than gospel music and on gossip rather than the gospel. They also feed on being conformed to this world rather than being transformed. Christian junk food junkies have no real effect in the building of God's kingdom, except to hinder others from becoming part of it. Psalm 119:1 says, "Blessed are the undefiled in the way, who walk in the law of the Lord."

MY SPIRITUAL JOURNEY

Am I a Christian junk food junkie? In what areas of my life am I a Christian junk food junkie?

_____

_____

_____

_____

REMOVE EXCESS BAGGAGE

Wherefore seeing we also are compassed about with so great a cloud of witnesses, let us lay aside every weight, and the sin which doth so easily beset us, and let us run with patience the race that is set before us. Hebrews 12:1

Imagine a race where one runner is 175 pounds and all muscles, but his opponent is 350 pounds and all fat. Who do you believe would win the race? The lean 175 pound man, of course. The same is true with the Christian race. Every weight that keeps us from running God's race with strength and endurance has to be laid aside. A Christian could be physically skinny but spiritually fat.

Whatever a Christian is doing that is not building him or her up in a Godly way is excess baggage. It needs to be removed. For instance, watching television on Wednesday nights instead of attending Wednesday night Bible study or listening to jazz music and not enough gospel are baggage. Whatever is keeping us from being sold out to God is hindering us from the plans He has for our lives.

MY SPIRITUAL JOURNEY
What is the weight I am carrying and how long will I allow it to weigh me down?

_____
_____
_____
_____
_____

CHRISTIANS USING DEAD WEIGHT

Thou shall not have in thine house diverse measures a great and a small.
-Deuteronomy 25:14

Sometimes we have to lift some weight in order to lose some weight. The word "weight" has two meanings. There is weight that makes us heavy and weight that makes us strong.

An athlete first begins with light weights, then moves on to heavy weights, and then moves to power weights. One sort of power weight in the Olympics is called dead weight. In the dead weight lift, the person grabs hold of the weights, snatches them up, and then pushes over the head. Likewise, Christians need to go to the weight room of prayer to lift off dead weight. Our dead weights are our distressed circumstances. The longer we hold on to dead weight, the heavier it becomes. God will lift it up for us if we will fast and pray. Then, we will be able to move forward by taking small or large steps.

MY SPIRITUAL JOURNEY

What dead weight am I carrying?

_____

_____

_____

_____

_____

CHRISTIANS BENCH PRESSING

I press toward the mark for the prize of the high calling of God in Christ Jesus.
-Philippians 3:14

When a body builder bench presses, he does it on his back. How much he can bench press depends on the strength of his muscles. When a Christian bench presses, he does it on his knees. How much we bench press depends on our fellowship and love for God. Christians who bench press often trust God more. The more we pray, the more we trust God. We trust God more because He proves Himself through answered prayer. God wants us to get rid of every weight that disables us from consistently bench pressing on our knees.

God wants to handle all our weight. When we learn to lay aside every weight to Him, we will run with patience to the finish line. When you find you can't let go and let God, go to Him in prayer and ask God to take it from you.

MY SPIRITUAL JOURNEY
What kind of weight am I attempting to handle alone?

_____

_____

_____

_____

_____

_____

_____

CHRISTIAN SQUATS

Evening, and morning, and at noon, will I pray and cry aloud: and He shall hear my voice.
Cast thy burden upon the LORD, and He shall sustain thee: He shall never suffer the
righteous to be moved. -Psalm 55:17, 22

When in the weight room with the "big boys" one has to learn to do squats. That's when the person bends his knees with heavy weights. There is power in bended knees. There are seasons when the believer needs to do squats. When life's problems come your way, get down on your knees and pray.

Sampson bent his knee and was able to push down pillars (Judges 16:26-30). The Hebrew boys went into the fiery furnace on bended knees (Daniel 3:23). Hezekiah bent his knees, and the Lord numbered his days (Isaiah 38:1-5). Jesus, in the garden of Gethsemane with the cup that was put before Him, went down on His knees (Matthew 26:36-39). There is power in bended knees because we are looking to the author and finisher of our faith for our strength.

MY SPIRITUAL JOURNEY

How often do I do squats?

_____

_____

_____

_____

_____

MORE THAN ENOUGH

If ye then, being evil, know how to give good gifts unto your children, how much more shall your Father which is in heaven give good things to them that ask Him. - Matthew 7:11

The Lord is my shepherd; I shall not want (Psalm 23:1). David knew if he relied on God for all his needs, God would also supply him with his wants. After all, Matthew 6:33 encourages us to first seek the kingdom of God and His righteousness. Then all these other things, our wants, will be added unto us.

When we seek the kingdom of God, we develop a spiritual relationship with God. God has more than enough anointing to supply our needs. He gives us life abundantly, joy unspeakable, peace that passes all understanding, and He gives us love unconditionally. God is Awesome! He always gives us more than we need.

MY SPIRITUAL JOURNEY

As I think on my daily life, can I honestly say that The Lord is my shepherd or am I leading myself?

_____

_____

_____

_____

_____

_____

_____

BECOME A SAUCER

Thou anointest my head with oil; my cup runneth over. -Psalm 23:5b

---

The question is often asked, "What is the anointing?" The anointing is the manifestation of The Holy Spirit operating in one's life. How does one get the anointing? One gets the anointing first by salvation, and of course through other miraculous ways that cannot be explained. One way to get the anointing is to be a saucer.

Psalm 23:5 talks about an overflowing cup. What is in this cup? It is the anointing. We get the anointing by hanging around a cup or someone who is already anointed. All one needs to be is a saucer. A saucer knows someone who has a cup that's overflowing. A saucer is a mentoree, and a cup is an anointed mentor.

If one wants to receive the anointing, then one should start associating with people whose cup is overflowing. God is in the cup-overflowing business. Be a saucer for someone whose cup is overflowing. You will start catching the drippings from their cup. Before long, God will make you a cup, and others will catch your drippings. Your disappointments will then become His-Appointments.

MY SPIRITUAL JOURNEY

Am I a cup or a saucer?

THE SHEEP AND THE SHEPHERD

The LORD is my shepherd; I shall not want. -Psalm 23:1

The sheep that knows its shepherd's voice will follow him and not strangers. The wolf knows that the sheep's weakest point is when it strays from the other sheep. The only way the sheep can know the shepherd's voice is that it spends time with the shepherd.

In John 10:27, Jesus said, "My sheep hear my voice, and I know them, and they follow me." Here, Jesus is referring to Himself as a loving shepherd who takes good care of His sheep, those who believe in Him and obey Him. When we are in consistent fellowship with Jesus, our shepherd, we are not confused about His voice, but we follow and obey Him. Being in fellowship with Him not only means praying to Him, but it also means studying His Word. We know God's voice through His Word. If we don't know Him, we can't fellowship with Him. When we don't fellowship with Him, we become fair game for the evil one.

MY SPIRITUAL JOURNEY

How would I describe my fellowship with God on a scale from 1-5, with 5 representing the best relationship?

Be ye not as the horse, or as the mule, which have no understanding: whose mouth must be held in with bit and bridle, lest they come near unto thee. -Psalm 32:9

Farmers tell me that when a mule has been trained to work only during the week, he won't plow on Sundays. They say that a mule can even be trained to stop working on Saturdays at 12:00 p.m. During the training process when the farmer pulls the reins a certain way and gives certain commands, the mule learns to respond to the commands.

To get our attention and to teach us, God sometimes has to hurt us. If a stubborn mule can be trained to respond to his master, the Christian ought to be able to be trained to fulfill the purposes of God. Mule education is driven by force, but Christian education is driven by love for God. The farmer says that when you can't get the mule's attention, you must hit him with force. Don't let God have to train you like a mule by forcing you to go the right way. I urge you not to wait to be hit by the force from God.

MY SPIRITUAL JOURNEY
What is keeping me from doing God's will?

_____

_____

_____

_____

_____

_____

KEEPING THE MAIN THING THE MAIN THING

…But one thing is needful: and Mary hath chosen that good part, which shall not be taken away from her. -Luke 10:41-42

Choose the main thing and do it. As Christians, we must choose what's important to us and who we really love.

Jesus teaches us in his visit to the village where Martha, Mary, and Lazarus lived to keep the main thing the main thing. When Martha noticed Mary wasn't helping to prepare and serve dinner, she became upset with Mary and said to Jesus, "Lord, doest thou not care that my sister hath left me to serve alone? Bid her therefore that she help me." Jesus told Martha that her service to Him was a good thing, but she hadn't kept the main thing, the main thing (Luke 10:38-42).

Many of us are serving and sometimes feel overwhelmed. We keep asking other people for help to fulfill our tasks instead of stopping to sit at the feet of Jesus. The main thing is Jesus, and until we put Him first, we will never keep the main thing, the main thing.

MY SPIRITUAL JOURNEY

Is sitting at Jesus' feet a priority in my life?

_____

_____

_____

_____

_____

SACRIFICING TIME

See then that ye walk circumspectly, not as fools, but as wise,
Redeeming the time, because the days are evil. -Ephesians 5:15-16

Keeping the main thing the main thing means sacrificing the time necessary to be trained. If we want to grow closer to God, there must be some sacrifice. Sacrificing may mean going to bed early so that we rise up early to pray. Sacrificing may mean giving up book club night for Bible study night. Sacrificing may mean having to miss football games or our other favorite television shows to worship God.

The main thing is what's important to God, and what He desires of us. Sacrifice is necessary for training to keep the main thing the main thing. God desires to make some of us anointed leaders, but we can't get out of bed. Some of us are too tired to keep the main thing the main thing. Some of us get to church after the message has been given or after the praise and worship have gone forth. We can't fulfill the purposes of God on Sundays if we stay up late on Saturdays.

MY SPIRITUAL JOURNEY

What am I willing to sacrifice in order to receive the training God wants me to have?

_____

_____

_____

_____

SUBMISSION IS NECESSARY

Submit yourselves therefore to God. Resist the devil, and he will flee from you.
-James 4:7

Not only is sacrifice needed in keeping the main thing the main thing, but submission is also necessary. Every believer has been commanded to submit to the authority over them (Ephesians 5:21-22, James 4:7, 1 Peter 5:5, and 1 Peter 2:13-14). Submission training is simply humbling oneself to receive instruction or to learn from someone else. According to Proverbs 15:32, the one who refuses to receive instruction is a fool.

Mary submitted herself to the teachings of Jesus Christ. To sit at someone's feet means to submit to them. Sitting at someone's feet is also an act of love, adoration, and honor. Mary adored and worshipped Jesus, and her love for Him was demonstrated.

MY SPIRITUAL JOURNEY

Do I have a problem with submission? At whose feet am I sitting?

_____

_____

_____

_____

_____

_____

_____

_____

WHEN YOUR BLOCKS FALL

Pride goeth before destruction and a haughty spirit before a fall. -Matthew 7:24-25

One of the most frustrating experiences as a child was watching my blocks fall. Blocks fall because we stack unstable blocks too tall and too soon. Though we rarely stack blocks as adults, there is still the frustration of falling blocks in our lives due to stacking things too tall and too soon. Some of us want to go from A to Z, skipping everything in the middle. It's like wanting to run before we crawl or walk.

I remember as a college football quarterback wanting to play first string. Though I was good enough, my coach would not let me. He didn't want me to stack my blocks too tall, too soon, and get the "bighead", so to speak. We usually stack our blocks too tall, too soon because of pride. Pride wants to lift itself up instead of waiting patiently for God to exalt us. "Pride goeth before destruction, and an haughty spirit before a fall" (Proverbs 16:18).

MY SPIRITUAL JOURNEY

What are the things in my life I am most proud of? Am I stacking them too tall and too soon?

_____

_____

_____

_____

_____

_____

Submit yourselves therefore to God. Resist the devil, and he will flee from you.
-James 4:7

Another most frustrating childhood remembrance for me was recess time with a boy named Henley. Instead of shooting marbles, Henley would spend all recess pretending to drive a car. It seemed as if whenever it was my time to shoot marbles, Henley would jumble my marble ring and shift his gears, making the marbles go everywhere. Just as Henley would jumble my marbles, there are times when something or someone comes along and knocks over our blocks.

Blocks fall because of some outside force knocking them down. The believer has an outside force knocking its blocks down today, and his name is Satan. Sex, gangs, drugs, violence, prejudice, alcohol, and sickness are all outside forces Satan uses to try and knock our blocks down. Most of all, he uses all these things to try and tear down THE WORD OF GOD. Yet, the Bible declares that if we resist the devil, he will flee from us (James 4:7).

MY SPIRITUAL JOURNEY

What am I willing to do to keep Satan from knocking down my blocks?

_____

_____

_____

_____

BUILD A SOLID FOUNDATION

And the rain descended, and the floods came, and the winds blew, and beat upon that house; and it fell not; for it was founded upon a rock. -Matthew 7:25

The major reason blocks are unstable is because they were not built on a solid foundation. Upon watching children build blocks, one thing I noticed is that they are so eager to get them built up, that they don't take the time to make sure their foundation is solid. The same is true with many of us in our Christian walk.

Blocks fall when we don't build them on a solid foundation. Some try to build upon their popularity. Others try to build on their good looks and their opinion. Others try to build on man's wisdom, education, and career achievements. All these things are good, but none is the source of our strength. It is only on Christ, the solid rock, we can stand. All other ground is sinking sand. "For no one can lay any foundation other than the one already laid, which is Jesus Christ" (1 Corinthians 3:11 NIV).

MY SPIRITUAL JOURNEY

Thinking on every area of my life, family, work, church, etc., what is the foundation of each of them?

_____

_____

_____

_____

_____

31

THE EAGLE LEADER

Behold, he shall come up and fly as the eagle... -Jeremiah 49:22

It has been stated that there are three types of leaders: chicken, turkey, and eagle. When a storm comes, a chicken leader will scratch, because he doesn't know what to do. When a storm comes, a turkey leader will hop because of confusion and not know which way to go. Similarly, a leader unprepared or not called by God will flee when the storm comes. When a storm comes, an eagle leader smells it coming. He doesn't run from the storm but prepares for it instead. In fact, he flies into the eye of it. During a storm, an eagle actually raises its wings and lets the storm push it higher and higher until it rises above it.

A called and prepared leader of God will do the same. Why? He knows that he has been called by God to lead. Not only does he know that he has been called, but he also knows how to call on his leader – the all mighty God. And because he calls upon Him daily, God tells him when the storm is coming and guides him through the storm to safety.

MY SPIRITUAL JOURNEY

Which type of leader am I; chicken, turkey, or eagle?

_____

_____

_____

_____

_____

…and your young men shall see visions, and your old men shall dream dreams:
-Acts 2:17

J oseph was a dreamer who dreamed many dreams of which his father and brothers rebuked (Genesis 37:5,9). One day Joseph's father sent him to check on his brothers who were tending the flock. When they spotted Joseph from a distance, they plotted to harm him (Genesis 37:13-34). Throughout the remainder of Genesis, though they succeeded in causing much harm to come upon him, they didn't destroy him.

Joseph's brothers failed to know that their fight wasn't against him but against God. The fight against a Godly dreamer is a fight against God, not the dreamer. Joseph was part of God's providential plan, and was called and anointed. Joseph eventually became the governor of Egypt (Genesis 41:39-36). In Genesis 42:6, when the brothers finally bowed before Joseph, they were actually humbling themselves to the plan of God. Joseph's brothers sought to kill Joseph's dreams, but Godly dreams cannot be killed.

MY SPIRITUAL JOURNEY

Am I a Godly dreamer? What is God speaking to me through my dreams?

_____

_____

_____

_____

FAILURE TO STAND UP FOR WHAT IS RIGHT

In that day I will perform against Eli all things which I have spoken concerning his house; when I begin, I will also make an end. -1 Samuel 3:12

According to 1 Samuel 2:12, the sons of Eli were sons of Belial. They knew not the Lord. When the people brought meat sacrifices as offerings to God, Hophni and Phinehas, the sons of Eli, had servants take from the people more than what they should have. They abhorred God's offering. Eli knew about their sin and confronted them about it; however, he failed to chastise them.

One day God sent a prophet to tell Eli that not only would his sons die but his entire family would also die. No one would be left from Eli's family to carry out the Levitical priesthood. One of our greatest failures is to not stand up for what is right. Eli failed to stand up for what was right. Why? According to verse 29, not only did Eli's sons sin, but Eli sinned as well. He benefited from the greed of his sons. In fact, Eli died a fat man. Eli and his sons failed to be honorable priests who glorified God, therefore causing His glory to leave them. Failure to stand up for what is right may cause God's glory to leave us.

MY SPIRITUAL JOURNEY

Have I ever failed to stand up for what is right?

_____

_____

_____

WHAT HAPPENS WHEN SYMBOLS ARE WORSHIPPED

Ye shall not go after other gods, of the gods of the people which are round about you; (For the LORD thy God is a jealous God among you) lest the anger of the LORD thy God be kindled against thee, and destroy thee from off the face of the earth. -Deuteronomy 6:14-15

First, the people of Israel worshipped the Ark of the Covenant. The Ark of the Covenant was symbolic of God's presence. They lost the battle because of their disobedience to God in how the Ark of the Covenant was to be carried (by the priest only). However, the priests had failed to live holy before God and were not worthy of carrying the Ark of the Covenant.

Symbols are useful but should never be worshipped. Many people today are worshipping the church building and not God. Others worship the Bible but not the God of the Bible. When we worship symbols, we are doomed for failure.

MY SPIRITUAL JOURNEY

How can I know if I'm a worshipper of God or the things of God?

RESULTS OF OBEDIENCE TO GOD

Behold, I set before you this day a blessing and a curse; A blessing, if ye obey the commandments of the LORD your God, which I command you this day: And a curse, if ye will not obey the commandments of the Lord your God. -Deuteronomy 11:26-28

God's glory is with us when we come into His presence with obedience. Make no mistake about it, there can be no glory or anointing without obedience to God. A preacher may be a great speaker but without obedience to God there can be no anointing in his preaching. The same is true with a musician or a soloist. Singing and music will not result in God's glory coming down unless there is obedience to God.

There is a move in the Christian community to usher in the presence of God through praise and worship, but there will be no anointing unless those who are worshipping Him are in obedience to Him. The preacher cannot preach on tithing unless he is an obedient tither himself. Likewise, he can't preach on the sin of pride with an anointing if he is endowed by a spirit of pride. The same is true with fornication or any other sin. We must be obedient to God's will, way, and purpose if we want to see His glory.

MY SPIRITUAL JOURNEY

Am I now the priest of the New Testament, housing The Holy Spirit?

_____

_____

_____

_____

POWER NOT FEAR

*For God hath not given us the spirit of fear; but of power, and of love,
and of a sound mind. -2 Timothy 1:7*

Luke 24:48 reads, "And ye are witnesses of these things." We are called and commanded by God to tell of salvation through Jesus Christ. If we are going to tell the story effectively, however, we must be hooked up to God's Holy Ghost power. The natural man doesn't share Christ very well, but when he gets hooked up to the power, he's much more effective.

We can't share what we are not sure we have. When sharing Christ, we must have a sense of His presence in our lives. He told us to go and that He would be with us. God has given us the assurance that the Holy Ghost precedes our witness. Still, many of us are scared that we don't have His power within us. Remember, God has not given us the spirit of fear but of power, and of love, and a sound mind. Therefore, we must use the power that dwells in us to ignite power in others who are in need of salvation. People need Jesus. How can they know about Him if we don't tell them about Him?

MY SPIRITUAL JOURNEY

Am I sharing Jesus Christ with unbelievers?

_____

_____

_____

_____

_____

SOW GOOD SEEDS

But this I say, He which soweth sparingly shall reap also sparingly; and he which soweth bountifully shall reap also bountifully. -2 Corinthians 9:16

In Matthew 13:3-9, Jesus tells an earthly story that has heavenly meaning. It's about a sower who goes out and plants seeds. In this story there was never a seed problem. The seed was always good. The problem was good seed falling on bad soil. The seed in this story represents The Word of God, and the soil represents The Church.

We are like wayside soil: we don't study God's Word enough to conquer Satan's false doctrine. We are like stony soil: as soon as trials and tribulations come, we stop trusting God and begin to complain about The Church. We are like thorny soil: materialism and riches become more important to us than a relationship with God.

MY SPIRITUAL JOURNEY

Am I sowing good seeds? Name them:

_____

_____

_____

_____

_____

_____

_____

HOOK UP TO THE POWER

But ye shall receive power, after that the Holy Ghost is come upon you: and ye shall be witnesses unto me both in Jerusalem, and in Judaea, and in Samaria, and unto the uttermost part of the earth. -Acts 1:8

The problem of being unprepared soil is a spiritual one. The problem is that too many Christians are not hooked up to the power. We can identify three ways to get hooked up to the power. First, we get hooked up by confessing our sins. 1 John 1:9 declares that if we confess our sins, God is faithful and just to cleanse us from all unrighteousness. God does not pile unconfessed sins on top of The Holy Ghost. As long as we have unconfessed sin, we will not have the anointing needed to bring in a harvest.

Secondly, we get hooked up to the power by praising God in faith. Hebrews 13:15 tells us to bring God sacrificial praise. Situations shouldn't matter. Connect praise to God's Word, and victory will come. Thirdly, we get hooked up to the power by praying in faith. When we pray in faith, we begin to act like what we desire has already happened.

MY SPIRITUAL JOURNEY

Am I hooked up to The Power?

_____

_____

_____

_____

_____

39

AS FOR ME AND MY HOUSE

And if it seem evil unto you to serve the LORD, choose you this day whom ye will serve; …
but as for me and my house, we will serve the LORD.
-Joshua 24:15a, 15c

If our focus is not on God, then it has to be on other things. What other things might our focus be on? Our focus might be on people, entertainment, jobs, organizations, material possessions, etc. Joshua called a meeting with the Israelites to find out where their focus was. Many of them were serving other gods in spite of what God had done for them. Joshua commanded them to destroy their idols and to serve God only (Joshua 24). When our focus is some place other than on God, we, like the Israelites, are guilty of worshipping other gods. When we worship other gods, we lose sight, direction, and focus.

Our families are deteriorating while we worship people, jobs, cars, homes, material possessions, organizations, entertainment, etc. Serving God is not just a Sunday event. Rather, it is a lifestyle. Unless we establish God as the chief aim in our lives, tomorrow will always move in the wrong direction. The only wise and reasonable thing to do is to serve the Lord who has brought us this far.

MY SPIRITUAL JOURNEY

Who or what do I worship?

_____

_____

_____

HOPE IN A MIRROR: FROM GLORY TO GLORY

…But we all, with open face beholding as in a glass the glory of the Lord, are changed into the same image from glory to glory, even as by the Spirit of the Lord.
-2 Corinthians 3:17-18

Hope for the believer is different from hope for the unbeliever. The unbeliever's hope is limited to things on this earth, whereas the believer's hope is eternal. The believer's hope begins with salvation through Jesus Christ. Our hope of glory is the foundation of our spiritual stability. We have a veil covering our hearts, keeping us from knowing God. Obeying the Ten Commandments does not lead us to being in the image of God.

After salvation, we change from glory to glory by studying God's Word, seeking His face, and daily praying to develop inner trust and determination to become mirrors that brightly reflect His glory. As the Spirit of God works within us, we become more and more like God. Moses followed God to the mountain, and His face shone like God. The closer we follow God, the more we will be like Him. Christ-likeness is a progressive experience. Salvation begins as an event but continues as a process.

MY SPIRITUAL JOURNEY

Can people see God in me? Why?

41

JOY INEXPRESSIBLE

Though you have not seen him; and even though you do not see him now,
you believe in him and are filled with an inexpressible and glorious joy. -1 Peter 1:8

In my observation, "Waiting to Exhale" was a story representing a panoramic view of the plight of black women in our society. The women in the movie shared their pain, struggles, and misfortune. They even cried, partied, and leaned on each other as they waited to exhale-waiting on that man who would take their breath away. It was a very realistic view of the black woman today, who has been uprooted, disfranchised, and deceived. Yet, she is smart, sexy, and often times painfully funny.

Many people today are waiting for a stronghearted, God-fearing spouse, but in their despair have become desperate and will probably marry the first man or woman who comes along. Many of us are doing some deep inhaling but some shallow exhaling. We are not letting go and letting God determine who our spouses will be. Not until we inhale a committed relationship with Jesus Christ can we find true joy.

MY SPIRITUAL JOURNEY

Who or what is going on in my life that I need to exhale?

_____

_____

_____

_____

_____

February 12
WAITING FOR THE ADOPTION

For not only they, but ourselves also which have the firstfruits of the Spirit, even we ourselves groan within ourselves, waiting for the adoption, to wit, the redemption of our body.
-Romans 8:23

The Samaritan woman at the well had been doing a whole lot of inhaling and very little exhaling. She was overly married. She had been married five times and had a man when Jesus met her at the well (John 4:7-29). Jesus had a predestined appointment to meet her at the well one morning. Like the woman at the well, many of us have made bad decisions in our lives and try to cover them up. But Jesus reveals who we really are. Just as He knew the past, present, and future of the woman at the well, Jesus knows our past, present, and future.

When our sins are uncovered, we become convicted, leading us to the opportunity to repent. Our sins must be uncovered before they can be covered by Jesus' blood. Like the woman at the well, we need to agree that we have sinned and then confess our sins. Confessing sin helps to get rid of sin. We confess it, exhale it, and God has the power to blot it out forever.

MY SPIRITUAL JOURNEY

Thinking on all the things that have bound me in the past, how does it feel to exhale?

_____

_____

_____

JESUS IS MR. RIGHT

Jesus saith unto her, I that speak unto thee am he. -John 4:26

Women today are still looking for Mr. Right. The woman at the well said to Jesus, I know that when the Messiah cometh, who is called the Christ, He will tell us all things. Jesus said to her, I am He. Jesus wanted the woman to know that she need not look any further. He is Mr. Right.

So many people today-single, married, saved and unsaved-need to know that Jesus is Mr. Right, Mr. Wonderful, The Lily of the Valley, and the Fairest of Ten Thousand. Trust in Him, and He will breathe on us. I believe the woman at the well was able to exhale for the first time in her life. The woman forgot why she had even come to the well and ran to tell the men to come and see a man, a real man (John 4:29). She told them to come see a man who designed us for more than sexual and carnal pleasure, a man who can take our breath away. This man provides living water. He is Jesus Christ, the only Mr. Right.

MY SPIRITUAL JOURNEY

Have I found Mr. Right yet? What does He do or what has He done to take my breath away?

_____

_____

_____

_____

_____

IT'S ALL ABOUT LOVE

Jesus said unto him, Thou shalt love the Lord thy God with all thy heart, and with all thy soul, and with all thy mind Matthew 22:37

The history of Valentine's Day is a mystery, but there are a few legends. One legend has it that during the time of the Roman Emperor Claudius II, men were prohibited from marrying in order to increase the strength of his army. However, a Roman priest named Valentine defied this order and secretly married the soldiers. Because of his defiant act, Valentine was thrown in jail and later killed. The legend goes on to claim that while he was in jail, he fell in love with the jailer's daughter and sent her notes saying, "Be my Valentine."

Though we are not certain of the authenticity of this love story, there is a love story that is authenticated in the Word of God. The story of God's love is the greatest love story ever told. God is love, and love is God, and nothing can separate us from His love, not even death. I'm glad that the scripture says that "God so loved the world" (John 3:16) and not "God so loved the church." Why? Because He didn't find me in the church.

MY SPIRITUAL JOURNEY
Where did God's love find me?

_____

_____

_____

_____

LOVE ACROSS BOUNDARIES

… Love your enemies, bless them that curse you, do good to them that hate you, and pray for them which despitefully use you, and persecute you; -Matthew 5:44

God's love is without prejudice; therefore, he loves perfectly. We hide our inability to love perfectly by making statements like, "I love them in the Lord, but I don't like them." God's love is about relationships with Him and with others. We are called to love all people in spite of their faults, and according to Matthew 5:44, in spite of how they treat us. God's love crosses all boundaries. If we are going to love like God, our love must be demonstrative and sacrificial.

We can't love God without demonstrating our love to others as God demonstrated His love for us when He sacrificed His Son. Perfect love went to the cross and died for us, who deserved no love at all. He was perfect and without sin while we were nothing but sin. God crossed the boundary of a sinless life for us to a death filled with our sins. Why can't we do the same for others? We have been commanded to love those who are bound and are poor. Instead, many of us look down on them. Christ told us that when we take care of the least of these, we are taking care of Him.

MY SPIRITUAL JOURNEY
Have I crossed any boundaries lately to show my love for others? Give details.

ANGELS HAVE CHARGE

For he shall give his angels charge over thee, to keep thee in all thy ways. -Psalm 91:11

The word "angel" means messenger. The term applies to every agent God uses to do His work of protecting, keeping, guiding, comforting, and correcting us.

A lady who lived alone was very sick, even unto death. She prayed for help. A doctor who lived in a distant county kept receiving persistent knocks on his door and phone calls to go and see about her. He kept replying, "I'm not making house calls tonight." But the knocks and calls kept coming. Finally the doctor gave in and went to see about the lady. He told her, "Looks like you called me just in time." But the lady said, "Doctor I don't have a phone in my house, nor a land line, and I sure don't have a cell phone."

The doctor was amazed. He told her that somebody had been knocking and calling him to come and see about her. The lady looked up and said, "All day and all night, angels have been watching over me." God still uses angels to accomplish His purposes through us and for us. God can send angels to whomever He wants to, but He has promised them to the righteous.

MY SPIRITUAL JOURNEY

Am I living in a way that angels will watch over me?

_____

_____

_____

THE ANGEL APPEARED

They shall bear thee up in their hands, lest thou dash thy foot against a stone.
-Psalms 91:12

It was the morning after a storm. A lady was traveling to work, and traffic lights were out everywhere. At the busiest intersection, she needed to make a left turn, but no one was being courteous. So instead of trying to go through the intersection on her own, like everyone else, she prayed for God to help her through the intersection. All of a sudden, a bus passed by her car. After it passed, a tall police officer stood signaling for her to come through. She had no idea, neither could she explain where the police officer came from; however, she knew that God had answered her prayer. In her heart, she believed that God had sent her an angel to guide her through that busy chaotic intersection.

When she arrived at work, little did she know that in the car behind her was not only one of her co-workers, but a Christian co-worker who had noticed the same thing. The co-worker was also amazed at the appearing of this very tall officer. Angels are watching over us.

MY SPIRITUAL JOURNEY

Have I had an angelic visitation in the past, but never stopped to consider it to be such until now? Think back.

BLESSED BY FEARING THE LORD

... Blessed is the man that feareth the LORD, that delighteth in his commandments. His seed shall be mighty upon the earth: the generation of the upright shall be blessed....
-Psalms 112:1-3

The fear of my father's blessed belt is what used to keep me from doing wrong. I didn't always understand the usage of discipline from my father's belt as a child, but now I know I was blessed by his discipline. My dad's rod blessed me to be who I am today. Many of the friends I grew up with who didn't fear the rod of correction are now dead, on drugs, or otherwise not living productive lives.

Fear means to reverence Him! Just as God's grace will cover our sins, the fear of the Lord will keep us on the right path and bless us. Fear of God's wrath produces a fearless and blessed life. God, in His word, constantly encourages us to let Him bless us. Those who fear the Lord are among the blessed ones. He not only blesses us, but He also blesses our seed. Yes, fearing God leads to our children having favor with God and man. When we fear God, we will never have to fear man or what tomorrow brings.

MY SPIRITUAL JOURNEY

As I look at my life, can I truly say that I reverence God in every aspect of my life?

Likewise also the cup after supper, saying, This cup is the new testament in my blood, which is shed for you. -Luke 22:20

A widowed farmer was called to war but was reluctant to go to war because he didn't want to leave his children. The town drunk said to him, "Well, I never did anything worthwhile. So, let me go for you." He did and died in action. The widower got his wagon, went to the battle line, brought the town drunk back to town, and gave him a hero's funeral. The question was asked, "Why would you do all this for this derelict?" The widower answered, "He may not have been important to you, but he died for me." We ought to feel the same way about Jesus Christ.

Jesus had no reason to die except for us. He died for the sin of the world. When something is given to us, we have a special relationship with it and it has a special place in our heart. Sometimes after a sermon, someone comes to me and says "That was for me". Jesus had all the prestige, fame, and honor he needed, leaving Him with no selfish motives to die. What Jesus did at Calvary's cross was "for me".

MY SPIRITUAL JOURNEY

Have I grasped the concept that the creator of all loves me?

_____

_____

_____

ACCEPT THE CALL

For the gifts and calling of God are without repentance. -Romans 11:29

God is always speaking and calling, but we are not always listening. Many think they are too unworthy to be called. Others think they are too young to be called. Samuel was a teenager when God called him into ministry (1 Samuel 3:4-10). There are no age restrictions for serving God. When I was called to preach, I thought I was too old, and some influential people thought so too. I had many vocations and was nearly forty years old when God called me the second time. He actually called me to preach at age twenty-one, but I didn't listen. I am so grateful that He didn't turn His wrath on me.

There are some Christians who think that only the preacher is called. There are those who think that when God calls them, it means they are to preach from a pulpit to Christians. God has called many to a ministry task that has nothing to do with the pulpit. There are different kinds of callings. All Christians are called to a relationship with Christ through salvation. All Christians are called to serve God through a predestined ministry task.

MY SPIRITUAL JOURNEY

Am I alert to the call of God? Do I even know His voice?

_____

_____

_____

_____

PARENTING GOD'S WAY

Children, obey your parents in all things: for this is well pleasing unto the Lord.
Fathers, provoke not your children to anger, lest they be discouraged. -Colossians 3:20-21

O ur families are too often guided by personal opinion and secular standards rather than by Biblical truths. Some of us are in bondage because of how we were parented, continuing in generational curses.

In the late 1990s, there was a record being played on the R & B radio stations entitled, "That's Just My Baby's Daddy." This is a picture of the disgusting and deplorable sign of the times in which we live. It depicts a man with the title of father only biologically, not lovingly.

Parents should be role models of the church in their homes. God has set parental standards for us throughout His Word and wants to lead us in His way relative to parent and child relationships. Christian fathers should relate to their families the way God relates and responds to His family – the Church. God, the Father, provides for His children. He takes care of us and supplies all our needs according to His riches and glory. Our parenting should resemble God's parenting.

MY SPIRITUAL JOURNEY

Are my parenting skills guided by personal opinion, secular standards, or biblical principles?

THE SALT OF THE EARTH

Ye are the salt of the earth: but if the salt have lost his savour, wherewith shall it be salted?
-Matthew 5:13

When a farmer slaughters a hog, he preserves it by placing it in salt. This process also gives and intensifies flavor. Salt is still used to preserve many food products today. Jesus said that if the salt loses its flavor, it is good for nothing.

Christians have a responsibility to remain unique and peculiar. When we try to blend in with the world, we become boring and stale. In other words, we are the flavor needed on the earth. Without flavor, the earth is in turmoil with wickedness. Being the flavor of the earth is being the light of it.

"The LORD preserveth all them that love him: but all the wicked will he destroy" (Psalm 145:20). God preserves all Christians who love Him. He has made us the salt so that when Satan tries to destroy us, he will be defeated. Again, all who are covered in salt are kept by God. To lose our covering is to lose our protection and our witness.

MY SPIRITUAL JOURNEY

Do I bring flavor to the earth?

_____

_____

_____

_____

TRUSTING AN ON TIME GOD

But, beloved, be not ignorant of this one thing, that one day is with the Lord as a thousand years, and a thousand years as one day. -2 Peter 3:8

On time means the right time. When the time was right, God demonstrated that He was an on time God by sending His son to save us. Jesus Christ freed us from bondage of the law so that we may have joy and all the other privileges that come with salvation.

Many of us don't trust God because we limit Him to time. We pray and believe, but we don't trust His timeline. We try to resolve the situation ourselves and often make things worse than they were. God is not limited to our timeline. Time is only necessary for us, not God.

God comes when we've done all we know to do. He comes after we surrender all to Him. He knows how much we can bear. "In the beginning was the Word, and the Word was with God, and the Word was God" (John 1:1). God was ahead of time. Jesus was old when He was born because He was as old as His daddy. God had already worked out our problems before we ever knew we had them. We are required to just trust and obey.

MY SPIRITUAL JOURNEY

In what areas of my life do I become frustrated while waiting on God?

That all the people of the earth might know the hand of the Lord, that it is mighty: that ye might fear the Lord your God forever. -Joshua 4:24

We don't always acknowledge the providential hand of God; therefore, we think our accomplishments are due to luck or good fortune. It is not an accident that we are in our current positions. Even though we can't see God's providential hand, He is always at work.

When I look back over my life and I take account of all the blessings God has credited to my blessing account, I don't have to see Him to know He is there. We are where we are so that the work of God can be manifested (John 9:1-3). The blind man was blind so that God's work could be manifested in him. We may have disabilities or wayward children. Still, God can work a mighty work through us and even them. We may not understand the providential hand of God now, but we will understand it by and by.

MY SPIRITUAL JOURNEY

Have I ever faced a situation where I couldn't see the providential hand of God? Can I now see how His hand was in it all along?

_____

_____

_____

_____

_____

February 25

WHAT IF YOUR TOMORROW IS CANCELLED?

For where your treasure is, there will your heart be also. -Matthew 6:21

Luke 12:16-21 tells the story of a rich farmer who stored up his riches. The rich man had great success and thought about what he should do since he had no room for all he had. What shall we do when we can't put more money in our 401K? What shall we do when we have achieved the highest degree of education? Will we do like the successful man and store up all that we can and then sit back and say, "you have enough stored away for years to come. Now sit back and take it easy!" "But God said unto him, Thou fool, this night thy soul shall be required of thee..." (Luke 12:20a) His soul was not required of him in three weeks, but "this night."

Why was the rich man's tomorrow cancelled? His tomorrow was cancelled because he was not rich toward God. He was selfish and believed his soul to be his own, when in actuality, his soul belonged to God. His riches should have been used towards the purposes of God and not his own selfish gain. 1 Corinthians 3:13 declares that every man or woman will be judged according to his or her work. The decision that the rich man made for his life was not pleasing to God.

MY SPIRITUAL JOURNEY
How do I know I'm rich toward God?

STARVE THE FLESH AND FEED THE SPIRIT

This I say then, Walk in the Spirit, and ye shall not fulfil the lust of the flesh.
-Galatians 5:16

According to Galatians 5:25, if we live in the Spirit, we should walk in the Spirit. Our behavior must become consistent with our belief. We have been set free from sin, but we continue to sin. One who walks after the flesh is a slave because he has not been set free from the bondage of his selfish desires. If we sow flesh, we will reap flesh. If we sow Spirit, we will reap Spirit. Paul asked and answered a question in Romans 6:1-2, Can a man be saved and live in sin? God forbid. Sin city doesn't have to be the believer's foreign address.

God urges us to be transformed by the renewing of our mind (Romans 12:2). We have to think differently if we want different results. If we are to walk in the Spirit, then we need to starve our flesh and feed our Spirit. The fruit of the Spirit (Galatians 5:22-23) is evident in one who consistently walks in the Spirit.

MY SPIRITUAL JOURNEY

Walking in the Spirit means acting like I am saved. Which fruit of the Spirit is not consistent in my life?

A LIFE OF LIBERTY

And that because of false brethren unawares brought in, who came in privily to spy out our liberty which we have in Christ Jesus, that they might bring us into bondage.
-Galatians 2:4

There are three methods of living a Christian life. Two won't work or are no good and will send us to hell. They are a life of legalism and a life of license.

A Life of Legalism is thinking that we can be saved by keeping the law (10 commandments) or doing perfectly everything Jesus told us to do. We can't do it, and even if we could, there is no salvation in the law.

A Life of License is thinking that because of grace we have a license to do whatever we want. It is cheapening grace. Grace does not give us a license to sin.

A Life of Liberty gives Christians power over sin but does not free us to sin. Furthermore, because we love and accept Jesus Christ as Lord and Savior, we will be guided by the Holy Spirit with our mind, selfless action, and behavior.

MY SPIRITUAL JOURNEY

Which of the above methods personally refers to me? How can I be certain?

_____

_____

CHRISTIAN CANNIBALISM

But if ye bite and devour one another, take heed that ye be not consumed one of another.
-Galatians 5:15

The Church should not be involved in a Life of Legalism or a Life of License. Paul warns of the results of a Church involved in legalism and license in Galatians 5:15. "But if ye bite and devour one another, take heed that ye be not consumed one of another." I call it Christian cannibalism when we judge and gossip about each other. It all stems from religious legalism. An example of legalism is judging and gossiping about others because they don't look like us. We assume, therefore, that they must not be one of us.

Legalism makes us try to change outwardly in others what God is gradually changing inwardly. An example of religious license is preachers and deacons thinking that because of grace, they have the license to have affairs with the women in the church. Another example is older women judging the attire of younger women because they don't dress or wear their makeup like them. From the pulpit and everywhere, we must not destroy one another. To the contrary, we must stand up and live a life of truth so we don't lead others astray from eternal life.

MY SPIRITUAL JOURNEY

Am I am holding on to a Life of Legalism?

REMAIN FAITHFUL (NO SHACKING UP)

... for I have espoused you to one husband, that I may present you as a chaste virgin to Christ. -2 Corinthians 11:2

Many years ago in this country, lots of couples began to move in together, or as some folks call it "shacking up." A shacking relationship is a non-committed relationship. As Christians, we know that a relationship with God is just the opposite.

God's love is complete, unwavering, and without question. Yet, we tend to "shack" our relationship with Him. We are committed to Him as long as things are going well for us. When things go awry, we are ready to walk away from our relationship with Him.

God is calling us to have a monogamous faithful love relationship with Him. Paul encouraged the Christians to be faithful to the true Jesus on whom they had built their salvation. In the church today, people preach of a Jesus of prosperity, thus lacking the full commitment to Jesus as Lord over every area of their lives. We would rather shack with Him and take His money than prepare ourselves to be a perfect bride for the perfect bridegroom. God wants all of us, not a portion on a given day.

MY SPIRITUAL JOURNEY

Is my marriage to God monogamous or a non-committed, shacking relationship?

DUMPING THE GREAT WHORE

…for he hath judged the great whore, which did corrupt the earth with her fornication, and hath avenged the blood of his servants at her hand.
-Revelation 19:2

In Hosea 1:2, God told Hosea to marry the prostitute, Gomer. He told Hosea that some of Gomer's children would be his and some would be from other men. God had Hosea to marry Gomer to illustrate the way the Israelites were being untrue to Him, committing open adultery against Him by worshipping other gods. Gomer's lifestyle represented the whoredom of Israel to other gods.

Many Christians are still in a relationship with the great whore of the earth. What is the great whore? The great whore is anything or anyone who is not part of God's kingdom and stands contrary to His purpose. We must dump the great whore if we expect to return with Jesus and His virgin bride. In Revelation 19:1-5, God reminds us that the day will come when the great whore will be destroyed.

MY SPIRITUAL JOURNEY

Who or what can be identified as the great whore in my life? What must I do to rid myself of the great whore in my life?

HANG WITH JESUS

I am the vine, ye are the branches: He that abideth in me, and I in him, the same bringeth forth much fruit: for without me ye can do nothing. -John 15:5

Fruit-bearing deals with hanging. When we look at a tree with fruit, the good fruit is always still on the tree. When fruit is on the ground, something has happened to it too quickly. Maybe the wind came and blew it down or someone came and shook the tree. Once it hits the ground, if it is not picked up quickly, it will perish and won't be good for eating.

Sometimes the storms of life come around in our lives and blow our fruit down, leaving it on the ground. Don't give up, because Jesus says that He is the vine and we are the branches; and, if we abide in Him, or if we hang with him, He will hang with us, and we will bear fruit. Fruit trees that bear fruit don't have limbs separated from the trunk. Limbs don't walk around doing their own thing, like some of us who have left the vine. We must hang with the vine, Jesus Christ, in order to be a productive branch.

MY SPIRITUAL JOURNEY

How do I know I'm "hanging" with Jesus?

_____

_____

_____

_____

_____

BARE GOOD FRUIT

For the fruit of the Spirit is in all goodness, righteousness and truth.
-Ephesians 5:9

In reading Galatians 5:22-23, we find the "fruit" of the Spirit and not "fruits" of the Spirit. It reads as a grammatical error, but in the Greek language "fruit" is singular because there is only one root fruit. The root fruit is love. Joy, peace, longsuffering, gentleness, goodness, faith, meekness and temperance are manifestations of love. Finally, a loss of the love fruit results in the loss of all.

Bearing good fruit is evidence of our operating in the fruit of the Spirit. As Christians, we believe we are to be fruit inspectors and often make remarks like, "You will know a tree by its fruit." Though this is true, too often, it gives us an excuse to examine other believers' faults rather than examining our own faults.

MY SPIRITUAL JOURNEY

After examining Galatians 5:22-23, are all the fruit of the Spirit evident in my life? If so, how?

_____

_____

_____

_____

_____

_____

_____

LOVE THE ROOT FRUIT

But the fruit of the Spirit is love, joy, peace, longsuffering, gentleness, goodness, faith.
Meekness, temperance: against such there is no law. -Galatians 5:22,23

The first fruit of the Spirit to be examined and the first to be mentioned in Galatians 5:22 is LOVE. Let's examine our love branch to see if we are hanging.

The love root is the very nature of God; therefore, the love root definitely refers to agape love, which is unconditional as well as demonstrative. Love is mentioned first because it is the main fruit from which every other fruit should stem. There are three things concerning those of us who believe we are hanging on love that we must demonstrate:

1. We must be able to demonstrate love to the ungodly. Romans 5:6 says, "for when we were yet without strength, in due time Christ died for the ungodly."

2. We must demonstrate love to the unworthy. Romans 5:8 says, "But God commendeth his love toward us, in that, while we were yet sinners, Christ died for us."

3. We must demonstrate love to the undeserving enemy. Romans 5:10 says, "For if, when we were enemies, we were reconciled to God by the death of his Son, much more, being reconciled, we shall be saved by his life."

MY SPIRITUAL JOURNEY
Am I hanging on the branch? Show some evidence.

THE JOY BRANCH

But the fruit of the Spirit is love, joy, peace, longsuffering, gentleness, goodness, faith.
Meekness, temperance: against such there is no law. -Galatians 5:22,23

Joy is the second fruit of the Spirit. Joy is not the same as happiness. Happiness is temporary and depends on our circumstances. Joy means inner joy at all times, regardless of the situation. Joy is internal and eternal. Joy means that in spite of my circumstances, God still is. Joy comes through knowing God. Joy means that regardless of my material possessions, the spiritual blessings of God are more important.

To know that Jesus died for us, chose us, saved us, adopted us, made us heirs to His throne, and sealed us with His Holy Spirit is joy. Once we give our lives to God, we receive His joy. He will not take it back. It is everlasting.

MY SPIRITUAL JOURNEY

Am I hanging on the joy branch? Show some evidence.

_____

_____

_____

_____

_____

_____

_____

THE PEACE FRUIT

But the fruit of the Spirit is love, joy, peace, longsuffering, gentleness, goodness, faith. Meekness, temperance: against such there is no law. -Galatians 5:22,23

The third fruit of the Spirit listed is PEACE. Philippians 4:7 reads, "And the peace of God, which passeth all understanding, shall keep your hearts and minds through Christ Jesus." According to this passage of scripture, the fruit of the Spirit peace is peace that cannot be understood. Why can't it be understood? It cannot be understood because the one who hangs in it, hangs in it all the time. That means that no matter what the person who is hanging in peace is going through, he or she will continue to be peaceful. Examples are when a loved one is lost, peace; when a job is lost, peace; when sickness and disease hurt the body, peace. Those who hang in the peace of God trust God even though they may be in the midst of trouble.

MY SPIRITUAL JOURNEY

Am I hanging on the peace branch?

_____

_____

_____

_____

_____

_____

_____

_____

_____

LONGSUFFERING

With all lowliness and meekness with longsuffering, forbearing one another in love.
-Ephesians 4:2

The fourth fruit branch is longsuffering. Let's examine our longsuffering branch to see if we are hanging.

Longsuffering means patience, trying to understand the other person's point of view and continuing to love them even if you disagree.

To walk in the Spirit of longsuffering means that we can't go off on people when they don't do what we want them to do or they don't do it as fast as we want them to do it. Longsuffering never strikes back or throws a punch, not even verbally. Longsuffering never gives in to pressure or hard work. When disease, accident, old age, etc. afflict, longsuffering suffers longer. When discouragement or disappointment attack, long-suffering continues to live with patience.

MY SPIRITUAL JOURNEY

Am I hanging on the longsuffering branch?

_____

_____

_____

_____

_____

_____

GENTLENESS

Take my yoke upon you and learn of me, for I am meek and lowly in heart: and ye shall find rest unto your souls. -Matthew 11:29

The fifth fruit branch is GENTLENESS. 1 Thessalonians 2:7 reads, "But we were gentle among you, even as a nurse cherisheth her children." Paul describes his gentleness for the church at Thessalonica as a good mother nursing or caring for her children. A good mother treats her children gently. To treat something or someone gently is to handle it or them with care as though they are very fragile.

Someone hanging in the fruit of the Spirit of gentleness is always kind and considerate in all their endeavors. When others are unpleasant and unloving, the person hanging in the Spirit of gentleness continues to be kind. On the other hand, a person not hanging in the fruit of gentleness would respond negatively to the same situation.

MY SPIRITUAL JOURNEY

Am I hanging on the gentleness branch?

_____

_____

_____

_____

_____

_____

_____

GOODNESS

Be of good courage, and let us play the men for our people, and for the cities of our God: and the LORD do that which seemeth him good. -2 Samuel 10:12

The sixth fruit branch is GOODNESS. The doing of good deeds should follow those who hang on the branch of goodness. Matthew 19:16-26 tells the story of a young man who came to Jesus seeking salvation. In verse 16, the young man referred to Jesus as "good." In verse 21, Jesus instructs him to sell all his possessions and give them to the poor as doing so would be storing treasures in heaven. In verse 22, the young man chose earthly treasures over heavenly treasures.

Since God is the one who is good, and He is the one who lives within us, then the fruit of the Spirit, goodness, also lives within us. The young man could not see the rewards of goodness beyond his riches because he did not have goodness living within him. Those who hang on the branch of goodness know that heavenly treasures are far better than earthly ones.

MY SPIRITUAL JOURNEY

Am I a doer of good deeds? Do I expect rewards for the good deeds that I do?

_____

_____

_____

_____

_____

FAITH

For as the body without the spirit is dead, so faith without works is dead also.
-James 2:26

The seventh fruit branch is FAITH. We demonstrate our faith in God by doing works that honor Him. Whatever works He has called us to do, we should do them faithfully. Those hanging on the branch of faith respond to God's Word with action. They are not just hearers of the Word, but doers of the word, also. James 2:26 declares that faith without works is dead. Saving faith is seen in the good works of believing people.

Many have been called, but only a few have gone to do the works of God. Some he called to the work of ministering to single mothers, but they haven't because they are afraid to share their own personal testimony. God has called all of us to the work of evangelizing. We failed because of the fear of rejection and embarrassment. If we are to hang on the branch of faith, we must trust God to help us complete the work He has called us to do.

MY SPIRITUAL JOURNEY

What work am I doing that honors God?

_____

_____

_____

_____

_____

_____

_____

MEEKNESS

Blessed are the meek: for they shall inherit the earth. -Matthew 4:5

The eighth fruit branch is MEEKNESS. Have you ever said about yourself, "I'm an humble person?" If so, that's exactly when you fell off the branch of meekness. Humility is meekness. When we think we have it, that's when we've lost it. Some of us are hanging so loosely on the branch of meekness that if we were to get a promotion or a little extra money, we would fall completely off! Others are hanging so loosely on the branch of meekness that if we were to graduate with a degree or obtain some other type of achievement, we would fall off completely.

Being prideful is the opposite of being meek. Pride is what will make one say that he or she is humble. We can get so full of pride that we become too heavy for the meekness branch and fall off and rot.

MY SPIRITUAL JOURNEY

How did Jesus show Himself humble? How can I relate?

_____

_____

_____

_____

_____

_____

_____

_____

TEMPERANCE

For the drunkard and the glutton shall come to poverty:
and drowsiness shall clothe a man with rags. -Proverbs 23:21

TEMPERANCE means control of our desires or control of our appetite. It's the master control of our passion and appetite for food, cigarettes, beer, sex, etc.

Are we hanging? What happens when our temperance tree gets shaken? Teenage pregnancy is at an all time high. Latest statistics in one state reflects that 38% of those who enter school get pregnant before they finish. That's nearly four out of every ten students. Many church girls are having sex with church boys. Six out of ten high school boys admitted that they had sex and had taken a drink before they got out of Jr. High School. We are out of control.

What about the statistics on adults? Are we faking holiness on Sundays? Fornication does not have an age limit. Fornication is having sex outside of marriage. There is nothing in the Bible about consenting adults or safe sex.

MY SPIRITUAL JOURNEY
Are my personal desires in line with God's desires for me?

_____

_____

_____

_____

March 13

JUST CAN'T KEEP IT TO MYSELF

And they, when they had testified and preached the word of the Lord, returned to Jerusalem, and preached the gospel in many villages of the Samaritans. -Acts 8:25

The chief of the temple had Jeremiah beaten for preaching. Jeremiah took the whipping then got up and complained to God about the day he was born. He told God that he didn't want to do His work anymore. If he could have, he would have shut up, but he couldn't because it felt like fire was shut up in his bones. (Jeremiah 20)

Once while out witnessing with my church, we knocked on the door of a self-sufficient, argumentative man. When the man came to the door, he said, "I don't believe in organized religion." I said, "I don't either." After reasoning with the man, we were able to lead him to Jesus Christ. We ought to always share Jesus. I could have let the man's first comment intimidate me, but I couldn't let it keep me from speaking to him because of the fire shut up in my bones. I just couldn't keep it to myself. The Holy Ghost fire shut up in my bones outweighed any feeling brought on by intimidation.

MY SPIRITUAL JOURNEY

Have there been times I 'kept it to myself' because I felt intimidated?

_____

_____

_____

_____

LIKE FIRE SHUT-UP IN MY BONES

But his word was in mine heart as a burning fire shut up in my bones...
-Jeremiah 20:9b

God is the master user of hot stuff. Jeremiah described the infilling of The Holy Spirit as fire shut up in his bones. In Revelation, John, on the Island of Patmos, told us that God would not have us lukewarm. Before He does, He will spew us out (Revelation 3:14-16). We need to be either hot or cold. God wants us to be on fire for Jesus.

At the Day of Pentecost (Acts 2:4), God used hot stuff to usher in His Church. There was wind and fire. God used hot stuff when He got ready to call Isaiah to be His servant preacher. Isaiah felt he was unworthy because he had unclean lips and was among unclean people. One of God's Cherubim flew down to the altar, picked up a hot coal, and purged Isaiah's tongue. Afterward, Isaiah told God if He needs somebody, send him (Isaiah 6: 5-8).

God wants Christians on fire in ministry. We cannot be effective in ministry without the Holy Ghost fire.

MY SPIRITUAL JOURNEY

How is God's Holy Ghost fire helping me to be effective in ministry?

_____
_____
_____
_____

CATCH ON FIRE

And when Paul had laid his hands upon them, the Holy Ghost came on them; and they spake with tongues, and prophesied. -Acts 19:6

Duringuring my earlier years of preaching, on a quiet day of worship, a brother came up to me and shook my hand. I asked him the usual small talk question, "How are you doing?" Usually people respond, "Fine." But this brother wasn't doing fine and proceeded to share with me that he wasn't well at all. As the conversation lingered on, I said to him, "I've seen you around and you seem to keep coming back." Then I asked him, "Are you enjoying the sermons?" A bold question it was to ask. The man responded, "I haven't heard a thing you said."

A bold question was asked and a bold response was given, which made me even more inquisitive. So I said to him, "Brother, why do you keep coming every Sunday?" He said to me, "I just come to see you catch on fire. I just need to see somebody who feels as good as you do. So every Sunday, I come to watch you burn with fire."

Thanks to that brother, I've been asking God to let me burn up every since. I just can't keep it to myself. It feels like fire shut up in my bones.

MY SPIRITUAL JOURNEY

Do others see the fire in my life?

CHRISTIANS DREAM TEAM

But his word was in mine heart as a burning fire shut up in my bones….-Jeremiah 20:9b

---

If we want to accomplish something, we need to get a dream team together. When America wanted to beat the Russians in Olympic basketball, we formed the American dream team. God has put the responsibility upon us, the empowered believers, to share Jesus. We are partners on His dream team. The other players on His dream team are The Word and The Holy Spirit. The Word compels, convicts, and draws people to Jesus. The Holy Spirit empowers and precedes the witness. The empowered believer, the witness, then goes forth sharing Jesus.

After the day of Pentecost, Peter and John were still on fire with the Holy Ghost. Peter preached full of the Holy Ghost and The Word, leading 3000 people to salvation (Acts 2). On one occasion a man, who was saved and healed, was leaping, jumping, and praising God. Peter and John were then asked to stop speaking in the name of Jesus. They challenged the church folks to judge for themselves if it was better to obey them or God. Peter and John explained that they could not help speaking about what they have heard and seen (Acts 3). They were on the Christian Dream Team.

MY SPIRITUAL JOURNEY

What is my testimony?

_____

_____

_____

THE WISE ONE

Who is wise, and he shall understand these things? Prudent, and he shall know them?
For the ways of the LORD are right, and the just shall walk in them:
but the transgressors shall fall therein.-Hosea 14:9

Wisdom is defined as fear of the Lord. Scripture suggests that not all of us are wise. He said, Brethren, I would not have you ignorant about this mystery, less you be wise in your own conceit (Romans 11:25). Many of us are wise in our own intellect, pride and braggadocios (who we are).

I know a young man who thinks he knows everything. He played on the basketball team with me in high school and in college. Once I went home and was told he was in jail. God laid it on my heart to visit him. As I talked to him between the bar window, I listened as he was trying to tell the jailer how to run the jail. He believed himself to be wise. Worldly wisdom is ignorance compared to the wisdom of God. Some of us are so wise in our own conceit that we can't see a place for God in our lives even though we have accepted Him as Savior. When the final word has been preached and the last invitation has been given, who will be found wise? Will you be found wise?

MY SPIRITUAL JOURNEY

Am I wise enough to receive the joy of salvation?

_____

_____

_____

GOD'S REDEMPTIVE LOVE

In whom we have redemption through his blood, even the forgiveness of sins.
-Colossians 1:14

Many of us wonder why God would save certain people? At the beginning of my pastorate, I had a counseling session with a new member, who was remembering her father who was an alcoholic and a wife and child abuser. Her mother's role was a lot like Hosea's role.

One day the woman called her mother, and her mother said, "Your 65-year-old daddy got saved today." The woman told me that she went home to see for herself. When she arrived home, her dad was at the hospital visiting the sick, which was now a common thing for him to do every Saturday and Sunday.

However, the woman just couldn't handle the fact that her abusive father qualified to receive God's forgiveness. The daughter became angry and dropped out of church. After much prayer, she forgave her father and returned to the church. She realized that God's redemptive, unreasonable love is available to all.

MY SPIRITUAL JOURNEY

Can I think of anyone who I believe is not deserving of God's redemptive, unreasonable love?

_____

_____

_____

SHARE CHRIST – THE LAST INVITATION

But watch thou in all things, endure afflictions, do the work of an evangelist, make full proof of thy ministry. -2 Timothy 4:5

What is man that God is mindful of him? Martin Luther said that if he were God, he would kick the whole world to death. Jonah must have felt this way about the city of Nineveh because he thought the people were too bad and too mean to be forgiven by God.

What are we going to do about this last invitation of accepting God's unreasonable love? There have been other last invitations in the Bible. There was a last invitation in Noah's day, but only Noah and his family accepted it. There was a last invitation in the days of Sodom and Gomorrah, but only Lot and his daughters got out of town. Invitations were made to be shared. Today could be the last invitation for unreasonable redemption for someone. Have you been wise in sharing it? Today could even be our last time to share it with a lost person.

MY SPIRITUAL JOURNEY

If today was my last day on earth, who would I invite to Christ? Then do it.

WALK WORTHY – GROW TALL

…beseech you that ye walk worthy of the vocation wherewith ye are called.
-Ephesians 4:1

I can recall coaching basketball in South Alabama. The chant for encouraging the team was 'grow tall'. When the game was in the heat of action and the players were jumping for the ball, the cheerleaders and fans on the bench would yell, "grow tall!" Soon it became like the "wave" of today at a football or baseball game. It was amazing to me that when everyone would yell "grow tall," players who didn't look like they were big enough to jump high were jumping all over the rim and snatching balls.

God is pleading with us today to "grow tall." He desires for us to grow up and walk worthy of the vocation to which He has called us. The basic premise of the book "Growing Up to the Head" is that Christ is the head of the Church. Christ is a perfect head, and we, the believers, make up the imperfect body that needs to grow up to Him. We are challenged to grow up to His fullness, completeness, and perfection. The Head desires to function with the body, but the body cannot function without the Head. The Head has a plan in His Word for us to grow tall to His expectations. Are you growing up?

MY SPIRITUAL JOURNEY

What is the vocation God has called me to?

_____

_____

WALK WORTHY OF YOUR CALLING

That you would walk worthy of God, who hath called you unto his own kingdom and glory.
-1 Thessalonians 2:12

Christians cannot and should not act or live like non-Christians. God has called us to walk in a certain way. He teaches us how to grow up in our walk throughout His Word. Non-believers can only guess at right and wrong, but the Holy Spirit within us tells us right from wrong.

Ephesians 4 warns us to stray from lying to each other because when we lie, we hurt each other. Many of us claim not to be liars but really are. We have become more sophisticated in lying by leaving out certain details.

Ephesians 4 warns us against sinning because of anger. If and when we get angry, we are to get over it quickly. When we are angry, we invite the devil to take over our being. Many husbands and wives go to bed angry at each other, giving the devil a foothold on their marriage. Don't give the devil too much play; he will gladly break up your family.

MY SPIRITUAL JOURNEY

Am I guilty of walking in lying and anger?

_____

_____

_____

_____

WALK WORTHY

For he that will love life, and see good days, let him refrain his tongue from evil, and his lips that they speak no guile. -1 Peter 3:10

Many Christians claim not to be thieves, but they are always looking for ways to try and get over on others. Even in church, we tip God and sign commitment cards pretending to be tithers.

Ephesians 4:29 warns us against using bad language, and urges us to say only what is good. We are encouraged to be a blessing to those we are talking to so that we may minister grace unto the hearers. We shouldn't use profanity. Neither should we say bad things about anybody. Not controlling the tongue could lead to someone not coming to Christ. Words are bullets. We don't condone guns and shooting but our tongues are fired guns, shooting out deadly words. Some of us have tongues that should be classified as automatics and others as oozies. Automatics are those who are expected to say whatever spews out, and they do it often. Oozies are those who don't fire often, but when they do, they fire with a bang. Christians have no excuse for walking in theft, bad language, lying, or stealing.

MY SPIRITUAL JOURNEY

Am I guilty of walking in theft and bad language?

_____

_____

_____

DON'T GRIEVE THE HOLY SPIRIT

And grieve not the holy Spirit of God, whereby ye are sealed unto the day of redemption.
-Ephesians 4:30

Ephesians 4:30 warns us against grieving the Holy Spirit. We need to understand that God the Holy Spirit is not an object but a subject. He is a person. He is just as much a part of the Trinity as God the Father and God the Son. He is not a wind. He is grieved when we do the things He warns us against like failing to walk worthy of the vocation to which He has called us. We grieve the Holy Spirit when He sees us lying, gossiping, and stealing. We shouldn't cause the Holy Spirit sorrow in the way we live. Remember, He is the one who will mark us to be present on that day when salvation from sin will be complete.

Ephesians 4:31 warns us against quarreling and having dislikes for each other. "I can't stand her" shouldn't be a part of our vocabulary. It is not of God. We are called to love each other even when the other person is wrong. When we dislike someone for doing something wrong, God is displeased with us. We should be kind to one another.

MY SPIRITUAL JOURNEY

At what times have I been guilty of grieving the Holy Spirit?

_____

_____

_____

_____

TUMBLEWEED CHRISTIANS

That we henceforth be no more children, tossed to and fro, and carried about with every wind of doctrine, by the sleight of men, and cunning craftiness whereby they lie in wait to deceive.
-Ephesians 4:14

Tumbleweeds blow here and there, wherever the wind tosses them. Too many of us are tumbleweed Christians. We should not remain infants or children tossed back and forth by every wind and every cunning and deceitful scheme of man. The wind represents the world. What the world is telling us is contrary to God's will. Violence on television, sitcoms portraying sex outside of marriage, and beer commercials are unacceptable in God's sight. The world has made alcohol legal, socially acceptable, and okay, but God says our bodies should be Holy and a temple for Christ.

The Head has plans but needs the Church to carry out His plans. It is a mystery to understand how God in all His sovereignty would choose an imperfect people as His body, but He did. What an awesome thought that God needs us, but to be used by Him, we have to stop following false doctrine and doing other things that grieve Him.

MY SPIRITUAL JOURNEY
In what areas of my life do I live like a tumbleweed Christian?

FAITH TESTED

I know thy works, and tribulation, and poverty,...
be thou faithful unto death, and I will give thee a crown of life. -Revelation 2:9a, 10d

God teaches us how and why we should remain faithful through an example of a poor yet rich church that was under persecution in a city called Smyrna. The church of Smyrna was one of the seven churches God addressed in the book of Revelation. Smyrna was a proud, beautiful city known for exporting goods. It was here that the Church was sanctioned, ostracized, and ridiculed by both Jews and worshippers of Caesar.

It was for this reason they may have been so financially poor and were referred to as the persecuted church. Interestingly, Jesus did not reprimand them like He did the other churches, but encouraged them to remain faithful. God is going to give us a crown, the crown of life. It will not be sent by US mail, Federal Express, or UPS, but Jesus Himself will give to each of us the crown of life.

MY SPIRITUAL JOURNEY

Can I recall specific times when I remained faithful to God? Has fear ever overruled my faith in God?

_____

_____

_____

_____

HEART TRANSPLANT

A new heart also will I give you, and a new spirit will I put within you.
-Ezekiel 36:26a

A change of mind may only reflect a change of opinion, but a change of heart reflects a complete turn in how one lives. The heart is a place of conviction and affection. Saul, on the road to Damascus, had a change of heart-conviction. Jonah, in the whale's belly, had a change of heart-conviction.

God told Ezekiel to tell the people that He was going to give them a new heart, a right spirit within them so that when they returned to Him, they would desire to be His people again.

God is still in the heart-changing business. Just as He promised to change the hearts of the Israelites under Babylonian captivity, He promises to change our hearts as well, if only we repent. Today is a good day for a heart transplant.

MY SPIRITUAL JOURNEY

What is my heart convicting me of today?

_____

_____

_____

_____

_____

_____

IN THE HOUSE

And straightway many were gathered together, insomuch that there was no room to receive them, no, not so much as about the door: and he preached the word unto them. -Mark 2:2

When Jesus was in the house, my son, a young child named George Orman McCalep, III, sick with spinal meningitis, was kept alive over 40 years ago. The illness left him a deaf person, but he now works as an electrician, married a beautiful woman, bought his own car and house, and signs to people telling them if they don't stop smoking and drinking and serve the Lord, they are going to Hell.

When Jesus is in the house, others will want to get in the house too, even the unsaved. When Jesus was in the house (Mark 2:1-5), there was a man sick of the palsy who wanted to get in the house so that he could be healed, but the house was full. Determined, his friends found an alternate route into the house. They clawed and scratched through the roof and lowered him down safely. Jesus saw their faith and said to the man sick of palsy, "Son, thy sins be forgiven thee" (Mark, 2:5b). This is what happens when Jesus is in the house.

MY SPIRITUAL JOURNEY

Do I have the heart of God? How do I know? Is there evidence of a heart for others?

_____

_____

_____

A CLEAN HEART

Create in me a clean heart, O God; and renew a right spirit within me.
- Psalm 51:10

Many of us have heart trouble, but some of us have hard and cold hearts.

Hard-hearted people feel no compassion for others and are usually stubborn and stuck in their ways. It was a hard heart that made Pharaoh resist Moses, the man of God, refusing to set the Israelites free. It was the cold heart of King Nebuchadnezzar of Babylon that threw the boys into the fiery furnace. Hard and cold hearts are unresponsive and feel no emotion or sensitivity to anything. A transplant is needed.

Before we can be deemed a worthy transplant recipient, bad spirits must be eliminated through much prayer. David asked God in Psalm 51:10 to create in him a clean heart and renew a right spirit within him. We must also ask God to take away our wrong spirits and to fill us daily with His right Spirit.

MY SPIRITUAL JOURNEY
What bad spirits are keeping me from getting a heart transplant?

_____

_____

_____

_____

_____

March 29
HEALING

He healeth the broken in heart, and bindeth up their wounds. -Psalm 147:3

When Jesus is in the house, the healing we need is there. In Mark 1, Jesus cleansed a man of leprosy and charged him not to tell anyone. The man couldn't keep it to himself. Afterwards, Jesus was pursued by throngs of people desiring healing and His teachings.

When Jesus is in the house, it will be a full house. In order for anyone to know that He is in the house, however, someone has to testify to the fact. For others to receive Christ, our lives must testify that He is in the house. When the house of God is empty, it is because Jesus is not present. When Jesus is in the house, people will come forth and testify of never having seen church done in such a way before. They will testify of their many healings, deliverance, and blessings, and praise will break out.

MY SPIRITUAL JOURNEY

Is Jesus present in my house (my body)? What is the evidence?

_____

_____

_____

_____

_____

_____

_____

KEEP GOING TO GOD

Praying always with all prayer and supplication in the Spirit, and watching thereunto with all perseverance and supplication for all saints; -Ephesians 6:18

No matter what our children go through, we want to know about it all. We want to know about all their joys and all their sorrows. Why? We want to know in order to make things better for them. God is our Spiritual parent, and He wants to know all of our joys and sorrows, just like a good earthly parent.

We go to God through prayer. We don't know what or how to pray, but The Word of God and the Holy Spirit will teach and guide us. The Holy Spirit will help to purify our prayers from all the junk we bring to God. Our prayer life with God should be habitual. Just like a child needs to tell everything to a parent, we need to tell everything to God. We need to pray to Him always (1 Thessalonians 5:17) and cast all our cares and our victories upon Him. He loves us and wants to commune with us. God wants to hear from us throughout our day so that He can order our steps and lead us into the right path He has chosen for us. Without God's directions, we will get lost.

MY SPIRITUAL JOURNEY

Do I take everything to God in prayer?

_____

_____

_____

LOOK ON US: RISE UP AND WALK

Then Peter said, Silver and gold have I none; but such as I have give I thee:
In the name of Jesus Christ of Nazareth rise up and walk. -Acts 3:6

Crack being sold in elementary schools is an ugly sight. Children having babies is an ugly sight. Homeless people living in cardboard boxes are an ugly sight. Acts 3:2 is the picture of an ugly sight, a man sitting at the gate called beautiful begging for money from Peter and John, two Spirit-filled disciples.

Peter said to him, "Look on us" (Acts 3:4b). Many of us don't want ugly sights to look on us. We want to point the ugly sight in another direction, like United Way, welfare, and self-help groups. The Church is the beautiful gate that needs to get bold and say, "Look on us." Peter first told the man of his deficit but then focused on his supply. Peter said, Silver and gold have I none but such as I have I give to thee. The Bible tells us that the man not only stood up but he began to jump, leap, and walk. He became a portrait of praise at the beautiful gate.

MY SPIRITUAL JOURNEY

If someone were to look on me, what should I expect them to see?

_____

_____

_____

_____

SERVING A RISEN SAVIOR

He is not here: for he is risen as he said, Come, see the place where the Lord lay.
-Matthew 28:6

What is your reason or alibi for not serving the risen Savior seven days a week? Has the world paid you off like the guards who were paid off and told to lie about what they had witnessed on Resurrection morning (Matthew 28:11-15)?

To believe that God is risen is to act like He is risen. We live in the most God-seeking religious age since the beginning of time. More people are seeking meaning to their lives by involving themselves in some sort of spirituality than ever before.

So how do we serve a risen Savior? To serve a risen Savior, we must learn to live in the between time. Some of us live pretty good on Sundays, but it's the in-between time that no one knows we are Christians. In other words, many Christians are in the closet Monday through Saturday. However, we are called to serve him at all times, everyday.

MY SPIRITUAL JOURNEY

What is my reason for serving the risen Savior?

_____

_____

_____

92

STAMPED: PAID IN FULL

But he was wounded for our transgressions, he was bruised for our iniquities: the chastisement of our peace was upon him; and with his stripes we are healed.

-Isaiah 53:5

H as there ever been a time in your life when you paid a bill in full? I can remember paying off my first car note. What a load off my back! Debt holds us down. It is a burden to us. When we have debt, it seems like the bills never stop coming.

We do foolish things that keep adding to a bill that Jesus has already paid in full. So, what makes resurrection day such a joyous occasion? It reminds us that our sin bill has been paid in full. Each time we think on the empty cross, we should be reminded that our debt has been settled. Our sin bill has been paid in full. We have a zero balance. Jesus paid it all!

MY SPIRITUAL JOURNEY

Thank God that my sin bill has been paid in full. Now, what personally can I do to stay out of debt?

_____

_____

_____

_____

_____

_____

_____

…Ye seek Jesus of Nazareth, which was crucified: he is risen;
he is not here: behold the place where they laid him.- Mark 16:6

Jesus is alive! Many of us have a problem getting to the point of Jesus being alive. We are still seeing images of the crucifix. A crucifix is a symbol of Jesus hanging on the cross. But Jesus is no longer hanging on the cross. Some of us are still mentally, spiritually, and physically wearing a crucifix. We are leaving Jesus on the cross daily rather than picking up our crosses to follow Him. Some of us still have a crucifix burden hanging around our hearts.

I remember preaching on a Passion Sunday. I was intense with dramatizing the suffering of Jesus. I went home that afternoon feeling like something was wrong. Gloom had taken over our home. We couldn't figure out what was wrong. Our house had changed. The problem was that I had forgotten to get Jesus up from the grave. I thought maybe I would get Him up on Resurrection Sunday. For the entire week preceding Resurrection Sunday, we were mentally and emotionally burdened down because we were still seeing Jesus on the cross. We need to remove the crucifixes from around our hearts and necks and throw them away, because the cross is empty. He is risen!

MY SPIRITUAL JOURNEY

Do I see an image of the crucifix or the risen savior? Why?

OUR SIN DEBT IS PAID

And when they looked, they saw that the stone was rolled away; for it was very great. -Mark 16:4

The empty cross and vacant tomb of Jesus should remind us to keep the faith. There is hope in spite of our bad decisions and failures. We may not know what tomorrow holds, but we know who holds tomorrow.

The empty cross and the empty tomb should also remind us that we have the potential for peace. Isaiah declared that the chastisement of our peace was upon Jesus.

The empty cross and the empty tomb should also remind us that we are healed. Isaiah declared that by Jesus' stripes we are healed. If Jesus was still hanging on the cross, we could not be healed, delivered, or saved. Our sin debt is paid. Our balance is zero.

MY SPIRITUAL JOURNEY

How do the empty cross and tomb remind me that I have hope?

_____

_____

_____

_____

_____

_____

_____

TELL THE WHOLE STORY

Now when Jesus was risen early the first day of the week, he appeared first to Mary Magdalene out of whom he had cast seven devils. -Mark 16:9

Those of us who have had that burden of sin lifted from us and have met the risen Savior should go and tell the whole story and tell it straight. If we are still wearing the crucifix around our neck, we are not telling the whole story because Jesus is no longer on the cross.

Jesus came into my life when I was eleven years old because I wanted to go to Heaven to live with Him and the other members of my family. I prayed hard and loud for a long time. I was determined not to get up until I was saved. Jesus heard my cry and delivered me. It made joy and happiness come into our home, but since I had not accepted Him in the sanctuary, my mother and I walked the dirt roads to tell all the neighbors who happened to be my relatives.

MY SPIRITUAL JOURNEY

What is the story I need to tell? Write it here.

_____

_____

_____

_____

_____

_____

IS ANYTHING TOO HARD FOR GOD?

Is any thing too hard for the LORD? At the time appointed, I will return unto thee, according to the time of life, and Sarah shall have a son. -Genesis 18:14

What is troubling you today? Name it. Have you lost or are about to lose your job or home? Are you broke financially, spiritually, and perhaps emotionally? Are you struggling with some type of drug addiction, child abuse, or domestic violence? Have you lost a loved one? Believe it or not, none of these situations is too hard for God. God can give us victory over anything. We only need to believe that He is able and that He can.

In Genesis 18:12, Sarah laughed when the angel of the Lord told her that she would give birth to a son at her old age. According to Genesis 21:2, Sarah had a son just as God had promised. There is nothing too hard nor is it ever too late for God, who created the heavens and the earth, parted the Red Sea, dropped manna down from heaven, healed the sick, and raised the dead. The only hard part is believing that He can.

MY SPIRITUAL JOURNEY

With what in my life have I not trusted God? Do I believe it to be too hard for Him?

_____

_____

_____

_____

MAKE ROOM FOR THE CHILDREN

But when Jesus saw it, he was much displeased, and said unto them, Suffer the little children to come unto me, and forbid them not: for of such is the kingdom of God. -Mark 10:14

Jesus said in Mark 10:15, "Whosoever shall not receive the kingdom of God as a little child, he shall not enter therein." Children are special to Jesus because they come to Him with honesty and humility.

Matthew 18:10 informs us that the angels of the children get to go before God before any others. Abraham sent Hagar and her son away with only bread and water. When it was gone and they could wander the wilderness of Beersheba no longer, she sat down and began to cry. It was not her cries, however, that moved God according to Genesis 21:17, "And God heard the voice of the lad." We need to learn to make room for our children. Teach them to love God with all their heart, soul, and mind. We need their prayers, too. It may be their voices that get us our break through.

MY SPIRITUAL JOURNEY

Does my intellect keep me from being honest and humble with God like a child to a parent?

_____

_____

_____

_____

_____

_____

LET THE HIGH PRAISES OF GOD BE HEARD

Let the high praises of God be in their mouth, and a two-edged sword in their hand; to
execute vengeance upon the heathen…this honour have all his saints.
-Psalms 149:6, 9b

Praising God is an honor. It is a powerful and victorious weapon to use against our enemy. Praise is such a piercing weapon that the psalmist describes it as a powerful two-edged sword. How can praising God help me to fight a battle against the attacks of Satan? It sounds like such a silly idea. Silly it may sound, but it works. It worked in helping Joshua and the Israelites to take down the walls of Jericho. It is the weapon of praise that takes vengeance against the heathen; not a gun, knife or some other tangible device.

Our God is an awesome God and worthy to be praised! So let the high praises of God be heard. If we want to overcome the wiles of the devil, then we must let the high praises of God be heard. When Satan tries to steal our home and our health, we must let the high praises of God be heard. We shouldn't walk around with dull-bladed swords, but we should sharpen up our swords with much praise. Praise ye the Lord! There is victory in praising God.

MY SPIRITUAL JOURNEY

List my current struggles and praise God for the victory over them right now.

_____

_____

_____

Verily, Verily, I say unto you, He that believeth on me, the works that I do shall he do also; and greater works than these shall he do; because I go unto my Father. -John 14:12

Employers cannot afford to have employees who do not do their jobs. In order for a job to function properly and productively, everyone must do their respective parts. The same is true with the body of Christ. God has given us all a job to do, and if one of us goes slacking, the entire body becomes weak. Jesus said in John 14:12 that the works He did, we shall do even greater.

What were the works that Jesus was doing? He was tearing down the walls of tradition. He was healing the sick and diseased. He was casting out demons. He was teaching the good news of the kingdom of God.

Christ is the head of the body, and we are the arms, legs, feet, hands, etc. that need to make "a hundred" in doing the work of the Ministry. Remember, 99 ½ won't do. No more slacking; it's time for the body of Christ to get to work and strive for a perfect score.

MY SPIRITUAL JOURNEY

Am I doing a good job with the assignment He has given me or am I causing the body of Christ to be weaker?

THE BIG PICTURE

Hear, ye deaf; and look, ye blind, that ye may see. -Isaiah 42:18

According to Esther 5:9-11, Haman, Prime Minister of Media-Persia, bragged to his wife and friends about his fame and riches, but he complained because a Jewish man named Mordecai refused to bow to him. He said that all his fame and riches were nothing because Mordecai refused to bow to him. Haman missed the big picture simply because of one little picture. He couldn't focus on his blessings because he was too focused on his pride.

We today are a lot like Haman. We become so focused on the things in front of us, that we are not able to see the purposes of God. For instance, someone says something bad about us and we get lost in what they said, causing us to lose focus on what God is trying to accomplish in us. We miss the opportunity to witness or counsel. Not seeing the big picture can prohibit us from moving to the next level in Christ Jesus.

MY SPIRITUAL JOURNEY

At what times have I failed to see the big picture? How do I plan to handle it differently?

_____

_____

_____

_____

GOD NEVER SLEEPS

He that keepeth thee will not slumber. Behold, he that keepeth
Israel shall neither slumber nor sleep -Psalms 121:3b-4

It is not good for human beings to go without sleep. A lack of sleep can be very dangerous and even put us at risk for developing illnesses. But the God we serve does not need sleep. God is the creator of all things, including sleep. He doesn't need sleep just as He doesn't need time. Such things were made for our benefit, not His.

In Esther 6:1, King Ahasuerus could not sleep. The scripture reads, "On that night could not the king sleep," which is an indication that he usually slept well. So on that night, King Ahasuerus decided that he would honor Mordecai, who had saved his life, by letting him ride his royal horse and wear his royal robe and crown while a prince led him through the streets shouting, "What shall be done unto the man whom the king delighteth to honor?" (Esther 6:6b) It was during this time that Haman, the prime minister, was about to ask the king if he could have Mordecai killed for not bowing to him. We, too, should be glad that God never sleeps because just as he made a way for Mordecai, He continues to make a way for us when we are asleep or awake.

MY SPIRITUAL JOURNEY

At what times has God proven Himself to be awake when I thought He was asleep?

102

REPETITIOUS PRAYER

But when ye pray, use not vain repetitions, as the heathen do:
for they think that they shall be heard for their much speaking. -Matthew 6:7

In Matthew 6:7, Jesus teaches us not to pray using vain repetition. Many confuse this verse to believe that once we ask God for something, we are never to regard it again. Jesus had nothing against repetitive prayers. He had a problem with praying in vain. To pray using vain repetition is to place focus on self. This type of prayer has no purpose and doesn't come from the heart. Jesus referred to those who pray in that manner as hypocrites and had this to say about them in verse 5, "They love to be seen so that they get their glory from men."

Luke 18:1-6 tells of a woman who continuously went to an unfair judge asking him to avenge her adversary. Because she wouldn't stop bothering the judge about her problem, he decided to avenge her. Jesus responded in Luke 18:7-8a, "And shall not God avenge his own elect, which cry day and night unto him, though he bear long with them? I tell you that he will avenge them speedily." Be persistent in prayer. He will answer.

MY SPIRITUAL JOURNEY

Am I guilty of praying in vain?

_____

_____

_____

_____

OUR FATHER WHICH ART IN HEAVEN

But thou when thou prayest, enter into thy closet, and when thou hast shut thy door, pray to thy Father which is in secret; and thy Father which seeth in secret shall reward thee openly.
-Matthew 6:6

One of the ways He taught us to pray is known as what we call "The Lord's Prayer" (Matthew 6:9-13.) However, the Lord's Prayer has become vain repetition. Many of us recite it repetitively, but have no idea of its meaning. The Lord's Prayer is purposeful and should be prayed from the heart with meaning and understanding.

Jesus taught the disciples to pray The Lord's Prayer, beginning with, Our Father which art in heaven. Why did Jesus begin His prayer this way? He is teaching us to honor and acknowledge God. When people worship other Gods, they are very specific in whom they are talking to, e.g., Satan or Buddha. God wants us to be clear about who He is, and He deserves to be addressed properly. Many demand a proper greeting, but God deserves it.

MY SPIRITUAL JOURNEY

What are some ways in which I can address or acknowledge God as I begin to pray?

_____

_____

_____

_____

HALLOWED BE THY NAME

Rejoice in the LORD, ye righteous, and give thanks at the remembrance of his holiness. -
Psalm 97:12

Jesus taught the disciples to pray, Hallowed be thy name. The word "hallowed" means holy. Holy is the name of Jesus Christ. To speak of God as holy is to praise Him. Here Jesus teaches us to give adoration or praise to God. God is great and greatly to be praised. Most of us have no problem coming together in corporate worship and praising God in the sanctuary. Before we begin to ask Him for anything in our prayers, we should tell Him how great He is by blessing His holy name.

Praise Him in the sanctuary. Praise Him in the prayer closet. Praise ye the Lord! Praise Him in the morning, evening, and in the midnight hour. Praise Him even when the sun goes down. Praise Him and His glory forever at all times, and in all circumstances. Psalm 30:4 says "Sing praise to the Lord, you saints of His, and give thanks at the remembrance of His Holy Name." (NKJV)

MY SPIRITUAL JOURNEY

Now that I have a better understanding of Hallowed be thy name, what are some ways in which I can praise God in my prayer?

_____

_____

_____

_____

105

HIS WILL BE DONE

Thy kingdom come, Thy will be done in earth, as it is in heaven.

-Matthew 6:10

Jesus teaches us that His desire is for us to do His will, and His will is for souls to be added to His kingdom. If we put what God wills before anything else, we will then see that God's will includes our desires. According to Ephesians 5:8, His will is that we be filled with The Holy Spirit. Then we are more susceptible to doing His will.

According to 3 John 1:2, His will is that we prosper and be in good health, even as our soul prospers. Our soul is made up of our mind, will, and emotions; therefore, the prosperity God has in mind for us is spiritual, mental, and physical. We need also to seek what God's will is for each of us personally. He has given us spiritual gifts and ministries. It is His will that we walk worthy of our vocation. Matthew 6:33 teaches us to seek the kingdom of God before anything else and all those other things will be added.

MY SPIRITUAL JOURNEY

What is God's will for me?

_____

_____

_____

_____

_____

OUR DAILY BREAD

For the bread of God is he which cometh down from heaven and giveth life unto the world.
-John 6:33

Jesus taught the disciples to pray, Give us this day our daily bread. Daily bread not only means the food that we consume, but it also means, most importantly, tasting of Jesus everyday. Jesus said that I am the bread of life. The psalmist tells us, "Oh taste and see that the Lord is good, blessed is the man that trusteth in him" (Psalm 34:8). Do we actually pray for our daily bread or do we pray for tomorrow, next year, or twenty years from now?

Just as we want to eat daily for our physical food, we need to taste of Jesus through prayer and meditation daily for our spiritual, mental, and social food because tomorrow is not promised.

However, when we pray purposefully and speak our desires, it gives God an opportunity to see how much more and in what areas He needs to groom us for our blessing.

MY SPIRITUAL JOURNEY

For what am I praying?

_____

_____

_____

_____

_____

_____

If we confess our sins, he is faithful and just to forgive us our sins,
and to cleanse us from all unrighteousness. -1 John 1:9

Jesus taught the disciples to pray, And forgive us our debts, as we forgive our debtors. Here, He teaches us to forgive. He teaches us first to ask forgiveness of our sins. 1 John 1:9 reads, "If we confess our sins, he is faithful and just to forgive us our sins, and to cleanse us from all unrighteousness." Confession of sin improves our relationship with God. Then, He teaches us to forgive others. First we are to get our relationship with Him in order and then with others.

Many times people will proclaim that "I will forgive him or her, but I won't forget." That is not true forgiving. When you actually forgive someone, you can't recall exactly what happened: you are not holding the incident in your memory bank. The sting from the hurt is gone, and you will actually thank God for His mercy. It is God's way of maturing you and growing you up in His likeness.

MY SPIRITUAL JOURNEY

For what do I need God to forgive me? Who do I need to forgive?

_____

_____

_____

_____

_____

TEMPTATION

And when he was at the place, he said unto them, pray that you enter not into temptation.
-Luke 22:40

Jesus taught the disciples to pray, And lead us not into temptation, but deliver us from evil. Here, Jesus is teaching us to pray for protection against the wiles of the devil. There is a game show called "The Weakest Link." In reality, the weakest link for someone can be alcohol, beer, pornography, lying, gossip, etc. Whatever our weakest link is, Satan finds it and seeks to kill and destroy us through it.

We need to learn to pray protection over our spirit because our spirit desires to commune with The Holy Spirit. We need to learn to pray protection over our body because it houses The Holy Spirit. If Satan can keep our house dirty, then he knows he doesn't have to worry about a clean, pure, and holy God dwelling in a filthy house. If our prayer lives line up with the word of God, then Satan is blocked from destroying us.

MY SPIRITUAL JOURNEY

How can I pray more specifically regarding protection? What is my weakest link?

POWER and GLORY

Then he called his twelve disciples together and gave them power and authority over all devils and to cure diseases. -Luke 9:1

Jesus taught the disciples to pray For thine is the kingdom, and the power, and the glory: forever. Amen. Here, Jesus teaches us to close our prayer, praising God, just as we began it. We are to close our prayer, focusing on the creator of heaven and earth, not on what we want, what we asked forgiveness for, what we need protection for, etc., but on God.

We praise God because we believe that He will do all those things that are good and perfect for us. We praise God because it is our weapon that will defeat the enemy and give us victory. We praise God because He said to praise Him and because He is worthy of our praise. We praise God until our praise turns into worship. Praise ye the Lord! Amen.

MY SPIRITUAL JOURNEY

How can I praise God today? How often shall I praise God?

_____

_____

_____

_____

_____

_____

_____

April 20
EVERLASTING JOURNEY

For God so loved the world, that he gave his only begotten Son, that whosoever believeth in him should not perish, but have everlasting life. -John 3:16

We are on a spiritual journey. For each mile we travel, Satan keeps putting up blockades in the road trying to convince us that our journey has ended. God keeps building a bridge of hope that we must keep crossing. How does God build a bridge of hope for our journey? He reminds us in His word.

Too often we give in to the tactics of Satan, believing our journey has come to an end. If we, however, believe the word of God as we say we do, we know that the journey can never end because the story is never-ending. When Satan attacks our bodies with sickness and diseases, we are quick to believe that our journey has come to an end, but if we believe what God said, then we know that healing is always ours, whether it be here on earth or in heaven with God.

Salvation is the never-ending story that we must hold on to as we travel this Christian journey. It began with our salvation and it will end in eternity –forever, Amen!

MY SPIRITUAL JOURNEY

In what ways has Satan tried to end my journey?

111

April 21
DEALING WITH OPPOSITION

The way of the wicked is an abomination unto the LORD; but he loveth him that followeth after righteousness. -Proverbs 15:9

When we are faced with opposition, we tend to talk back instead of listening. Being still puts us in a position to better hear and obey God than when we are constantly talking. There have been many times in my life when I have been persecuted, belittled, and put down. I was not prepared to deal with the situation; I either had a self pity party or didn't say what I should have said. But once I got home and talked it over with my husband, he encouraged me by saying, "It's okay. You will have an opportunity to redeem yourself. Just wait". Be still. God will give you a better opportunity to deal with the enemy at another time and another day.

He delivered me after over twenty years of working in an environment where Satan was in control. I didn't quit when times were tough. I cried, prayed, and kept going. Now I am reaping a good retirement check because God has provided for me.

MY SPIRITUAL JOURNEY

When dealing with opposition, do I tend to be still and listen to God or keep talking?

_____

_____

_____

_____

LOVE GOD

Jesus said unto him, Thou shalt love the Lord thy God with all thy heart, and with all thy soul, and with all thy mind. -Matthew 22:37

Many of us are cheating on God. Can we say that we are in a monogamous relationship with God? Cheating on God is putting people or things before Him. What people or things do we serve before we serve God? We can answer this question by determining where our time, money, and resources are spent and who they are helping. We give most of our time to the people or things that we love.

Some of us are like the lyrics: if our love for sports is wrong, we don't want to be right. If our love for fornication is wrong, we don't want to be right. If our love for food is wrong, we don't want to be right. If our love for television and movies is wrong, we don't want to be right. The list could go on and on. Only we know who or what is our first love. How many of us can declare that if loving God is wrong, we don't want to be right?

MY SPIRITUAL JOURNEY

What's in my life that I have refused to give up for God? What do I enjoy more than working for the ministry of Jesus Christ?

_____

_____

_____

_____

THE POWER OF A TESTIMONY

And they overcame him by the blood of the Lamb, and by the word of their testimony; and they loved not their lives unto the death. -Revelation 12:11

When Ashley gave her testimony of how God healed her from breast cancer, little did she know that there were several other women in the congregation who had been diagnosed with the same disease, some of whom had even been healed. When Carlton gave his testimony of how God had delivered him from cigarette smoking, he did not know that there were several other people in his class seriously thinking about stopping. When Jean gave her testimony of how God paid her mortgage on the day she was to be evicted, she did not know that there were several other people in the congregation facing almost the same dilemma.

When we refuse to share our testimony, we refuse to walk in victory. When we share our victory, we help inspire others to live victoriously. We should know that Christ defeated Satan at Calvary's cross, and from His blood that was shed, we have victory over any circumstance we encounter. Our victory over Satan is first in the **blood** and then in our **testimony**.

MY SPIRITUAL JOURNEY

How did it make me feel to know that God was using me to inspire others?

A BLESSED MAN

Blessed is the man that walketh not in the counsel of the ungodly, nor standeth in the way of sinners, nor sitteth in the seat of the scornful. But his delight is in the law of the LORD; and in his law doth he meditate day and night. -Psalm 1:1-2

What does a blessed man look like? To answer this question, we must first know what he doesn't look like and Psalm 1 tells us just that. In verse 1, the psalmist tells us that the blessed man doesn't walk in the counsel of the ungodly. In other words, he doesn't go searching for advice from those who don't know God. The psalmist continues to tell us in verse 1 that he doesn't stand in the way of sinners. In other words, he doesn't behave in such a way that it would keep the unsaved from coming to Christ. Lastly, in verse 1, the psalmist tells us that he doesn't sit in the seat of the scornful: he doesn't sit around ridiculing or belittling others.

In verse 2, the psalmist tells us that a blessed man's delight is in the word of God, and in God's word he meditates day and night. As a result of his taking in of the word of God daily, whatever ministries God has called him to do will prosper. Everything he does will prosper.

MY SPIRITUAL JOURNEY

Am I like the blessed man in verses one and two? Why do I think so?

_____

_____

_____

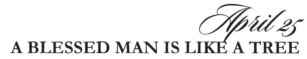
A BLESSED MAN IS LIKE A TREE

And he shall be like a tree planted by the rivers of water, that bringeth forth his fruit in his season; his leaf also shall not wither; and whatsoeer he doeth shall prosper. -Psalms 1:3

A blessed man is like a tree planted in the right position. If we want to be blessed, we must be planted in the family of God. We will miss some of our blessings if we decide to be planted on an island by ourselves to worship God.

A blessed man is not just planted, but he is planted with purpose. If we are planted right, we are to magnify God no matter the circumstances, and God will do the watering. A tree doesn't produce all the time, but it brings forth its fruit in its season. Christians should never give up because our season is coming. Today may be someone else's season, but keep serving God. All God's children have a season. Keep walking by faith. Your season is coming.

Finally a blessed man is like a tree because he is preserved to produce fruit for the kingdom of God. The Word of God says a blessed man's fruit will be preserved later and forever.

MY SPIRITUAL JOURNEY

Am I planted or positioned right?

_____

_____

_____

_____

_____

THE POWER OF THE EYE

The light of the body is the eye: if therefore thine eye be single, thy whole body shall be full of light. -Matthew 6:22

The man at the beautiful gate (Acts 3:2) could not see, just like the two men sitting on the side of the road when they heard Jesus was coming their way (Matthew 20:30). Before their healing, they were blind in two ways, physically and spiritually.

Matthew 6:22 tells us that the eye is the light of the body. In verse 23, Jesus tells us that if the eye looks on things that are good, then the whole body is good. How does what the eye look at make us good or bad? Our body desires what the eye sees. The eye sees everything: food, people, etc. The rest of the body sees nothing; therefore, it is subject to follow the eye. It's what the eye lusts for that causes the rest of our body to lust after good or evil. So, if the eye sees or seeks the things of God, we are in good shape. Similarly, if it seeks the things of the world, it is leading us astray. Keep your eyes focused on Jesus, and your body will be full of light.

MY SPIRITUAL JOURNEY

What do I see or seek?

_____

_____

_____

_____

SOLID AS A ROCK

And I say also unto thee, That thou art Peter and upon this rock I will build my church; and the gates of hell shall not prevail against it. -Matthew 16:18

Peter was always getting into trouble by saying or doing what he thought before he checked to see what Jesus wanted him to say or do. Yet, his intentions were good. Jesus knew that the day would come, after He had ascended into heaven, that Peter would become the leader of the Christian community in leading souls to Christ. Peter would stand boldly and firmly sharing the gospel of Jesus Christ. Peter was unstable in the beginning because he hadn't yet been baptized in the Holy Ghost. Once the Holy Ghost came upon him in Acts 2, he became solid as a rock.

Jesus didn't intend for Peter alone to be a rock for Him after He ascended into the heavens. He intended for all who believe to be rocks and to continue to build His church. He wants all of us to stand boldly and share the gospel in all the earth.

MY SPIRITUAL JOURNEY

How solid am I when it comes to being bold for Jesus? Am I a soft cushioning pillow, an orthopedic mattress, or solid as a rock?

118

April 28

A JOB WITH BENEFITS – PART I

Bless the LORD, O my soul: and all that is within me, bless his holy name. Bless the LORD, O my soul, and forget not all his benefits. -Psalm 103:1-2

Christians working for God are assured many benefits. David, in Psalm 103, inspires us not to forget them. In verse 3, David declares that He forgives all our iniquities. As many sins as we have, God forgives us for not some but all of them. He forgave us for them at Calvary's cross. Even now, if we confess our sins, He is so faithful and just that He will forgive us and cleanse us from the sins we don't even know we have committed (1 John 1:9).

David further declares that our health benefits are covered because God can cure all our diseases. In our benefit package, according to verse 4, God provides a life of peace and not destruction, a life of love and kindness. When we make mistakes, His mercy endures forever. Lastly, in verse 5, He pleases my taste with the good foods of the earth so that they keep me young. He alone is the secret to the fountain of youth. With benefits like these, why would we want to work for anyone else?

MY SPIRITUAL JOURNEY

What benefits does David declare in this lesson that I am not receiving?

_____

_____

_____

119

A JOB WITH BENEFITS – PART II

Bless the LORD, O my soul: and all that is within me, bless his holy name. Bless the LORD, O my soul, and forget not all his benefits. -Psalm 103:1-2

If working for God comes with such great benefits, why am I not receiving them? Many of us are not reaping the benefits of working for God because we are not blessing Him with all our soul. To bless God is to make Him happy or to honor Him. How do we bless Him with all our soul? What is the soul? The soul is made up of our mind, will, and emotions. Our mind is what we think. Do our thoughts bless God? Our will is what we want. Does what we want bless God? What we want ought to line up with what God wants or wills for us. Our emotions are what we feel.

What stirs us to bless God? When we are sad, happy, and excited about the same things as God, we bless Him. God is sad about the lost. God is happy about those of us who share salvation to the lost. God is excited about those who come to know Jesus as Lord and Savior. Bless the Lord, O my soul; and all that is within me, bless His holy name! Bless His name forevermore and receive all His benefits!

MY SPIRITUAL JOURNEY

What is keeping me from receiving God's benefits package?

IN HIS IMAGE

I will praise thee: for I am fearfully and wonderfully made: marvellous are thy works; and that my soul knoweth right well. -Psalm 139:14

The earth is God's and everything in it. It is God who is the maker of the heavens and the earth. He knows every star by name. It was God who created everything, including man, and then said about His work, "It is good." If it was good enough for God, then why isn't it good enough for us? God says that marvelous are His works, no matter how big or little, tall or short. He made our frames. The problem is not in God's craftsmanship. Rather, the problem is in our not realizing that we were created in the image of God.

God has made each temple beautiful and wonderful for His purpose. Our problem is that we keep letting society, and not God, decide our purpose. It is society, and not God who determines that we must look a certain way, wear certain clothes, hair styles and accessories, and have certain jobs to be recognized. If God gave you skinny legs, walk well in the spirit. If God gave you a big nose, hold it up high. If God gave you nappy hair, style it and go. If God gave you big eyes, seek out things that are good. Every person and every thing that God has made are fearfully and wonderfully made.

MY SPIRITUAL JOURNEY

How has society made me feel?

A WAY OUT

There hath no temptation taken you but such as is common to man: but God is faithful, who will not suffer you to be tempted above that ye are able; but will with the temptation also make a way to escape, that ye may be able to bear it. -1 Corinthians 10:13

As believers in Christ Jesus, it is good to strive to live a life holy and pleasing to God, but no matter how hard we try, there will be temptations. It is Satan's job to kill and destroy us with temptations. We need to know that we have victory over every temptation he tries to use against us. Paul said that every temptation we face would be common to us. "Common" here means that whatever temptations we face would be ordinary, general, or everyday, and that others would be facing the same temptations.

Paul concludes that with the temptation, God will make a way for us to escape. With every temptation, God has given us an exit door, if we want to escape. The answer to escaping temptations is through God. We can escape alcohol, drugs, fornication, pornography, gossip, lying, cheating, stealing, hatred, etc., if only we believe and accept the truths of God.

MY SPIRITUAL JOURNEY

What temptation have I faced and thought it was not common?

_____

_____

_____

_____

PAUL'S THORN

And lest I should be exalted above measure through the abundance of the revelations, there was given to me a thorn in the flesh, the messenger of Satan to buffet me, lest I should be exalted above measure. For this thing I besought the Lord thrice, that it might depart from me. -2 Corinthians 12:7-8

The apostle Paul had been given such a great vision from God that God allowed Satan to put a thorn in his flesh in order to keep him humble. No one knows for certain what Paul's thorn was, but we do know that he was in pain. Often times when Christians are ill, they refer to the illness as their thorn in the flesh. Paul's thorn is not everybody's thorn. He asked God three times to take the thorn away. According to verse 9, we know that God did not remove the thorn because He wanted Paul to remain humble.

Paul didn't just accept this thorn in the flesh without question, but he fellowshipped with God. In other words, he communicated with God, and God's answer was "no." Those who have fellowship with God hear His voice and obey. Those who don't are confused and stray.

MY SPIRITUAL JOURNEY

What are ailments in my life that I am certain are thorns from God?

_____

_____

_____

_____

PRAISING THE HELL OUT OF YOURSELF

Let the high praises of God be in their mouth, and a two-edged sword in their hand . . . this honour have all his saints. Praise ye the LORD.
-Psalm 149:6, 9b

Indeed, Christ died on the Cross for the forgiveness of our sins. Yet, the presence of sin, evil, and wickedness is still with us. However, God has given us a weapon to combat evil. Praise is an antidote for the anti-Christ. Praise and evil cannot exist in the same location. So, we can literally praise evil and wickedness away. We can praise the hell out of ourselves!

Many saints are most comfortable praising God when others praise along with them, but we need to be able to stand alone and praise the hell out of ourselves, all by ourselves –in spirit and in truth. Praise should not be done as a tactic to draw attention to oneself, but it should be done to glorify God. Praise should even be a part of our quiet time. Praising God should be a natural part of our everyday prayer and worship experience with God.

MY SPIRITUAL JOURNEY

Is praising God daily on my agenda?

Let them praise his name in the dance: let them sing praises unto him with
the timbrel and harp. -Psalm 149:3

Psalm 149:3a invites us to praise God with the dance. Again, praise should not be done as a tactic to draw attention to oneself, but it should be done to glorify God. If our focus is on others and what they think, then we need to stop and remember David's experience with his wife Michal (2 Samuel 6:16, 23). Michal was punished for her attitude about David praising God with the dance.

When attempting to praise God with the dance, Satan uses the spirit of intimidation, which is employed by the spirit of fear, to whisper things in our ears such as, "it doesn't take all that." Rebuke Satan and continue dancing.

Missing out on the opportunity to praise God in dance may have several consequences. First, it may limit our opportunities to enter into God's presence or may cause us to miss the joy of being truly liberated. Secondly, it may cause deadly sins of pride to exist in our lives. Thirdly, it may cause us to miss a joyful experience to literally shake the devil off.

MY SPIRITUAL JOURNEY

What are the benefits of my dancing before the Lord?

UPLIFTED HANDS

"Thus will I bless thee while I live: I will lift up my hands in thy name." -Psalm 63:4

Can the lifting of hands be an acceptable form of praise to God? According to Psalm 63:4, yes, it can. Other passages of scripture also speak of the lifting of hands as an instrument of praise to God. The lifting of hands is a universal sign of surrender. Someone who has not surrendered his or her life to God will not lift his or her hands in submission to Him. This person would rather continue using the hands for survival. Coming into God's presence with uplifted hands is like coming to His party with a pleasing gift. Refusal to bring uplifted hands to God's party is like being a party pooper. Party poopers don't get to fully enjoy the party favors. Party favors are part of the party's fun.

What are some of the party favors at God's party? Some of the party favors are singing, shouting, clapping, etc. Reaching up is just as important as reaching out. So lift those hands up and bless the Lord!

MY SPIRITUAL JOURNEY

Has praising God with uplifted hands been like going to His party? Will I continue to be a party pooper at His party?

_____

_____

_____

_____

WITH THANKSGIVING

"Enter into his gates with thanksgiving; and into his courts with praise: be thankful unto him, and bless his name. -Psalm 100:4

D on't run the risk of serving God with sadness. Be thankful unto Him and bless His name. Thankfulness to God is a result of an attitude of gratitude. What better way to show gratitude to God than to praise Him with thanksgiving? Thank Him for His goodness. Thank Him for His mercy. Thank Him for His kindness. Thank Him when Satan tries to tell you that it was all your doing and not God's doing.

Satan has a tendency to try and put the spirit of pride in us regarding accomplishments. Satan's spirit of pride says to us, "Why are you thanking God for that? He didn't make it possible. You worked hard and did that all by yourself." "Why are you doing all that; it doesn't take all that." It is left up to us to give God the thanks He is due. We are to thank Him for the good and the bad.

MY SPIRITUAL JOURNEY

For what am I thankful? Thank You God for:

.

_____

_____

_____

_____

_____

_____

_____

Praise ye the LORD. Sing unto the LORD a new song, and his praise in the congregation of saints. -Psalm 149:1

Singing is eternal. Start practicing on this side to prepare for the other side. Bible study will be over one day, but singing will never end. Singing is not limited to those who have the talent to sing, it is universal. God instructed us to make a joyful noise unto Him, not a beautiful noise. Someone with the talent to sing can make a beautiful noise without it being joyful. Singing is the most user-friendly form of praise.

Music and singing are God's primary means to praise and worship Him. Failure to praise God with a song may cause us to miss out on the most convenient way of showing love to God.

Singing to God is just as appropriate in private worship as it is in corporate worship. What freedom it is to make a joyful noise unto God in the privacy of our own homes.

MY SPIRITUAL JOURNEY

Is singing a regular part of my everyday lifestyle or do I wait for the choir on Sunday?

_____

_____

_____

_____

_____

Bring all the tithes into the storehouse, that there may be food in My house, and prove me now therewith saith the Lord of hosts, if I will not open you the windows of heaven, and pour you out a blessing, that there shall not be room enough to receive it. -Malachi 3:10

Tithing is just as demonstrative and important to God as uplifted hands, singing, and clapping. Malachi 3:10 commands us to bring the tithe (10%) into God's house. Tithing is about trusting God, and not our paycheck, as our provider. The question is often asked, "Do I tithe on the gross or on the net?" And the answer is, "Do you want to be blessed on the gross or on the net?" Tithing is a weapon available to all saints to be used in spiritual warfare. God has even promised that if we praise and worship Him through the tithe, He will rebuke the devourer from our resources (Malachi 3:11).

Failure to use tithing as a form of praise and worship is an indication of our not being in a perfect relationship with God. Not tithing says to Him that we do not trust Him. It also forfeits our opportunity to be a participating partner in business or personal finances with God. Lastly, we miss the marvelous opportunity to praise the spirit of doubt out of ourselves.

MY SPIRITUAL JOURNEY

How has tithing been a praise experience for me?

Praise ye the LORD. Praise, O ye servants of the LORD, praise the name of the LORD.
Blessed be the name of the LORD from this time forth and for evermore. -Psalm 113:1-2

"Remember, your name is McCalep" was a reminder from my father that my name meant that I was expected to be respectful and well behaved. Mighty is the name of God. It is in His name that we find out who He is and discover His manifold nature and character. God wants us to know Him through His names as listed:

Jehovah-Jireh   He is our provider.

Jehovah-Rophe   He is our healer.

Jehovah-Nissi   The Lord our banner.

Jehovah-M'Kaddesh   The Lord our sanctifier.

Jehovah-Shalom   The Lord is our peace.

Jehovah-Saboath   The Lord of hosts.

Jehovah-Rohi   The Lord is our Shepherd.

Jehovah-Tsidkenu   The Lord of our righteousness.

Jehovah-Shammah   The Lord is present with us.

God's name is so powerful that we can praise the hell out of ourselves in His name alone.

MY SPIRITUAL JOURNEY

How can I personally say that I know God?

HALLELUJAH!

Then I heard what sounded like a great multitude, like the roar of rushing waters and like loud peals of thunder, shouting: "Hallelujah! For our Lord God Almighty reigns. Let us rejoice and be glad and give him glory!
-Revelation 19:6-7a

Hallelujah holds the honor of denoting the highest praise to God. Like gold, hallelujah has universal value. It has no language or cultural boundaries. It can be integrated into singing, dancing, the lifting of hands, and physically bowing down before the Lord. Any way we choose to come into God's presence, we can come in with hallelujah.

The word "Halla" means to brag or boast, and the word 'jah' means God. The only noun missing is you. We are the ones who need to begin bragging and boasting about God. We need to boast on who He is and brag on what He has done. To participate in an assured universal communication and common denominator with Christians all over the world, simply shout Hallelujah! Hallelujah!

MY SPIRITUAL JOURNEY

Is hallelujah a part of my daily worship experience? Why?

_____

_____

_____

_____

_____

JOY DOWN IN MY SOUL

Thou wilt shew me the path of life: In thy presence is fullness of joy; at thy right hand are pleasures for evermore.-Psalm 16:11

What is joy? Holman's Bible Dictionary defines joy as "The happy state that results from knowing and serving God...The fruit of a right relationship with God." It is not something people can create by their own efforts. Joy in the Christian life is in direct proportion to a Christian's walk with the Lord. In Ephesians 1:3, the apostle Paul revealed his excitement about the worthiness of God. God has blessed us with spiritual blessings; therefore, we, too, must become excited and testify about what God has already done.

Paul understood what it meant to have joy. This man was one who was able to sing songs of praise while in jail. Paul got "caught up" in his praise. A believer who understands what it means to have joy knows that joy can only come from God. Joy has nothing to do with our circumstances, but it has everything to do with who God is in our lives. A believer who understands what it means to have joy also knows that spiritual blessings far outweigh material blessings because material blessings are temporary and spiritual blessings are eternal.

MY SPIRITUAL JOURNEY

How does knowing God give me joy?

DEPENDENT GRACE

For by grace are ye saved through faith; and that not of yourselves: it is the gift of God. -
Ephesians 2:8

Once a father and daughter's boat capsized. The father swam back to shore. Before he left his young daughter, he asked her, "Do you remember when Daddy taught you how to float?" She replied, "Yes, Daddy, I remember." Her father instructed her to float on the water until he returned for her. After searching and not finding the young girl, the Coast Guard presumed her to be dead. However, the father convinced them to go out looking for her once more. This time they found her. She was alive and content singing a song! Why so content they asked? She replied, "My Daddy told me he would come back and get me. My Daddy always keeps his promises."

Grace is God's unmerited favor, or undeserved goodness, a gift that we receive from Him. As we grow up in grace, we become more dependent upon God, not independent. Until we become dependent upon our heavenly God, like the little girl in the story was dependent upon her earthly father, we will never fully experience God's grace.

MY SPIRITUAL JOURNEY

In what ways do I depend upon God?

May 13

TEAR DOWN THOSE WALLS

And that he might reconcile both unto God in one body by the cross, having slain the enmity thereby. -Ephesians 2:16

When Jesus saved us, He created a new personhood. He made a new being: one body, the Church. God melted down every barrier and raised up a new being -one person, one body, one baptism, one Spirit (Ephesians 4:5-6).

Walls of denominationalism divide good Christians, preventing fellowship and praise together to the one true God. Walls of tradition separate us and keep people from coming to God.

How many Christians are fighting to hold on to meaningless, church traditions simply because "it's always been that way"? God is calling the church to break down the walls of racism, traditionalism, denominationalism, or any other obstacle that would prevent a person from being saved. Let's remember that Christ tore down every wall that separates us from Him. We should not create new ones because they would not be of Christ.

MY SPIRITUAL JOURNEY
What needless walls have I built up that keep me from loving others? What am I willing to change in order to correct my behavior?

_____

_____

_____

_____

A LIFE WITH PURPOSE

According to the eternal purpose which he purposed in Christ Jesus our Lord.
-Ephesians 3:11

L iving to fulfill God's purpose is the key to being fruitful and fulfilled. When we have His purpose in our lives, we have joy, peace, and contentment.

To fulfill God's purpose for us, we must direct our lives to seek and share the saving knowledge of Jesus Christ to unsaved people. Jesus' focal purpose was to seek and to save. It should be ours as well. Jesus directed us to be a witness of Him (Matthew 24:14).

How can we witness to the lost? First, we must develop a sincere burden for lost people. Look for opportunities to share the gospel everywhere we go. Secondly, we must learn to love sinners more and tell them what Jesus has done for us. Thirdly, we must not be afraid of not knowing the answer to all questions. We must seek answers in the word of God and be prepared for the next time. Fourthly, we must invite someone to church regularly. Fifthly, we must participate in evangelistic efforts at our church.

MY SPIRITUAL JOURNEY

Do my individual purposes align with God's purpose for the Church?

IMITATORS FOR CHRIST

And that ye put on the new man, which after God is created in righteousness and true holiness. -Ephesians 4:24

In the movie, "The Color Purple," the character played by Oprah Winfrey, Sophia, was recalling a day when Miss Celie, played by Whoopie Goldberg, came to her aid. Sophia explained, "When I see'd you ... I know'd the'y is a God." Miss Celie had shown God's love to Sophia at a time when she could not see it on her own. As Christians, people should see us and know there is a God because we have imitated Him so well. We can never be Him, but we can continue to grow in His likeness. God uses us to reveal Himself.

We should live and conduct ourselves in a way that causes others to see the love of God in us. If we imitate Him, as we grow in His likeness, we will do what He does. Imitators of Christ are 'knock-offs' of the original, or very good imitations. There are well-made "knock-offs" and poorly made "knock-offs" within the body of Christ. People should see us and know that God exists because we have imitated Him so well.

MY SPIRITUAL JOURNEY

Who do people say I look like? Does anyone ever say I look like Jesus?

_____

_____

_____

_____

May 16

HIS SPIRIT LIVES WITHIN ME

And be not drunk with wine, wherein is excess; but be filled with the Spirit.
-Ephesians 5:18

When the Holy Spirit fills us, He consumes, empowers and uses us for the purposes of God. Luke 1:15, reveals to us that John the Baptist and his mother Elizabeth were filled with The Holy Spirit. After John's birth, old, doubting, mute Zacharias was filled with the Holy Spirit! God opened his mouth, and Zacharias began to bless the name of the Lord. Peter, the Disciple, and Stephen, the Great Deacon (Acts 6:5a), were also filled with the Holy Spirit. Paul, the Apostle, was filled with the Holy Spirit on the road to Damascus (Acts 9:17), and Jesus, the Son of God, was also filled with the Spirit when He returned from the Jordan (Luke 4:1).

When we surrender our lives to Christ and stay on the spiritual journey, God will fill us with the Holy Spirit to abide in us forever.

MY SPIRITUAL JOURNEY

Does God's Spirit live within me? What is the evidence?

_____

_____

_____

_____

_____

_____

LOVE GOD AND MAN

Jesus saith unto him, Thou shalt love the Lord thy God with all thy heart, and with all thy soul, and with all thy mind. This is the first and great commandment. And the second is like unto it, thou shalt love thy neighbor as thyself. —Matthew 22:37-39

Jesus clearly stated in Matthew 22:36-40 that relationship is the essential principle to individual, spiritual, and Church growth. We have a responsibility to establish a relationship with God and man. Our relationship with God is vertical, as our relationship with each other is horizontal. There are six necessary relationships relative to spiritual growth:

(1) Pastor and God – The head of the church leadership should have a personal relationship with God. (2) Members and God - Personal relationship with God. (3) Pastors should – Work to mend relationships with members. (4) Members and Pastor – Don't fight but pray for their pastor. (5) Members and Members – Don't dislike, but love each other. (6) Church and Community – Be proactive with the community and mission field relative to relationships.

MY SPIRITUAL JOURNEY

As I examine my own relationships, which do I believe may be causing an imbalance?

_____

_____

_____

_____

SUBMISSION- HUSBAND AND WIFE

Submitting yourselves one to another in the fear of God. -Ephesians 5:21

Ephesians 5:22-33 deals primarily with the marriage relationship. Our problem is that most of us want to skip past verse 21, which tells us to honor Christ by submitting to one another. Husbands are quick to point out to their wives that they are supposed to submit to them. In their haste to point out the wife's failure, husbands sometimes overlook where they have fallen in the area of mutual submission. Mutual submission means acknowledging one another's gifts and putting egos aside so that the marital relationship can grow. That means, for example, if a husband is not as knowledgeable about money management as his wife, he should not hold to a sense of false interpretation of head of household.

Verse 22 says for wives to submit to their husbands. This is a self-chosen Spiritual submission that cannot be forced upon her by the husband or anyone else. When done in the Spirit, it has nothing to do with superiority or inferiority. It is equal submitting to equal for the harmony of the marriage and the family, just as it is with Christ and the Church.

MY SPIRITUAL JOURNEY

Am I honoring verse 21 by submitting one to another?

_____

_____

_____

FAMILY SUBMISSION

Children, obey your parents in the Lord: for this is right. Honour thy father and mother;...
That it may be well with thee, and thou mayest live long on the earth...fathers, provoke not
your children to wrath: -Ephesians 6:2-4

E phesians 6:1-4 deals with the obligations of both parents and children to maintain family harmony. Children are reminded to obey their parents, but parents are reminded to carry themselves in a manner worthy of being obeyed. Parents are not to provoke their children. Family relationships are crucial to our ability to grow up spiritually. It is our responsibility to unify our primary relationships.

How can a preacher accept the authority to share God's Word from the pulpit yet ignore the role of provider and caregiver in his home?

How can a pastor preach to his wife when she knows he has been unfaithful to her? How can a youth minister prepare young people for adulthood when his own daughter barely speaks to him? The sad truth is that such relationships happen all of the time within our churches, and we ignore them rather than confront and try to mend them.

MY SPIRITUAL JOURNEY

What are some key Biblical principals I use to keep harmony in my home?

PROFESSIONAL RELATIONSHIPS

Submitting yourselves one to another in the fear of God. —Ephesians 5:21

It's easy to be loving and caring toward those who demonstrate love, care, and concern toward us. Christians who work in environments where religion is suppressed or frowned upon have been given a great responsibility to show love where there is none. Establishing professional relationships in the workplace can be done by following God's word.

Paraphrasing what Paul says about master/slave relationship, employees are to be obedient to employers. Work for employers as though we are working for God Himself; Work for employers with a cheerful heart; God will repay us for doing good to our employers. The employee should yield to the employer, the higher authority, but the employer, the one holding that authority, must not abuse the privilege. Employees and Employers – submit yourselves one to the other (Ephesians 5:22).

MY SPIRITUAL JOURNEY

What is my work environment like?

_____

_____

_____

_____

_____

_____

DOING GOOD WRONG

Take heed that ye do not your alms before men, to be seen of them: otherwise ye have no reward of your Father which is in heaven. -Matthew 6:1

Jesus uses the word "alms" to teach us how to give. The word "alms" is not a term we use often, but it means righteous acts. It means giving financial duties and service without an expectation of receiving money. If we are going to fulfill the purposes that God has given us, saints must step up to the plate to give their service without the expectation of getting paid.

Jesus says there are three things we must do, and they are to give, pray, and fast. Giving, praying, and fasting are Christian duties. He even warned us to be careful to not do these things for the wrong reasons, thus forfeiting our blessings. Simply put, we should not do good just to be seen by others because when we do so, we receive our reward from men. Nor should we sound the trumpet as the hypocrites do in the synagogue and in the streets so that we get glory from men. The good we do should be in secret. Our Father, who sees in secret, will then reward us openly.

MY SPIRITUAL JOURNEY

What is my motive in giving?

_____

_____

_____

_____

PRAYING WRONG

And when thou prayest, thou shalt not be as the hypocrites are: for they love to pray standing in the synagogues and in the corners of the streets, that they may be seen of men. Verily I say unto you, they have their reward. -Matthew 6:5

J esus teaches us in Matthew 6:5-15 that our prayers can be wrong and hypocritical. We can even become addicted to praying. Being addicted to praying is to allow prayer to become habit-forming. We begin to love the sound of our own prayers.

We can love to pray so much that we love to pray more than we love our God to whom we're praying. Praise is also a part of prayer. Some people can praise until it becomes habit forming to the point that it becomes self glorifying. One problem with our prayers is empty repetition. Yet another is not thinking about what we are saying because our mind may be somewhere else.

There are three great rules for praying outlined in verse 7. One, don't speak too much. Two, don't use vain repetition. Three, trust God when praying.

MY SPIRITUAL JOURNEY

How repetitive am I when I pray and why?

_____

_____

_____

_____

_____

PRAY RIGHT

*Likewise the Spirit also helpeth our infirmities: for we know not what
we should pray for as we ought: but the Spirit itself maketh intercession
for us with groanings which cannot be uttered. -Romans 8:26*

God answers all prayers with either, "yes", "no" or "wait",
but not all prayers have the right motive. The Holy Spirit
knows our motives. When our motives are wrong, the
Holy Spirit intercedes on our behalf and prays to God for what
we really need (Romans 8:26).

A man prays, "Lord, I need a fancy new car. My neighbors have
new cars, and they aren't even saved." He's not ready. His motive
is wrong so God's answer is "wait." His car breaks down so he has
to catch the bus, and he's getting to work late. Suddenly the man
looks up towards heaven and says, "Lord, please send me a car."
Now he's ready to be blessed. The Father's answer now is "yes"
and includes some of the trimmings like a sunroof. God didn't
have a problem with the man being specific, but he did have a
problem with his motive.

MY SPIRITUAL JOURNEY
Are there times when I pray, and I don't have the right motive?

_____

_____

_____

_____

_____

RIGHT POSITION

And when thou prayest, thou shalt not be as the hypocrites are: for they love to pray standing in the synagogues and in the corners of the streets, that they may be seen of men. Verily I say unto you, they have their reward. -Matthew 6:5

Having the right position before God is just as important as the prayer we pray. You may stand, fall down, or turn toward the wall. The stance is not the most important thing; it is the position of the heart. Our hearts should be free of debris so we can openly confess all to Him, whether physically bowing or using other manners of turning towards Him.

Being spiritually naked before God is coming before Him as an empty vessel, ready to fulfill His purposes. God wants us to go into our closet and get naked, take off our selfishness, pride, and independence and fall down before Him. Don't be ashamed. Close the door. He's the Father who brought us into the world. He knows every sin we have committed. There is no need to put on a façade. God knows.

MY SPIRITUAL JOURNEY

In what position is my heart when I pray to God?

_____

_____

_____

_____

_____

Moreover when ye fast, be not, as the hypocrites, of a sad countenance:
for they disfigure their faces, that they may appear unto men to fast.
Verily I say unto you, they have their reward. -Matthew 6:16

Matthew 6:16 says, "When we fast," and not, "If we fast." Fasting is not optional for those of us who claim to be believers in Christ Jesus. It is imperative. Those who are medically challenged should consider sacrificially giving up something other than food.

Jesus urged us not to look sad or deprived of food when we fast so that others might feel sorry for us or think we are so holy for fasting. He urged us instead to anoint our head and wash our face so that no one knows we are fasting. When we fast to grow closer to God and for our prayers to be answered, fasting should be done without notice. Religious people fast before men, but Christians fast before God. We can't accept the praises of man and give God the glory at the same time. The more recognition or credit we seek or accept, the less glory God gets.

MY SPIRITUAL JOURNEY

Is fasting a regular part of my spiritual discipline? Why or why not?

_____

_____

_____

_____

May 26

FOUR TIMES TO FAST

Howbeit this kind goeth not out but by prayer and fasting. -Matthew 17:21

There are four times the believer should fast. The believer should fast when feeling an urge or pull to get closer to God. I believe it was fasting that caused me to be still and dependent enough on God so that I truly sought His will for my life.

The believer should fast when a special need arises. There are times when we desperately need to hear from God e.g. when we are seeking healing, deliverance, or are in financial crisis. Matthew 17:21 declares that some deliverances can only be cast out through fasting and praying.

The believer should fast when humility is needed. We sometimes get prideful. Pride is a spirit that is not of God. We sometimes need to fast so that God can convict us of pride, while restoring our humility. Finally, the believer should fast when there is a need for Holy Ghost power.

MY SPIRITUAL JOURNEY

Is there a reason for me to fast today?

____

____

____

____

____

BENEFITS OF FASTING

That thou appear not unto men to fast, but unto thy Father which is in secret: and thy Father, which seeth in secret, shall reward thee openly. -Matthew 6:18

There are great benefits in fasting. Fasting keeps us coming in the presence of God, bringing us closer to Him. Fasting humbles our soul before God. Fasting teaches us to be dependent on God. Fasting demonstrates to God our seriousness about loving and serving Him.

Fasting helps us refrain from being enslaved by a habit. I like to eat at night and from time to time top off my nightly eating habit with lots of ice cream. Fasting helped me to eliminate this habit.

God needs healthy and prepared vessels. We are called to be those vessels so that we may magnify God, but overall, the greatest benefit of fasting is to **glorify God**.

MY SPIRITUAL JOURNEY

What am I not willing to sacrifice in order to fast?

_____

_____

_____

_____

_____

_____

_____

A BLESSED CUP

Ye cannot drink the cup of the Lord, and the cup of devils: ye cannot be partakers of the Lord's table, and of the table of devils. -1 Corinthians 10:21

The Christian's alcohol drinking days should be over. Someone may be thinking, "There is no harm in having a little sip." There are two reasons why Christians shouldn't drink alcoholic beverages. First, God tells us that our bodies are the temple of the Holy Ghost. Jesus lives in us. We shouldn't want God living in an alcoholic environment.

Secondly, God tells us in 1 Corinthians 8:13 that we ought not eat or drink anything that causes someone else to stumble. We may be strong enough to take a little sip, but our drinking might cause someone not as controlled or responsible as we are to not stop at a sip. For these two reasons alone, Christians should neither sip, buy, nor sell alcoholic beverages.

MY SPIRITUAL JOURNEY

Am I still defiling the Lord's temple (my body) with alcoholic beverages?

_____

_____

_____

_____

_____

_____

A BLESSED CUP

Blessed be the God and Father of our Lord Jesus, who hath blessed us with all spiritual blessings in heavenly places in Christ. -Ephesians 1:3

There is a spiritual cup God wants us to have, but we don't obtain it through a whiskey bottle. The cup Jesus passed to us is a blessed cup, and everyone should want to drink from it.

The Israelite males were not smitten because God instructed Moses to take a lamb, sacrifice it, dip a hyssop branch in the blood, and mark it over the door of the Israelite homes so that the death angel when seeing the blood would pass over their homes, sparing their first born males.

Now, over 2000 years later, Jesus has become the ultimate reason for our Passover celebration. Jesus was the lamb crucified. He shed His blood, not just for the Israelites, but for all mankind. When death comes knocking on our doors, those of us washed in the blood will pass over into eternal life. Christ is our Passover. Christ is the reason we can now sit at the communion table called The Lord's Supper and drink from the Blessed Cup.

MY SPIRITUAL JOURNEY

Jesus has passed to me a blessed cup. How am I drinking from that cup?

And no man putteth new wine into old bottles; else the new wine will burst the bottles, and be spilled, and the bottles shall perish.   But new wine must be put into new bottles; and both are preserved. Luke 5:37-38

New wine needs to be poured into a new cup. The blood of Christ is the new wine that gets poured into the believer. When salvation is poured into the believer, he or she becomes a new cup. The Holy Spirit continuously pours new wine into the believer. The Holy Spirit is too good and too powerful for old cups. Pouring new wine into old cups is wrong (Luke 5:37-39).

Christians can't keep on drinking from the cup of the world which includes greed, lust, gossip, anger, or pride. We need a new cup for the power of the Holy Spirit for two reasons. The first reason we need a new cup is to handle the bubbling. When new wine gets in us, something starts moving. A transformation of fermentation starts to take place, but if we don't have a new cup, it will all spill out. The second reason we need a new cup is to keep the wine sweet. When new wine is poured into a vessel that has no foreign substances, it becomes sealed with the Holy Spirit until the day of redemption.

MY SPIRITUAL JOURNEY

What is in my cup that needs to be cleaned out?

_____

_____

_____

THE RIGHT CUPS

And be not conformed to this world: but be ye transformed by the renewing of your mind, that ye may prove what is that good, and acceptable, and perfect, will of God. -Romans 12:2

There are three cups the believer needs in order to keep our wine from turning sour. First, the cup of transformation represents change in our lives, changing our way of thinking. Romans 12:2 commands us not to be conformed to this world but to be transformed by the renewing of our minds. Being transformed means no longer flirting and getting high on the lusts of the world.

The second cup is the cup Jesus took in the Garden of Gethsemane. It was a bitter and sin-filled cup. All our lying, stealing, drinking, pot smoking, lust, and more are in this cup. This was the cup of forgiveness Jesus took, and He is asking us to take today.

The third cup is the cup of celebration which we take when we participate in the Lord's Supper. We should celebrate Jesus' death as often as we can until He comes again.

MY SPIRITUAL JOURNEY

From what cup am I drinking?

_____

_____

_____

_____

_____

AT THE TABLE

Thou preparest a table before me in the presence of mine enemies:
thou anoinest my head with oil; my cup runneth over. -Psalm 23:5

God doesn't serve little servings. When He serves, our cups run over. Not only has He prepared a table for us, but He also prepared it in the presence of our enemies, declaring us victorious. There is also a special anointing at God's table. He anoints our head first because oil drips, and when it drips, it does so from top to bottom, covering us from head to toe. This special anointing ushers in the infilling of the Holy Ghost so that when we come to God's table, we will be filled abundantly.

There is also contentment at God's table. The psalmist declares that he will dwell in the house of the Lord forever. Sometimes we run here and there looking for contentment and satisfaction in alcohol, drugs, work, and other people, but we leave discontented and empty each time. There is what I call, "a God hole" in each of us, and the only thing we can put into "a God hole" is God. We were created for His pleasure and purpose; therefore, trying to put something else in the "God hole" is like trying to put a square peg in a round hole. It will not fit!

MY SPIRITUAL JOURNEY

In what areas of my life have I refused all that God has offered me at His table?

CONQUERING THE MOUNTAINS

And Joshua spake unto the house of Joseph, even to Ephraim and to Manasseh, saying,
Thou art a great people, and hast great power: thou shalt not have one lot only.
-Joshua 17:17

Many of us believe ourselves to be a great people, and we want a bigger piece of the pie. God is saying, "Yes you are a great people, a Royal Priesthood because I have made you great, but the free land has already been handed out." (Affirmative Action, welfare, and food stamps have been handed out and are about to die).

If we want the mountaintop, we have to prepare and work for it. How do we work for it? We work for it by using the skills and talents to the best of our abilities while trusting God more. We prepare for it by increasing our spiritual capacity (reading the bible daily, praying and fasting) to fight against the wiles of the devil. We've got to get over the hill of fear, doubt and unbelief, pride, and self-righteousness and trust God to do great things.

MY SPIRITUAL JOURNEY

What are some of the struggles I have encountered or am avoiding that are keeping me from reaching the mountaintop?

_____

_____

_____

_____

_____

A SPIRITUAL JUMPSTART

Not slothful in business; fervent in spirit; serving the Lord; -Romans 12:11

Do you recall how we were on fire for the Lord when we first got saved? We were on fire because we were excited about what God had done for us, but then life's problems started to weigh down on our spiritual battery. Spirit killers of the world began to work on and drag our battery down, and now we need a jumpstart; we need our hearts to be regenerated.

When corrosion gets on a car battery, it has to be cleaned off with acid or a cola. Then there are times when a battery only needs water to make it run more effectively. There are other times when we need to pull out jumper cables and give the car a jumpstart. Once we properly connect the cables and give the car some gas, the car runs smoothly.

The same is true with the Christian faith. There are times when we only need to begin to praise God and to give Him thanks in order to get our spiritual batteries charged and going again. There are other times when we have to hook up our spiritual battery with God's spiritual cable, the Holy Spirit.

MY SPIRITUAL JOURNEY
At what times have I had to jumpstart my spiritual battery?

June 4
GETTING HOT FOR GOD
Not slothful in business; fervent in spirit; serving the Lord. -Romans 12:11

The problem of many Christians is the sin of apathy. Apathy means to be indifferent, unresponsive, sleepy, and lethargic. Apathy comes from a Greek word meaning no feeling, the same as anesthesia. Anesthesia is used in the dentist's office for the purpose of numbing. Satan is gradually putting the church in a state of numbness. Some of us have overdosed and are literally in a coma. Fire in the pulpit and frost in the pews is a sign of apathy. Lukewarm giving and witnessing is also a sign of apathy.

Satan's drugs have us in a schizophrenic state that says, "If you praise God, everyone is going to be looking at you." It's time to take our Holy Ghost pills at home so that we can come into the sanctuary with boldness and courage, surrendering true praise to our God. It's time for the body of Christ to get hot for God. It's time to rebuke the devourer and praise the hell out of ourselves. God created us for the purpose of praising and worshiping Him. One Christian on fire will light up another.

MY SPIRITUAL JOURNEY
Do I allow Satan to hinder my praising God? If yes, how will I overcome? Perfect love casts out fear.

_____

_____

_____

_____

HEARKEN AND BE BLESSED

… if thou shalt hearken diligently unto the voice of he LORD thy God, to observe and to do all his commandments which I command thee this day, that the LORD thy God will set thee on high above all nations of the earth. -Deuteronomy 28:1

God is the promise keeper who has signed a contract with us to bless us and supply all of our needs, if we obey His commandments. The "ifs" and "buts" of disobedience prevent us from receiving His promises.

In Deuteronomy 28, God gave to Moses and the Israelites a promissory covenant to bless them, and it is valid for us today. God promises **first** of all to bless us in the city and in the **fields** in obedience to Him. Secondly, God promises to bless our **produce**. Whatever we produce, He will increase if we just keep sowing and planting. He promises to bless our basket in the store. Thirdly, God will bless our travel, if we remain obedient to Him. Fourthly, He promises to bless our coming in and our going out. Lastly, He promises that if we hearken to Him, He will cause our enemy to be smitten in our face. He will say to the devil, "In your face," and send him running. Hearken to the voice of God and be blessed. Obedience is better than sacrifice.

MY SPIRITUAL JOURNEY

What "ifs" or "buts" of disobedience are keeping me from receiving the blessings of God?

Being justified freely by His grace through the redemption that is in Christ Jesus.
-Romans 3:24

O ur second response to the fact that Jesus has provided us a note with a zero balance is to be moved with fear and with joy. I stayed out of a lot of trouble not because I was so good but because I was scared of my daddy's left hand belt strap. Not only was I scared of my daddy's belt strap, but I also feared hurting him because I knew that he was one of the few people in the world who loved me.

Knowing the wrath of our heavenly Father should do the same for us. We ought to be afraid of the wrath of God. I'm scared not to tithe. God loves us. We ought to be scared of hurting Him. What a marvelous mix of emotion it is to tremble because we fear the Lord but in the midst have joy. I'm scared, but I'm happy. He died, but He lives. Let's take that heavy debt from our shoulders and be glad that God has given us a zero balance.

MY SPIRITUAL JOURNEY

Am I fearful of the wrath of God? Do I even believe that God punishes me?

_____

_____

_____

_____

_____

And thus are the saints of his heart made manifest; and so falling down on his face,
he will worship God and report that God is among you. -1 Corinthians 14:25b

---

Our third appropriate response to the fact that Jesus has provided us a note with a zero balance is to worship Him. When the Marys met the risen Savior, they grabbed His feet and worshipped Him. When the disciples met the risen Savior, they held his feet and worshipped him.

When we realize we can't add to that zero balance of the shackles having been taken off our feet, setting us free from the pit of hell, we need to cry out, "Hallelujah!" When we think about God's merciful kindness and love and all He had to do to become the risen Savior, we ought to fall down and worship Him. Worship Him because He is worthy to be worshipped. Revelation 19:10 says, worship God: for the testimony of Jesus is the spirit of prophecy.

MY SPIRITUAL JOURNEY

How do I worship God?

_____

_____

_____

_____

_____

_____

God declares that the effectual fervent prayer of the righteous avails much. One of our problems is not believing ourselves to be the righteous. When people refer to us as righteous, though they may mean it negatively, we sometimes become shy or offended. Instead, we should stand boldly and proclaim that to be righteous is our goal and desire because of the love we have for our Lord and Savior.

Many of us think God does not hear our prayers because we are not right with Him, but the blood of Jesus is what makes us right with God. There is nothing we can do to earn being right with God other than to accept Jesus Christ, His son, as our Lord and Savior. There are times when we fall away from God, but 1 John 1:19 tells us that if we confess our sins, we serve a God who is faithful and just to cleanse us from all unrighteousness, restoring us back into a right relationship with Him through our prayers of confession and repentance.

MY SPIRITUAL JOURNEY
How do I feel about being called or considered righteous?

_____

_____

_____

_____

FERVENT PRAYER

The effectual fervent prayer of the righteous availeth much. -James 5:16b

---

Another problem we have is not praying prayers that are fervent. According to scripture, our prayers need to be effectual and fervent. Prayers that are effectual are powerful. The word "fervent" means hot or intense. Our prayers need to be powerful, hot, and intensified.

An effectual prayer should have an effect on someone. Too often, we recite prayers that sound good and affect others, but God is not moved by them. He is the one who should be affected by our prayers. God wants to hear from our heart, just as He heard from Hannah's in 1 Samuel. Hannah desired to have a child. Because she prayed with such fervency, her prayer had an effect on God, causing Him to grant her request. Hannah's prayer availed much.

MY SPIRITUAL JOURNEY
The word "effectual" means working. Are my prayers working for me?

_____

_____

_____

_____

_____

_____

_____

PRAYER THAT AVAILS MUCH

If ye abide in me, and my words abide in you, ye shall ask what ye will, and it shall be done unto you. -John 15:7

When the righteous pray, our prayers ought to accomplish a lot. However, many of us are accomplishing very little, if anything, because our prayers need to be effectual and fervent by praying the word. John 15:7 reads, "If ye abide in me and my words abide in you, ye shall ask what ye will and it shall be done unto you." The key is to have God's word embedded in our hearts. When the word is embedded in our hearts, we will pray it back to God.

The Holy Spirit is our guide and teacher. Just as a teacher gets excited when she knows her pupil learns what she is trying to teach, I believe The Holy Spirit gets excited when we speak the word of God that He has been trying to teach us. Praying the word of God with intensity will get His attention. When we pray the specific word of God, and not a generalized prayer, we accomplish much.

MY SPIRITUAL JOURNEY

Is there a prayer I normally pray, when I pray? Write it here.

_____

_____

_____

_____

_____

SPECIFIC PRAYERS

Confess your faults one to another, and pray one for another, that ye may be healed.
-James 5:16a

God has given us instructions on how to handle circumstances. We have been taught that when trouble arises, we are to pray. The problem is that most Christians don't know what to pray for. We tend to pray the same thing over and over regardless of the circumstance. If we want to avail much, then we need to be specific in our prayers.

When we are in trouble, many of us get on our knees and pray, "Lord have mercy on me. I need your help Lord. I just can't make it without you." Perhaps your prayer is not the same as the above example, but it may be quite similar. God will honor it due to the fact that we asked and trusted Him enough to help us with our circumstance. However, if we want our prayers to accomplish much, then we must learn to pray specific prayers that address our circumstances. Remember, Jesus said in James 4:2d, "You do not have, because you do not ask God."(NIV)

MY SPIRITUAL JOURNEY

What circumstance am I facing right now about which I need to be specific?

163

Hear my prayer, O Lord, and let my cry come unto thee. -Psalm 102:1

When doctors announce we have an illness or disease, they are specific about ailments. We need the doctor's facts to gain knowledge of how we should pray. Though his diagnosis may be factual and true, the **truth** lies within the word of God.

I had cancer, but I didn't just pray to be healed of cancer. I prayed for my body to line up with the Word of God that declares by His stripes I am healed. I prayed that I never be attacked by any cancerous disease again or any other type of disease, but that I be restored to wholeness, like the woman with the issue of blood. I reminded God of His will that I prosper and be in good health, not for my sake, but so that He be glorified by my continuing in the building of His kingdom. I also prayed for the healing of others who were sick.

I reminded God of the benefits of serving Him, for He is the God who forgives all my sins and heals all my diseases. Praise ye the Lord. And finally, but foremost, I prayed in Jesus' name. Amen.

MY SPIRITUAL JOURNEY

My prayer for healing is (If healing is not what's needed, list another prayer):

ONE DOLLAR BILL BLESSINGS

But this I say, He which soweth sparingly shall reap also sparingly;
and he which soweth bountifully shall reap also bountifully. -2 Corinthians 9:6

When it comes to giving to God's storehouse, we sometimes give little. When it comes to giving to other places, we tend to give more liberally. These tendencies apply not only to monetary giving but to other areas as well. When it comes to serving in the church, we feel there is no reward; therefore, we put forth little effort in giving of our time to serve God. When it comes to praising God, we are afraid of how others perceive us. Consequently, we give little or no praise. When we go to games or other sources of entertainment, we praise hilariously.

Entertaining man seems to be more important to us than entertaining God – our Lord, our help, our strength, our shield, the horn of our salvation, and the supplier of all our needs. If we expect God to bless us bountifully, we must give bountifully, not of necessity, but out of love for Him. When we tip God a one dollar bill in the offering plate, we should expect a one dollar bill blessing in return.

MY SPIRITUAL JOURNEY

Am I reaping what I sow? Am I reaping sparingly or bountifully?

THE IDLE MINDED

Slothfulness casteth into a deep sleep; and an idle soul shall suffer hunger.
-Proverbs 19:15

We often hear of teenagers stealing cars, breaking in homes, abusing drugs, getting pregnant out of wedlock, and the like. These are usually not what we call 'bad' kids. In fact, many of them come from blessed families. What happened is they allowed their minds to become idle, giving place to the enemy to fill it with his desires.

We can overcome an idle mind by filling ourselves with the work, word, and Spirit of God. When we are filled with His work, word, and Spirit, we have no time to tarry with the enemy. We are diligently working out our salvation with recognition and anticipation of all of His promises.

MY SPIRITUAL JOURNEY

At what times do I usually fall trap to an idle mind?

_____

_____

_____

_____

_____

_____

_____

_____

A DECLARATION OF WAR

...neither be ye sorry; for the joy of the Lord is your strength.
-Nehemiah 8:10

The pastor can't declare war for us. We have to declare war for ourselves. The war we need to declare is not a physical fight against each other, but a spiritual battle between us and Satan and his demonic forces.

A mainline church in America was in disagreement about what hymns would be in their hymnal. Some wanted to take out the song "Onward Christians Soldiers." They thought it was too militaristic. Some people have become so educated that they don't believe in a personal devil or demons of the spirit world. Yet, these same folks believe in unseen, uncontrollable, and cosmic forces. Call a rose by any other name, and it's still a rose. Call the devil by any other name, and it's still the devil. It's time to declare war and use our weapon called praise.

MY SPIRITUAL JOURNEY

Why should I believe there is a spiritual battle going on?

_____

_____

_____

_____

_____

_____

PREPARE FOR WAR

For we wrestle not against flesh and blood, but against principalities, against powers, against the rulers of the darkness of this world, against spiritual wickedness in high places.
Ephesians 6:12

To declare war, we must prepare for it. In Ephesians 6, Paul tells us how to prepare for war. He instructs us to be strong in our God and in the power of His might. We can't fight spiritual wickedness with human ability. We can't get spiritual strength from working out in the gym, doing push ups, aerobics, Tae Bo, running, or other training. Spiritual strength comes from God.

Furthermore, Paul instructs us to put on the whole armor of God. We must put on the belt of truth, Jesus Christ, and the breastplate of righteousness. We must put on the shoes of the preparation of the gospel of peace and the shield of faith. We must put on the helmet of salvation and the sword of the Spirit, which is the word of God. There is no need to declare war against Satan if we are not dressed for battle. Get dressed with the armor of God and head for the battlefield. Fully dressed, you are certain to win.

MY SPIRITUAL JOURNEY

Am I prepared for war?

_____

_____

_____

_____

THERE IS VICTORY IN PRAISE

Let the high praises of God be in their mouth,
and a two-edged sword in their hand. -Psalm 149:6

Nehemiah declared that the joy of the Lord was his strength in Nehemiah 8:10. God has given us strength and power through the joy of rejoicing. To rejoice is to praise. There is victory in praise. Psalm 8:2 says, "Out of the mouth of babes and sucklings hast thou ordained strength because of thine enemies, that thou mightest still the enemy and the avenger." Strength and praise translate the same. They are secret weapons that God has given to us.

Aside from the armor Paul has instructed us to put on in Ephesians 6, Christians must also put on praise. The psalmist in Psalm 149:6 reads, Let the praises of God be in their mouth, and a two-edged sword in their hand. The sword of praise is a weapon to be utilized by all God's saints. God has already whipped Satan's behind and has given us praise just to whip it a bit more. We wouldn't have so much weakness and fear if every Christian knew that victory is in the praise.

MY SPIRITUAL JOURNEY

How often do I use praise on the battlefield?

_____

_____

_____

_____

RECALL YOUR VICTORIES

June 18

We will not hide them from their children, shewing to the generation to come the praises of the LORD and his strength and his wonderful works that he hath done. -Psalm 78:4

King Saul's armor was so heavy that David refused to use it. It was David's reflection on the joy of the Lord that caused him not to use King Saul's armor. He began to recall the victories he had won without this physical armor and decided to rely on His spiritual armor. David didn't use Saul's breastplate and sword because he remembered being on the other side of the mountain when a bear came up against him, and God protected him from the bear. He remembered when a lion came upon him and God stretched open the lion's mouth. David knew that the same God that saved him then would give him the victory against big Goliath.

God has given us victories, and we need to recall some of them. Each victory will help us to help another to win. We should remind ourselves that the same God who brought us out of obscurity and bondage is the same God who will deliver us forever.

MY SPIRITUAL JOURNEY

In what ways has God brought me victory over the enemy?

_____

_____

_____

_____

170

FULLY DRESSED IN SPIRITUAL ARMOR

Put on the whole armor of God that you may be able to stand against the wiles of the devil.
-Ephesians 6:11

Too many Christians try to go to war against evil without having on their full armor. We can say, "I rebuke you Satan," all we want to, but if we are not fully dressed for battle, we will be defeated. 2 Corinthians 6:7 says "by the word of truth, by the power of God, by the armor of righteousness on the right hand and the left."

We shouldn't overestimate Satan and his army. They owe their existence to God through whom they were created. Satan and his army launched an assault on the crucified Christ when they thought He was at His weakest, but they were defeated. Satan rebelled against God, trying to steal His praise and worship, but God didn't lie down. He fought back (Ephesians 4:8) and won, stripping Satan and his army of their armor. The devil is going to hell, and the only pleasure he can get is to take some of us with him. If we are fully dressed in our spiritual armor and ready for battle, we have victory over Satan.

MY SPIRITUAL JOURNEY

Am I certain I am on the winning team?

THE DAY OF EVIL

Wherefore take unto you the whole armour of God that ye may be able to stand in the evil day, and having done all, to stand. -Ephesians 6:13

A battle is a battle and a war is a war. It doesn't matter if we win or lose the battle, the war goes on. There is a critical position in every war. The Christian's critical position in battle over evil ought to be where we draw the line and say to the devil, "I have stood all I can stand, and I can't stand no more." It is time to declare war over evil and take back our children, our families, our communities, and our land.

Ephesians 6:13 cautions Christians about the day of evil. The devil is on our trail morning noon and night, only to leave for a season. Only when we prepare ourselves with the Word and fervent prayer can we withstand those times when Satan tries to have a hay day in our lives.

MY SPIRITUAL JOURNEY

During times of battle, what caused me to reach my critical position?

_____

_____

_____

_____

_____

_____

And I saw a new heaven and a new earth: for the first heaven and the first earth were passed away; and there was no more sea. -Revelation 21:1

Heaven and earth will pass away. The world as we know it will be gone. The moon, earth, stars, planets, and galaxy will all be gone. There will be a new creation. The heaven where Christians will live forever with Jesus does not yet exist except in the mind of God.

If God told us more about this new heaven, we would become too anxious to do our work for Him on earth. When we are anxious, we can't concentrate on anything else because of the expectation of the upcoming event. Many of us have that problem now. We are so heavenly-minded, we are no earthly good. Paul had to caution himself about being heavenly-minded. When he was taken up to the heavens above heavens he said, "And lest I should be exalted above measure through the abundance of the revelations…" (2 Corinthians 12: 7) Therefore, God gave him a thorn in his side that he might not even boast or relish what he felt and saw.

MY SPIRITUAL JOURNEY

How does it make me feel to know that one day earth as we know it will be no more?

_____

_____

_____

HEAVEN IS GOD'S THRONE

Heaven is my throne and earth is my footstool: what house will you build for me? saith the Lord: or what is the place of my rest? -Acts 7:49

What does God tell us about the new heaven? He pinned back the curtains of eternity and gave John on the isle of Patmos a peek, giving us a description of what He wants us to know. God calls it a new city, the New Jerusalem (Revelation 21:2). The foundations of this new city rest on this new earth, and it will be our heavenly home, a real city. When we think of a new city here on earth, we think of crowded streets and busy people.

We won't have to worry about that in the new city. We are told that the streets will be paved with gold. Today, we value, invest, and some people worship gold. We have gold everywhere. In the new heaven, we will walk on what was sometimes worshipped on earth. We will only worship God. He tells us specifically that the former things will be passed away, and that He will bring about a new creation. Pain, trials, and tribulation will be passed away. What a blessing!

MY SPIRITUAL JOURNEY

What trials and tribulations am I facing today that I look forward to knowing one day will pass away?

THE HOLY CITY

And I John saw the holy city, new Jerusalem, coming down from God out of heaven, prepared as a bride adorned for her husband. -Revelation 21:2

What more does God tell us about the new heaven? There won't even be the sun or the moon or the stars because they belong to the former things.

I can remember being in eighth grade science class discussing the power of the sun. We studied photosynthesis that told us that without the sun there would be no life. I remember learning that because of the sun, green plants with chlorophyll can manufacture their own food, but if the sun was cut off, there would be no life. Yet, in the new heaven, there will be no sun because the Son of all light will provide all the light we need.

The Bible also tells us that there will be no night. We all know that bad things tend to happen mostly at night. I've always tried to persuade my children that it's best to be home at night. Crimes, accidents, and death happen at night more than they occur in the day time. Revelation 21:27 tells us that there shall in no wise enter into anything that defiles it. It will be a safe city.

MY SPIRITUAL JOURNEY

What are my thoughts on Jesus being my light?

_____

_____

_____

175

Day and night they never stop saying: "Holy, holy, holy is the Lord God Almighty, who was, and is, and is to come." -Revelation 4:8b NIV

What more does God tell us about the new heaven? Revelation 21:22 tells us that there will be a city with no temple for the Lord God and the Lamb, our Savior, Jesus Christ, will be our temple.

There is a practical lesson in that we should not worship religion. We ought not be in competition for the biggest and the greatest church or worship our local congregation. We ought to be worshipping God.

There will be no more sea. There will be no more separation. There will be no more Africa, Asia, China and Europe. There will be no more Southern Baptist, Missionary Baptist, Methodist, Pentecostal, Church of God in Christ, etc. Zephaniah 3:9 tells us that there will be one pure language so that we can call upon the name of the Lord to serve Him with one consent. God will give us all the light we need, and we will praise Him all the time.

MY SPIRITUAL JOURNEY

How does it make me feel to know that one day denominationalism will be eliminated?

_____

_____

_____

A PREPARED PLACE

And I go and prepare a place for you, I will come again, and receive you unto myself; that where I am, there ye may be also. -John 14:3

There are several things we learn from this lesson on our prepared new heaven. First, heaven has been prepared for us. Secondly, in heaven and in hell, everybody will live forever. Remember the unbeliever who chooses to die without Christ will be cast into the fiery lake to live forever.

Thirdly, heaven and earth will pass away, but God's word will not. Therefore, we should fill our values on the word of God. Rearing our children, maintaining our marriages, building our lives, and doing our ministry, should be based on God's word.

Finally, this word of prophecy is a blessing in that it can set us free from the idol god of materialism. Clothes, houses, cars, even heaven and earth will all pass away because there will be a new heaven.

MY SPIRITUAL JOURNEY

Where will I spend eternity? Am I certain?

_____

_____

_____

_____

_____

_____

GRACE AND PEACE

*Grace and peace be multiplied unto you through the knowledge of God,
and of Jesus our Lord;-2 Peter 1:2*

People everywhere are searching for grace and peace. True grace and peace can be obtained only through knowing God, yet many Christians, like the rest of the world, are still searching for grace and peace in unfit places and people. In fact, Peter declared that grace and peace would be multiplied unto those who know God.

Grace is God's unmerited favor that is only given to those who believe in Him. Peace is God's unexplainable serenity that is given to those who believe in Him. God's favor and peace are given to us at salvation but are multiplied in us through learning of Him. The more we learn of Him, the more favor and peace we receive. He will even share His own glory and goodness with those who get to know Him (2 Peter 1:3).

MY SPIRITUAL JOURNEY

How well do I know God? How much grace and peace do I have in my life?

_____

_____

_____

_____

_____

ONLY BELIEVERS CAN ENTER

Who shall ascend into the hill of the LORD? Or who shall stand in his holy place? He that hath clean hands, and a pure heart: who hath not lifted up his soul unto vanity, nor sworn deceitfully. -Psalm 24:2-4

No one can enter into God's house except they go through His Son, Jesus Christ (Matthew 14:6); therefore, salvation must be a prerequisite. According to the Psalmist, not all people are allowed in God's presence. The Psalmist says that the ones who enter into God's presence must have clean hands and a pure heart. Not all Christians qualify or have grown in these areas.

God has set certain standards for entering into His house. He is concerned about what our hands touch, and what our hearts feel. There are people who are dishonest and deceitful. These are they who have not yet been transformed by the renewing of their minds. These are the ones who have not yet put their trust in God.

Those who go into God's house practice honesty in what they do and feel. They are the ones who will receive God's goodness. These are the ones who are allowed to stand before God and worship Him.

MY SPIRITUAL JOURNEY

Have I positioned myself to enter into God's house?

179

POWER OF THE TONGUE

Death and life are in the power of the tongue: and they that love it shall eat the fruit thereof.

-Proverbs 18:21

Life and death are in the power of the tongue. We can choose to speak life or death. When we speak positive, good thoughts towards others, we feed them good fruit. When we speak negative, bad thoughts towards others, we feed them rotten fruit. We can either build others up or tear them down.

When people are diagnosed with what we refer to as life-threatening illnesses, many of us tend to speak death over them. The doctor gives the person six months, and we will give them one. Some of us not only begin to speak negatively, but we also begin to make funeral arrangements. When people are faced with illnesses, it would be great if we began to speak healing and life instead of death.

A person who consistently speaks death is a negative person and has very little faith in God, if any at all. We cannot always avoid them but should not allow ourselves to be a receptacle to their negativity. When they speak death, we should speak life.

MY SPIRITUAL JOURNEY

Do I usually speak life or death?

_____

_____

_____

WISE OR FOOLISH

A fool uttereth all his mind: but a wise man keepeth it in till afterwards.
-Proverbs 29:11

Proverbs 21:20 says, "There is treasure to be desired and oil in the dwelling of the wise; but a foolish man spendeth it up." The wise man saves for his future, but the foolish man spends whatever he gets. Are you wise or foolish?

Proverbs 1:5 says, "A wise man will hear, and will increase in his learning; and a man of understanding shall attain unto wise counsels". Proverbs 1:7 says, "The fear of the Lord is the beginning of knowledge: but fools despise wisdom and instruction." A wise man loves instruction from those who are wise, but a foolish man refuses to hear it.

The book of Proverbs has a lot to say about a wise and foolish man. The one who is truly wise is the one who loves, trusts, and obeys God. The one who is truly foolish is the one who rejects Him.

MY SPIRITUAL JOURNEY

Am I wise or foolish?

_____

_____

_____

_____

_____

STAND WITH ME

Again I say unto you, That if two of you shall agree on earth as touching anything that they shall ask, it shall be done for them of my Father which is in heaven. For where two or three are gathered together in my name, there am I in the midst of them.

-Matthew 18:19-20

In times of trials, too many of us attempt to go through them alone. In times of adversity or trials, we need to learn to tarry with each other. Satan likes it when we are alone. It makes it easier for him and his army to gang up on us, but he knows that with another saint, we are unstoppable. God says that if just two of us will touch and agree, He will answer our prayer. Satan knows this, and that is why he tries to keep us apart.

Ecclesiastes 4:12 says, "And if one prevail against him, two shall withstand him; and a threefold cord is not quickly broken." One standing alone can be attacked and easily defeated, but two can stand together and conquer. Three is even better because a triple-braided cord is harder to break than a double-braided one. Together we stand, and divided we fall —one-by-one. The next time we go through something, we need to run to saints we trust, and ask them to stand and to tarry with us.

MY SPIRITUAL JOURNEY

In past situations, did I usually stand alone? Who do I trust to stand with me in the future?

_____

_____

_____

FORGIVE AND FORGET

Saying, Blessed are they whose iniquities are forgiven, and where sins are covered.
-Romans 4:7

Proverbs 21:20 says, "There is treasure to be desired and oil in the dwelling of the wise; but a foolish man spendeth it up." The wise man saves for his future, but the foolish spends all they have. Jeremiah 33:8 says, "And I will cleanse them from all their iniquity, whereby they have sinned against me; and I will pardon all their iniquities, whereby they have sinned, and whereby they have transgressed against me."

Even though Jesus forgives us, we have difficulty when it comes to forgiving someone who has treated us badly. We make it difficult for that person to enter our space again.

A story goes that a woman went to heaven and met St. Peter at the gate. He allowed her to enter heaven by spelling the word LOVE. He assigned her the task of watching the gate. As she kept watch over the gate, her ex-husband came to the gate. She had him spell one word, "Hippopotamus." God has forgiven us and nailed our past to the cross. We should likewise forgive others.

MY SPIRITUAL JOURNEY

Do I have a problem with forgiveness?

WHO SAVED US?

Neither is there salvation in any other: for there is none other name under heaven given among men, whereby we must be saved. -Acts 4:12

Most of us, in reading the Ten commandments, have come to realize that we have failed to keep them. Those who have read the Mosaic Law in its entirety would give up on trying to go to heaven if our salvation depended upon the law. The book of Leviticus alone would send us to hell. For centuries, people have struggled to try to please God by trying to keep the written law.

God's law is His Word, but He knew that we would not be able to keep it without the power of the Holy Ghost. That's why He sent His son, Jesus Christ, the perfect lamb. The law couldn't save us, but Jesus could. Jesus came to the rescue and nailed our sins to the cross, blotting them out forever. Our sins of using profanity, lying, lust, fornication, adultery, and pride, are all nailed to the cross. We are the guilty ones who should be nailed to the cross; instead, Jesus died in our stead.

MY SPIRITUAL JOURNEY

How have I failed to keep God's laws? How does being saved give me peace even in my failures?

_____

_____

_____

_____

NAILED TO THE CROSS?

Blotting out the handwriting of ordinances that was against us, which was contrary to us, and took it out of the way, nailing it to his cross. -Colossians 2:14

O nce a young boy said to his parents before being baptized, "I'm really not scared to be baptized, but is it going to hurt when they nail me to the cross?" In the beauty of innocence, the boy was willing to be nailed to the cross because he wanted to be like Jesus.

The ancient custom of erasing a debt was to nail the note to a tree. Once that was done, the debt could never be brought up again. Marriages are hurt when we keep bringing up stuff that happened a long time ago. A couple could be getting along fine and all of a sudden, when there is a confrontation, something comes up that happened ten years ago, adding fuel to the fire.

We have a tendency to bury the hatchet but leave the handle above the ground. However, once Jesus forgives our sins, they are forgiven forever. Jesus nailed all our fears, losses, failures, defeats, worries, and frustrations to the cross, and cast them into the sea of forgetfulness never to rise again.

MY SPIRITUAL JOURNEY

What sins am I carrying that I need to nail back to the cross?

A CONDEMNING SPIRIT

And Jesus said unto her, Neither do I condemn thee: go, and sin no more.

-John 8:11b

Many believers have an unforgiving and condemning spirit. We have this spirit because we have not yet internalized what Jesus did for us on the cross. It's amazing to me how those who are married can be so condemning of unwed mothers as surveys indicate that a great percentage of married people once practiced fornication. They just did not get caught.

Jesus illustrates so vividly how we can have unforgiving and condemning spirits when He spoke to us about a woman caught in adultery. She was caught in the very act. I always found it interesting that the woman was brought forth, but the man was not brought forth. When the religious people brought the woman to Jesus, they quoted the written law and asked Him, What do you say? Jesus, after several incidents of writing in the ground, looked up and said to them, He who is without sin cast the first stone. Each unforgiving and condemning spirit walked away in repentance (John 8:1-11). Jesus commanded the woman to go and sin no more.

MY SPIRITUAL JOURNEY

Am I bound by an unforgiving and condemning spirit?

NOT DEATH BUT LIFE

For the wages of sin is death; but the gift of God is eternal life through
Jesus Christ our Lord. -Romans 6:23

We all worked for sin before giving our lives to Christ. Sin was once our employer. When we work for somebody, we want to get paid. How much do we deserve? What level did we work for sin? Someone once testified that he was the CEO of sin's corporation. Look at how sin pays. Sin doesn't pay in monetary value. Sin's payoff is death. The wages of sin is death.

Death and life are two words with two different concepts. Both words describe a journey, two distinctly different journeys. Before salvation, we were all headed one way. Hotel Hell had a reservation for us. All the devil had to do was type our name in his database and a room was reserved for us. But something happened when we accepted Christ as our Lord and Savior. Our names were changed from being in the database of Hotel Hell to reservations at Hotel Glory -not eternal death but eternal life.

MY SPIRITUAL JOURNEY

Am I sure about my reservations?

_____

_____

_____

_____

_____

_____

THE WAGES OF SIN

*For the wages of sin is death; but the gift of God is eternal life through
Jesus Christ our Lord. -Romans 6:23*

Most people are afraid of death and dead people. Truth be told, we can't live fully because we are scared to die. We spend more time trying to figure out how to stay safe from harm and death than we spend seeking and fulfilling the purposes of God. We spend money on burglar alarms for our houses and cars, weapons to protect us from criminals, and larger facilities to house criminals. We do Internet surfing to make sure that criminals don't live next to us. We run from death, yet we deserve it.

The wages of sin is death, and we deserve the wages. The good news is that Jesus pocketed our wages. The blood of Jesus washed us white as snow and gave us life, not death. Not only did He pocket death, but He also gave us the free gift of eternal life. Life eternal means we don't have to be afraid of dying because we are going to live with God forever. To know Christ is to live, and to die is gain (Philippians 1:21).

MY SPIRITUAL JOURNEY

What am I doing to show that I live for Christ?

_____

_____

_____

_____

THE GREATEST LOVE OF ALL

For God so loved the world, that he gave his only begotten Son, that whosoever believeth in him should not perish, but have everlasting life. -John 3:16

When Christians hear hard core rap music, we flinch because we find it offensive, but there is a song called 'The Greatest Love of All' that we groove to because of its smooth sound. Do we really know what it says? It suggests that loving ourselves is the greatest of all. Christians should be offended by this song.

Proverbs 3:5 teaches us to lean not on our own understanding. God admonishes us to depend upon Him, not ourselves. Satan uses trickery in a simple song to trap our minds. Loving ourselves is not the greatest love of all. What Jesus Christ did at Calvary's cross is the greatest love of all. Christians have been called out of selfishness into the light of Christ that teaches us to love others. We have been called out of independence to dependence upon God.

MY SPIRITUAL JOURNEY

How have the misguided lyrics of "The Greatest Love of All" or other similar songs caused me to depend upon myself?

_____

_____

_____

_____

If we confess our sins, he is faithful and just to forgive our sins; and to cleanse us from all unrighteousness. - John 1:9

Christians have come to the realization that salvation is essential to receive life eternal and not death eternal. We further understand that accepting Jesus Christ as our Lord and Savior is the way to eternal life. In other words, we have no power to save ourselves. We are too weak. However, many Christians act as though we can overcome sin daily on our own. Jesus will help us when we starve the flesh and walk in the Spirit.

After repenting, one is saved for eternal life. After salvation, we sometimes slip back to our carnal ways. We must consistently starve the flesh. To live our lives for God at all times, we must allow our Lord and Savior to be in control. We must repent in order to keep God with us at all times (1 John 1:9).

MY SPIRITUAL JOURNEY

When I sin, do I tend to forget that I sinned or do I consistently repent?

_____

_____

_____

_____

_____

_____

July 9
PRAYING ON HIGHER GROUND
(Praying in Faith)

But Jesus, said unto them, A prophet is not without honour, but in his own country, and among his own kin, and in his own house. And he could there do no mighty work, save that he laid his hands upon a few sick folk, and healed them. And he marveled because of their unbelief. And he went round about the villages, teaching. -Mark 6:4-6

Praying on higher ground is praying in faith. There is a difference between praying and praying in faith. Praying in faith means believing God has already done what we are praying for Him to do. When we pray on higher ground, we are praying in faith with authority and power, based on the promises of God. If we are praying for someone to be saved, we ought to be treating that person as though they are already saved.

We shouldn't underestimate prayer power mixed with God's power. When we pray in faith, we don't have to wait for God's answer to give Him praise. A prayer on higher ground includes much praise. Prayer is God's ordained connected link to Him. He has given us the power and the victory.

MY SPIRITUAL JOURNEY
Is there anything in particular I need to pray in faith for today?

_____
_____
_____
_____
_____

191

SAVED BUT STILL A SLAVE

Stand fast therefore in the liberty wherewith Christ hath made us free,
and be not entangled again with the yoke of bondage. -Galatians 5:1

Two slaves decided to run away from their master. Their names were Faith and Doubt. The night before they were to run away together, Faith said to Doubt, "I have a boat hid down at the river. If ya wanna go wit me, meet me by that rock down yonda." On the night they were to run away together, Doubt didn't show up. By the time he decided to meet Faith down by the rock, Faith was gone and went on to enjoy a life of freedom. Doubt forever remained a slave.

Many of us are like Doubt. Our faith in God goes up and down like a roller coaster. However, without faith, it is impossible to please God (Hebrews 11:6). With faith we can move mountains, but without it our mountains will remain (1 Corinthians 13:2). If you want to please God, increase your faith. God has called us out of slavery into liberty. Not overcoming our doubts is Satan's tactic for keeping us entangled in bondage (Galatians 5:1).

MY SPIRITUAL JOURNEY

What is it that causes me to doubt God?

_____

_____

_____

_____

_____

SET THE ATMOSPHERE

And they were offended in him. But Jesus said unto them, A prophet is not without honour, save in his own country, and in his own house. And he did not many mighty works there because of their unbelief. -Matthew 13:57-58

Atmosphere can be the element of influence that sets the tone for the time being. In Matthew 13:53-57, Jesus had a hometown audience and an unpleasant atmosphere. Many of the people of Jesus' hometown were offended by His wisdom and miracles. They just couldn't believe that the boy who grew up as a carpenter's son could have so much wisdom about God. He wanted to heal, deliver, and save, but He was hindered by their unbelief. It wasn't that He wasn't able, but He didn't have the atmosphere He needed to perform the blessings He desired to bestow upon the people.

God doesn't go where He is not wanted. We're not seeing the move of God because of our unbelief. If we want to see a mighty move of God, we must set the atmosphere for His presence. The atmosphere must be inviting and filled with praise, worship, and prayer.

MY SPIRITUAL JOURNEY

How do I set the atmosphere for God's presence?

_____

_____

_____

_____

TRUE FREEDOM

Stand fast therefore in the liberty wherewith Christ hath made us free, and be not entangled again with the yoke of bondage. -Galatians 5:1

We sometimes categorize those who are slaves to addictions or those who are imprisoned as being in bondage. Bondage is whatever enslaves us and keeps us from being free. Jesus came to set us free.

Many are bound by the clothes they wear to church, worried about messing up their new suit or losing their new hat. They're not free to praise God because they're concerned about what others may think. Some are even bound by tradition and music. Bondage even affects our witness. We tend not to invite Christians of other races to our churches.

John 8:32 says that we shall know the truth, and the truth shall set us free. True freedom rests within the Word of God, not others or traditions. Until we come to know the freedom of living in Christ Jesus, we will remain entangled in sin. Stand in freedom, and if you are not the one who is bound, then be the one to proclaim liberty to the captives and open the prison gates to those who are bound (Isaiah 61:1).

MY SPIRITUAL JOURNEY

To what or whom am I entangled?

_____

_____

_____

IS THE HOUSE WORTHY?

And when ye come into an house, salute it. And if the house be worthy, let your peace come upon it: but if it be not worthy, let your peace return to you.
-Matthew 10:12-13

Many Christians are afraid of witnessing because we fail to realize the power of the Holy Spirit living within us. In fact, to assist us in witnessing, we have been anointed to bless others with the peace of God. The word of God instructs us when witnessing to go into a house and bless it, and if the house be found worthy, let our peace rest upon it.

What makes the house worthy? Those who receive the word of God are those He counts as worthy to receive the peace we have been anointed to give to them. For each home we enter, we take a welcoming gift basket filled with peace. The owners of the home have the choice to receive or reject this peace offering gift. We are such an anointed people that when we leave someone's home, we have the power to leave peace there. Yet, many of us are afraid to go. What power we have but fail to use. Oh what peace we forfeit.

MY SPIRITUAL JOURNEY

Am I sure of my peace?

195

SCARED TO DEATH

And fear not them which kill the body, but are not able to kill the soul: but rather fear him which is able to destroy both soul and body in hell. -Matthew 10:28.

Fear is false evidence appearing real. Sometimes, we are terrified about what could have been, but never was. Rosie was terrified about what could have been, but never was. This fear kept her from experiencing the peace of God. Many people, even Christians, are afraid of what man might do to them. We demonstrate fear by how we live each day. Our homes and cars are secured with burglar alarms. Some even live with twenty-four hour bodyguards. When we see young men dressed in baggy clothing, we cross the street because we think they will harm us.

Why don't we fear God like we fear man? Why don't we hide ourselves with fig leaves as Adam and Eve did in the garden? Jesus told us not to be afraid of man who could only destroy our bodies, but to fear Him who could destroy soul and body. It's God who we must face at the final judgment, not man.

MY SPIRITUAL JOURNEY

How do I live each day, in fear or in peace?

_____

_____

_____

_____

_____

July 15
DO YOU HAVE BREATH?

Let every thing that hath breath praise the Lord. Praise ye the Lord.
-Psalm 150:6

Psalm 150:6 commands everything breathing to praise God. Place your hand in front of your mouth and blow. Do you have breath? If you put your hand in front of your mouth, the answer has to be "Yes." If you didn't have breath, you wouldn't be reading this word for the day. Of all the things God has done for us, all He asks in return is that we praise Him.

Consider all that Christ endured before and at Calvary's cross. He was criticized for doing good. He was lied on by false witnesses. He was beaten senselessly. He had nails driven in his hands and feet while on Calvary's cross. He died for all of us, and all He asks in return is that every living thing praise Him. Animals are living things. So get this, if we don't praise God, the animals will. One way or the other, God is going to receive His praise. I don't know about you, but I don't want animals or rocks praising God for me.

MY SPIRITUAL JOURNEY

Am I a participant of God's praise party?

197

July 16
LOT'S WIFE

Remember Lot's wife. -Luke 17:32

Genesis 19:26 states, "But his wife looked back from behind him and she became a pillar of salt." As God was destroying the city of Sodom and Gomorrah, Lot's wife looked back. She looked back because she wanted to return to what she knew as home, a city that had plenty. As she ran from the city of Sodom and Gomorrah, all she could see in front of her was a wilderness, but behind her was a city that had plenty. She couldn't bear the thought of returning to the wilderness because she had struggled so hard to leave when she traveled with Abraham and his family.

Jesus told the disciples to remember Lot's wife because the time would come when they, too, would have to not look back but move forward. Moving forward is letting go of our selfish desires to fulfill the purposes of God. Moving forward can also lead to a wilderness experience, but know that when God leads us to the wilderness, He will bring us out greater than before.

MY SPIRITUAL JOURNEY

Why am I trying to avoid my wilderness experience?

_____

_____

_____

_____

_____

CROWNS AND CROSSES

Remember the word that I said unto you, the servant is not greater than his Lord. If they have persecuted me, they will also persecute you; if they have kept my saying, they will keep yours also -John 15:20

Many Christians want the crown but not the cross. Yet, crucifixion always precedes resurrection.

Everyone wants to be included in the rejoicing on Easter morning, but no one wants to stop by on Good Friday. It was on that day Jesus was spat on, mocked, pierced, crowned with thorns, bled, and died. We have to die with Him before we can be used by Him.

Many churches today teach on the blessings (the crowns) we receive because we are heirs of God. We hear very little about the persecution (the crosses) we will endure because we are His heirs. Jesus stated in John 15:20 that if we are His servants, we will endure persecution just as He did. When we declare Jesus is Lord of our lives, we will be persecuted. When we praise Him on our jobs, we will be persecuted. Don't be dismayed. Accept the persecution for our crown awaits us

MY SPIRITUAL JOURNEY

When is the last time I faced persecution for Christ?

And be not conformed to this world: but be ye transformed by the renewing of your mind, that ye may prove what is that good, and acceptable, and perfect, will of God. -Romans 12:2

S ome time ago I was flown up to Nashville to spend a day with a group of Biblical curriculum writers who wanted my input. The goal was to develop a curriculum that solved all life's problems based on scripture. The goal was very admirable. It would be wonderful to transform the Christian community to see everything through the eyes of God and not the world.

Christians are called to have a God-view of life. Romans 12:2 warns us not to think like the world, but to think with the new mind God has given us. We have been given the mind of Christ through the Word of God. When God's view really matters to us, we won't listen to certain music, watch certain movies, drink certain types of beverages, and use certain types of language. When God's view really matters to us, we will study and learn His Word so that we will not be ignorant in our walk with Him.

MY SPIRITUAL JOURNEY

How do I show that God's view matters in my life?

_____

_____

_____

_____

TRUE AMBITION AND GREATNESS

And whatsoever ye do, do it heartily, as to the Lord, and not unto men; Knowing that of the Lord ye shall receive the reward of the inheritance; for ye serve the Lord, Christ.

-Colossians 3:23-24

Being a servant is like being a bond slave. A bond slave is locked in to his job. Free men walk away from their jobs but bond slaves can't. He can't walk off when the sun gets too hot. If we want to be great, we must learn to serve others.

I am thankful for the respect I receive as a pastor, but I don't want to see any one standing up when I enter the room. If I'm going to be chief, I need to be slave of all, not the king, for He has already come. It's our human weakness to try to make an earthly deity and declare it to be God. True ambition and greatness do not exercise authority over people because true ambition seeks to be a servant. True ambition and greatness are doing the will of God.

MY SPIRITUAL JOURNEY

Am I ambitious about serving others?

FROM SATURDAY TO SUNDAY
Remember the Sabbath day, to keep it holy. -Exodus 20:8

There needs to be a time of meditation on Saturday before we get to church on Sunday. Back in the day, to prepare for Sundays, we would take our baths Saturday night so that all we had to do on Sunday morning was get dressed. It elevated God because it was a part of our preparation for worship.

There needs to be a time of invitation: inviting the Holy Spirit to meet us in the sanctuary. Without the presence of the Holy Spirit in the sanctuary, we meet in vain. Without the presence of the Holy Spirit in the sanctuary, we open the door to other spirits.

God will not meet us in the sanctuary if the spirits of gossip, grumbling, complaining, anger, and hatred exist in our hearts. Set the atmosphere for Sunday by preparing for worship on Saturday.

MY SPIRITUAL JOURNEY
How can I use Saturday to prepare for Sunday worship?

_____

_____

_____

_____

_____

_____

_____

_____

_____

THE RIGHT WAY

The steps of a good man are ordered by the LORD: and he delighteth in his way.
-Psalm 37:23

"There is a way that seemeth right unto a man, but the end thereof are the ways of death" (Proverbs 16:25). Have you ever made a decision about something that you thought was right, but it turned out to be wrong? Everyday as we work to find our way, we should not try and do it alone, but with God. Our choosing which way we should go can lead to either death and destruction or life and peace. Psalm 27:11 reads, "Teach me thy way, O Lord, and lead me in a plain path, because of mine enemies."

Following God's way keeps us safe. Thomas said to Jesus in John 14:5, "We know not whither thou goest; and how can we know the way?" And Jesus said in verse 6, "I am the way." When we are searching to find our way, we should follow Jesus. He is the way, the truth, and the light.

MY SPIRITUAL JOURNEY

Which way am I headed?

_____

_____

_____

_____

_____

203

WHO IS RICH

And again I say unto you, It is easier for a camel to go through the eye of a needle, than for a rich man to enter into the kingdom of God. -Matthew 19:24

Riches can be a spiritual drawback for us just as it was for the young ruler in Mathew 19:16-22. God cautions us about wealth, as He did with the young rich ruler. The young man turned down salvation because his wealth was more important to him. He had become self righteous, full of pride and the love of money. Wealth leads to greed, and greed leads to pride.

To keep Christians humble, God has entered us into a covenant relationship with Him through the tithe. We give to God 10% of what already belongs to Him. The young rich man was in covenant with no one, leaving him prideful and without a relationship and fellowship with God. To be rich is to be sold out to God. Those sold out to God trust Him with everything, including riches.

MY SPIRITUAL JOURNEY

Am I sold out to God with my finances, family, job, etc?

_____

_____

_____

_____

_____

_____

_____

HEAVENLY TREASURES

But lay up for yourselves treasures in heaven, were neither moth nor rust doth corrupt and where thieves do not break through nor steal. -Matthew 6:20

Those rich in the Lord set their minds on heavenly treasures (Matthew 6:20). What are some of the heavenly treasures we should have on our minds? According to John 14:2, there are many mansions awaiting us in heaven. Mansions await us in heaven built by the hand of God and not of man. These mansions are tax and interest free, with no mortgage. Jesus paid it all.

Revelation 21:21 lets us know that the streets alone in the heavenly city are paved with gold, not asphalt. The city is also rich in light. There is no need for electricity, for the glory of God and of the Lamb will illuminate it. We won't have to worry about a power outage. One of the richest treasures we will have there is the absence of sorrow and death. Most importantly, our richest heavenly treasure is to be in the presence of our God all day long (Revelation 21:22-23). He who sets his mind on heavenly treasures is rich indeed.

MY SPIRITUAL JOURNEY

Which treasures are more valuable to me right now, my earthly ones or my anticipated heavenly ones? Why?

_____

_____

_____

_____

THE LIVING SACRIFICE

I beseech you therefore, brethren, by the mercies of God, that ye present your bodies a living sacrifice, holy, acceptable unto God, which is your reasonable service.
-Romans 12:1

There are three types of sacrifices described in the Bible: the **insufficient**, the **sufficient**, and the **living**. The insufficient and sufficient sacrifices have fulfilled their purposes, leaving one to be fulfilled; the living.

The **insufficient sacrifice** was the yearly blood shed of unblemished animals offered unto God by the high priest of the Tabernacle. This was done for the purpose of cleansing the priest and the Israelites of their sins (Hebrews 9).

The **sufficient sacrifice** was the blood shed of Jesus Christ (Luke 22:20) offered up to God for all mankind for the purpose of cleansing us from our sins once and for all. His blood has made it possible for us to have a relationship and fellowship with God.

The **living sacrifice** according to Romans 12:1 is the body of the believer. A living sacrifice for God is a life that lives holy and acceptable to Him, which allows the Holy Spirit to dwell in us.

MY SPIRITUAL JOURNEY

Is my body an earthly tabernacle where the Holy Spirit would want to live?

OUTSIDE THE TABERNACLE

How much more shall the blood of Christ, who through the eternal Spirit offered himself without spot to God, purge your conscience from dead works to serve the living God?

-Hebrews 9:14

We are now the priests of God (1 Peter 2:9) and the blood of Jesus has already cleansed us so that we may enter into the presence of God freely. Jesus has paid it all, yet many Christians remain outside the tabernacle. Many of us are like a man who has been homeless for so long that when he is given a house, he still sleeps outside. Some of us still live outside the Tabernacle by doubting our salvation.

Others of us are still trying to wash our hands of the past sins we were forgiven for when we came to Christ. God has cast them into the sea of forgetfulness. It is Satan who doesn't want us to forgive ourselves. Everything on the outside of the tabernacle represented judgment and death. Those of us who don't believe that the blood of Jesus Christ is enough to save and cleanse us will remain outside the Tabernacle, never embracing the joy of salvation.

MY SPIRITUAL JOURNEY

Am I living inside or outside the Tabernacle?

THE HOLY PLACE

A tabernacle was set up. In its first room were the lampstand, the table and the consecrated bread; this was called the Holy Place. -Hebrews 9:2 (NIV)

Moses was instructed by God to build a room in the Tabernacle known as the Holy Place. Inside the Holy Place were a candlestick, and a table with shewbread (Hebrews 9:2). The candlestick, which was always burning, represented Christ who has brought light into a dark and dying world. The table was made with a golden crown representing Christ as King of Kings. Holy bread was kept on the table representing Christ, our bread of life. The Holy Place represented Christ in His fullness, the bread of life, and king of kings.

The Holy Place was a place of service unto God. This is where the priest worked, blessed the people, and instructed them of the law. We enter into the Holy Place when we find our place of service in God's house. Serving God is His will being done in our lives. Our service may not be the same as the priest in the Tabernacle, but believers are instructed to serve God using our spiritual gifts.

MY SPIRITUAL JOURNEY

Have I entered into the Holy Place of service?

_____

_____

_____

_____

_____

208

THE MOST HOLY PLACE

And after the second veil, the tabernacle which is called the Holiest of all. -Hebrews 9:3

Moses was instructed to build a room in the Tabernacle known as The Most Holy Place or the Holy of Holies. This was the most sacred place in the Tabernacle. On the lid of the Ark was the Cherubim of Glory, the Holy Angels of God shadowing the Mercy Seat. Most importantly, on the lid of the ark was the Mercy Seat. It covered the Ark in its entirety. The Mercy Seat was where God communed with Moses and Aaron.

Because of what Jesus Christ did, God's presence is no longer limited to one place, but His Spirit dwells in all Christians. The Most Holy Place was the place where Moses and Aaron pleaded for mercy for the Israelites. Today, all Christians have the opportunity to come running to the mercy seat and lay all on the altar. Christ has made this possible. God wants us to consistently go beyond the place of service, The Holy Place, and enter into the place of worship, the Holy of Holies.

MY SPIRITUAL JOURNEY

Have I entered into the Holy of Holies?

_____

_____

_____

_____

_____

BEYOND THE VEIL

And after the second veil, the tabernacle which is called the Holiest of all.
-Hebrew 9:3

The veil was a curtain in the Tabernacle separating The Holy Place and The Most Holy Place. When Christ died on Calvary's cross, the veil was literally torn from top to bottom, signifying we now have the opportunity to enter into the Most Holy Place. To enter into the Most Holy Place is to be daily in God's presence. Because of Christ's accomplishment, we can now be in both rooms at the same time, praising and worshipping God as we serve Him. Yet many Christians remain outside the veil.

One of the things that keep us outside the veil is sin. Sin robs us of the opportunity to be in the presence of God. If we desire to no longer live outside the veil and enter into the presence of God, then we must go before the mercy seat of God and confess our sins. He will forgive us and cleanse us from all unrighteousness (1 John 1:9).

MY SPIRITUAL JOURNEY

What's behind the veil that's keeping me from entering into the Most Holy Place?

WHY STUDY GOD'S WORD?

All scripture is given by inspiration of God and is profitable for doctrine, for reproof, for correction, for instruction in righteousness. -2 Timothy 3:16

We send our children to school and we sometimes return to school for advanced studies. We don't keep our educational text books on the coffee table and dust them off once a year, yet with the Word of God, many are guilty of just that.

We study God's Word for many reasons:

1. God has magnified His Word above His name (Psalm 138:2).

2. In the beginning was His Word, and one day the Word became flesh in Jesus Christ (John 1:14).

3. God's Word blesses the man who delights in His Word (Psalm 1:1-3).

4. God's Word increases our understanding and revelation (Psalm 119:98-104).

5. God's Word cleanses us from all unrighteousness (John 15:3, Psalms 119:9).

6. Finally, God's Word is a deterrent to sin which keeps us from sinning against Him (Psalm 119:9-11).

MY SPIRITUAL JOURNEY

How valuable is God's word to me?

THE HOLY SPIRIT IMPREGNATES

Now the birth of Jesus Christ was on this wise: When his mother Mary was espoused to Joseph, before they came together, she was found with child of the Holy Ghost.
-Matthew 1:18

Two young people were engaged to be married. The young man didn't know it but the young lady was pregnant already and he wasn't the father. This is the story of the miraculous birth of Jesus Christ. Mary was a virgin and untouched by man.

Many Christians desire to give birth to ministry, but are not ready to conceive. When we first got saved, we were spiritual virgins, untouched by Christian intellect, opinion, and church politics. The moment we became saved, we entered into marriage with Christ. At this stage, we become spiritually pregnant because God deposits spiritual gifts and ministries in our hearts. We have strong desires to accomplish something for the kingdom of God but are afraid to act on our passion. If we fail to act, Satan will use our mind, and will use others to convince us not to fulfill God's purpose.

MY SPIRITUAL JOURNEY

With what do I believe the Holy Spirit has impregnated me?

He that dwelleth in the secret place of the Most High shall abide under the shadow of the Almighty. -Psalm 91:1

D on't stay a spiritual virgin. Don't stay spiritually pregnant. Go into labor and give birth. Mary had a divine child, but she had to go into labor just like every other woman (Matthew 1:21). We cannot bring forth a ministry without labor. The Son of God had to be brought forth. To bring forth is labor. We, too, must go beyond pregnancy and into labor. Some of us want to skip labor and give birth, but labor comes before birth.

When God has spoken a ministry into our lives, we must begin to operate in it. Mary brought forth a son and called his name Jesus. Once we begin to labor in what we have heard God speak to us or labor in the vision He has given us, God will give birth to our ministry. After we give birth, we need to feed the baby and watch it grow until the next pregnancy. When God births our ministry, it will be given a name, and its name will speak for it.

MY SPIRITUAL JOURNEY

What labor have I put forth for the birthing of this baby?

_____

_____

_____

_____

_____

OBEDIENCE IS REQUIRED

For to this end I also wrote, that I might put you to the test, whether you are obedient in all things. -2 Corinthians 2:9

Queen Vashti and Esther both had the potential to give birth. Queen Vashti was queen to King Ahasuerus, emperor of Media-Persia. One day the king was having a party and requested Queen Vashti's presence. He wanted to show off her beauty, but she refused to go, causing the king to vanish her from his presence forever (Esther 1:10-12, 19). Queen Vashti aborted her potential.

Esther and Mary, the mother of Jesus, had something going for them that Queen Vashti did not. Queen Vashti's name means "to drink." Queen Vashti was too drunk with the wine of the world to know how to have a spiritual response to a drunken king. Esther and Mary were prayer warriors who had faith. They both walked in holiness and had the favor of God. Most importantly, they were both obedient. We too must walk in faith, holiness, and obedience to God if we expect to give birth to ministry. We must also fast and pray, expecting our ministry passions to come forth.

MY SPIRITUAL JOURNEY

Do I have qualities like Mary and Esther?

_____

_____

_____

_____

MY BODY, GOD'S TEMPLE

Know ye not that ye are the temple of God, and that the Spirit of God dwelleth in you?
-1 Corinthians 3:16

Christ ascended into heaven and sent the comforter, God the Holy Spirit, just as He promised. We are the temples where the Holy Spirit lives. The Holy Spirit doesn't want to live in a dirty house of sin. A clean house is holy and righteous and is where the Holy Spirit desires to live.

Paul warns us to flee from fornication. We tend to warn singles about sex, but many who are now married have never repented of past sexual sins.

Paul also warned us not to be idolaters and worshipers of other gods. Some worship cars, others, homes, and even education. Next, he warns us against adultery. Some of us are having affairs with others in the church. Failure to respect the body is failure to have a holy place of residence for the Holy Spirit.

MY SPIRITUAL JOURNEY

Have I swept my house lately?

_____

_____

_____

_____

_____

_____

WASHED, SANCTIFIED AND JUSTIFIED

But ye are washed, but ye are sanctified, but ye are justified in the name of the Lord Jesus, and by the Spirit of our God. -1 Corinthian 6: 11b

I n 1 Corinthians 6:9-10, Paul warned us against homosexuality. A homosexual person is one who enters into an intimate relationship with someone of the same sex.

Paul also warned us against theft. Thieves take things that belong to others. How many of us are stealing God's time and giving it to television or some other type of entertainment? Paul further warned us against being covetous or greedy, lusting after and wanting what others have. Many Christians are materialistic, living the opposite of Matthew 6:33, which tells to first seek God's kingdom and His righteousness and everything else will be added unto us by Him. We fail when we try to add "all these things" ourselves. Failure to allow the body to be God's temple is failure to allow the Spirit of God to have a holy place to reside.

MY SPIRITUAL JOURNEY

What room or rooms have I left dirty?

_____

_____

_____

_____

_____

_____

_____

MY BODY IS THE LORD'S

Now the body is not for fornication, but for the Lord and the Lord for the body.
-1 Corinthian 6:13b

God wants to reside in our bodies, but it has to be cleaned in its entirety. In 1 Corinthians 6:9-10, Paul warned us against being a drunkard, intoxicated. Aside from being literally drunk with wine, alcohol or other drugs, some of us are intoxicated with profanity, television, movies, obsessions, and fantasies. It's all about what's in our minds. Paul also warned us against slander revilers. Those who slander misrepresent others by lying and gossiping. Some are even lying and gossiping about the Church.

Paul further warned us against robbery, stealing with force or a weapon. Some are stealing God's word, using it for their own agenda. Our temples must be washed in the redemptive blood of Jesus so that all the filthy things that we have done in the past will be washed away. Then, we can go and sin no more as Jesus told the woman at the well.

MY SPIRITUAL JOURNEY

Is my house clean from social sins? Am I in a back-sliding position?

REBUILD THE TEMPLE

Go up to the mountain, and bring wood, and build the house and I will take pleasure in it, and I will be glorified, saith the Lord -Haggai 1:8

In Haggai 1:2-15, God told the people that if they rebuilt His physical temple, He would be pleased with it and appear before them in His glory. The people repented, obeyed, and were blessed with the glorified presence of God. Though God was referring to an actual building that needed to be rebuilt, I believe the message is the same regarding our bodies, the new temple of God. If we repent of our sins and obey God, He will dwell within us and bless us with His daily presence.

Why are sexual sins so abhorrent to God? Our sexual sins are sins against our bodies. In 1 Peter 1:16, God said, "Be ye holy for I am holy." We cannot expect our temples to be used by God if we are not living lives that are pleasing to Him. We should walk in the Spirit and not in the flesh.

MY SPIRITUAL JOURNEY

Is God dwelling in me?

_____

_____

_____

_____

_____

_____

STAY ANOINTED

You anoint my head with oil; my cup runs over. -Psalm 25:5

In Moses' first encounter with God, He told him to take off his shoes because the ground he was standing on was holy ground. Aaron the high priest and his sons had to be washed and anointed before entering into the Tabernacle of God. The Tabernacle and everything in it had to be anointed before the presence of God entered into it. Every time Aaron and his sons walked by the burnt offering altar (where the animal sacrifices were made) and into the Tabernacle, they had to clean their feet, hands, and garments.

Jesus on the cross exemplifies the fact that God is concerned about our holiness. Jesus said to His Father, "Why have thou forsaken me?" He was asking God, Why have you left me? Jesus had taken on all the sins of the world, and God cannot dwell in the same place as sin. If God departed from His Son because of sin, He certainly won't live within us because of our sin.

MY SPIRITUAL JOURNEY
If I could rate my spiritual temple on a scale from 0-10, with 10 being the highest score, what would be my score?

_____

_____

_____

_____

CALLED TO PRAY AND NOT TO PREY

Pray without ceasing. -1 Thessalonians 5:17

When a tiger seeks its prey, it sneaks up on it and waits for it to get nearer so it doesn't have to go through a long chase. A tiger is not the only animal that preys seeking its meal. Why do we prey on each other? We have difficulty changing from prey to prayer. Christians have been called to pray and not to prey. Spouses tell everyone except God when their spouse is not doing right. Even in the church, when someone doesn't treat us right, we tell others, hoping to establish a "can't be trusted" reputation for the person in question. Such behavior can be labeled as preying.

The Word of God tells us to confess our faults to each other to become healed (James 5:16). When we tell others about someone else, it doesn't heal us, it only leaves us miserable. We will remain that way until we learn to go to God in prayer. God wants to be our best friend, the one with whom we share everything. We must believe God to be our reality or we will never have an effective, powerful prayer life with Him.

MY SPIRITUAL JOURNEY

Is there any "preying" I need to confess?

_____

_____

_____

_____

ABIDING IN CHRIST THROUGH PRAYER

I am the vine, ye are the branches: He that abideth in me, and I in him, the same bringeth forth much fruit: for without me ye can do nothing. -John 15:5

Jesus is the vine and we, like a branch, must be connected to Him. Prayer keeps us connected to the vine. Without prayer, the branch will wither. Worldly things gain victory over us when we are not connected to Jesus Christ.

When a phone is turned on, it has power. The phone has power because it is connected, but if we never use it, it is useless to us. We must answer the phone in order to connect and communicate with the person on the other end.

We need to pick up the phone and dial JESUS continuously. We allow ourselves to get disconnected from Him because of our situations and circumstances. Our situations and circumstances could easily be taken care of if only we would abide in the vine. The branch cannot be effective without the God-given tool of prayer that connects us to Him.

MY SPIRITUAL JOURNEY

Do I allow myself to get disconnected from the vine?

_____

_____

_____

_____

_____

ABIDING IN CHRIST THROUGH HIS WORD

If ye abide in me, and my words abide in you, ye shall ask what ye will, and it shall be done unto you.-John 15:7

It is impossible to abide in God through prayer alone. We must include His Word and His Spirit. The Word of God needs to abide in us to make our prayer life more powerful and effective. When the Word of God abides in us, The Holy Spirit brings it to our remembrance. God's Word tells us that we have not because we ask not, and to ask in His will and it shall be given unto us. How can we ask without prayer? How will we know what to ask if we don't know the word of God and the guidance of His Holy Spirit?

How does one know if he is abiding? One helpful method is to keep a daily journal. In it, you can keep a record of your prayer time, bible study, and witnessing opportunities. When the branch abides in the vine, the branch can ask what it wants in the will of God, and the vine will give it to him. How does one know what he wants? When the branch abides in the vine, what the branch wants is what the vine wants.

MY SPIRITUAL JOURNEY

Does God's word abide in me?

_____

_____

_____

_____

NO MORE EXCUSES

The slothful man saith, There is a lion without, I shall be slain in the streets.
-Proverbs 22:13

When things don't turn out the way we planned or we fail to meet our desired goal, we sometimes make excuses. I once heard a wise man say, "The root of every failure is an excuse." Excuses are simply stepping stones to failure. Excuses keep us from bringing about necessary change in our lives. Excuses lead us to becoming like the man in Proverbs 22:13, lazy.

God is calling us to a higher level, but we keep making excuses. To make excuses when God calls us is not uncommon. Moses' excuse when God called him was that he couldn't talk. Jeremiah's excuse was that he was too young. Gideon's excuse was that he was too poor. God doesn't use us based upon our ability. Rather He uses us based upon our availability. George McCalep's excuse was that he was a sinful man. Sadie McCalep's excuse was that she talks in a whiney voice.

MY SPIRITUAL JOURNEY

What are my failures? What are my excuses?

_____

_____

_____

_____

_____

_____

And they all with one consent began to make excuse. Luke 14:18.

We often set goals that we fail to accomplish because of a lack of discipline. Discipline is training that develops self-control as well as treatment that corrects or punishes. How many times have we prayed prayers like, "Dear God, please make me eat right," "Dear God, please help me lose weight," "Dear God, please make me exercise." We even pray for God to make us disciplined, but God is not a "make us" kind of God. He is a "freewill God."

The discipline is left up to us. Paul urged us to discipline ourselves in Romans 12:2 when he said these words, "And be not conformed to this world: but be ye transformed by the renewing of your mind, that ye may prove what is that good, and acceptable, and perfect, will of God." The "ye" Paul is talking to is us. We have to do something different in our lives to make a difference in our lives. We will continue to fail to accomplish our goals if we fail to discipline ourselves. If we want to accomplish our goals, we must stop making excuses and start making plans.

MY SPIRITUAL JOURNEY
What are my goals, spiritual and otherwise?

_____

_____

_____

_____

August 12
BEING IDLE

And withal they learn to be idle, wandering about from house to house; and not only idle,
but tattlers also and busy bodies, speaking things they ought not.
-1 Timothy 5:13

Idleness tends to occur when there is a lack of discipline. Proverbs 22:12 describes a man who won't go to work because he has not been trained or disciplined to do so. To be disciplined is to rely on the Holy Spirit. When we sit around idly, doing nothing to enhance our knowledge and abilities, we lack discipline and are doomed for failure. When God wills something for us, He will help us through the discipline.

In addition, to be disciplined is to exercise faith and patience. According to James 1:3, faith helps us to grow in patience. Faith inspires the reason for continuing the discipline. The race is not given to the swift, but to the one that makes no more excuses and endures until the end.

MY SPIRITUAL JOURNEY
In what areas do I lack discipline? Will I continue to make excuses in this area?

_____

_____

_____

_____

_____

PROCRASTINATION

The slothful man saith, there is a lion without, I shall be slain in the streets.
- Proverbs 22:13.

God has left the body of Christ with a great work to do. Too many of us have not disciplined ourselves to do it. It's time for the body of Christ to get in spiritual shape, stop procrastinating, and discipline ourselves for building God's kingdom.

If we procrastinate about exercising the body, make excuses, and eat everything we desire, the results may be tiredness, obesity, diabetes and other infirmities and diseases. Also, if we procrastinate and do not study God's Word, pray and have quiet time with God, we will become spiritually bankrupt. If we don't witness for God, in our disobedience, we will be responsible for more people going to hell. If we spend every penny we earn, the results would leave us in poverty. Finally, if we make excuses and fail to go to work on time, we would be fired.

No more excuses. It's time to "just do" the will of God. We can do all things with Christ's strength.

MY SPIRITUAL JOURNEY

Will I 'just do it' today? What will I do?

_____

_____

_____

WHO WAS JEZEBEL?

And it came to pass, as if it had been a light thing for him to walk in the sins of Jeroboam the son of Nebat, that he took to wife Jezebel the daughter of Ethbaal king of the Zidonians, and went and served Baal, and worshipped him
-1 Kings 16:31

J ezebel was the daughter of King Ethbaal. She and her family worshipped the "little g" god Baal. Her name means, "where is the prince?" Jezebel was a woman of no remorse, a self-seeker, a murderer, a manipulator and a controller. When we look at her character, we see all that we are not to be. But there is something about her character that we can all learn. She worshipped, supported and followed her god well. She cared for and fed over 400 prophets of Asherah (mother god of the god Baal) daily. Of course she worshipped the wrong God.

What is the evidence showing that we love and serve the true and living God? We should be about making a "sold out" commitment to God so that the lost world can see a dedicated disciple of Christ. Everything that we do or say should be in God's will.

MY SPIRITUAL JOURNEY

Am I a supportive and dedicated follower to the true and living God?

LET GOD'S LEADER LEAD

And it came to pass, as if it had been a light thing for him to walk in the sins of Jeroboam the son of Nebat, that he took to wife Jezebel the daughter of Ethbaal king of the Zidonians, and went and served Baal, and worshipped him.

-1 Kings 16:31

Jezebel was married to Ahab, king of Israel, and the worst of all kings before him. 1 Kings 21 tells of a poor choice King Ahab made when a man named Naboth refused to sale him his land. He went to bed and refused to eat. When Jezebel asked why he was sad, he told her. Jezebel decided to handle King Ahab's affair by having Naboth stoned to death, thus giving her husband the vineyard he whined for.

What do we learn from Jezebel? What happened between King Ahab and Naboth earned Jezebel what is called today, the "Jezebel spirit" or "take over spirit." Jezebel took over because her husband refused to lead. We too must be careful in trying to take over what God has not called us to handle. We must learn to let God handle His leaders in His way and in His time or else we will find ourselves subject to the wrath of man and God.

MY SPIRITUAL JOURNEY

What am I trying to handle that God has not called me to handle?

_____

_____

_____

_____

WORSHIP IDOL GODS AND BE CURSED

And it came to pass, as if it had been a light thing for him to walk in the sins of Jeroboam the son of Nebat, that he took to wife Jezebel the daughter of Ethbaal king of the Zidonians, and went and served Baal, and worshipped him.

-1 Kings 16:31

Elijah built an altar to God, dug a trench around the altar, filling the altar and the trench with water. He then called out to God to prove that He was the God of Israel. God delivered and sent fire down. Elijah then had all the prophets of Baal killed. But when Ahab told Jezebel about all that Elijah had done, she was furious and vowed to kill Elijah for killing the prophets of Baal. But her husband humbled himself before God and his life was spared.

We worship idol gods: our cars, jobs, homes, children, wives, husbands, and, yes, even our lawns. We see people on Sunday cutting grass and attending their lawns rather than going to the house of worship.

If we continue to worship idol gods, we will be cursed. But when we find ourselves in the wrong camp, headed for destruction, we should stop, repent, turn right and God will bless us.

MY SPIRITUAL JOURNEY

Am I worshipping idol gods?

_____

_____

_____

COMPLETE YOUR ASSIGNMENT

And let us not grow weary in well doing, for in due season we shall reap, if we faint not.
-Galatians 6:9

We sometimes get stuck and don't complete tasks. Some get stuck and don't complete a college degree, and others get stuck cleaning out the closet or garage. There will always be incomplete work in our daily walk.

We must strive for the completion of the general tasks as well as the specific assignments given by our Father, who directs our path. There will always be lost people. Our task is to reach as many as we can to receive our reward. There will be broken homes that require our love and devotion to help mend.

As a matter of fact, we now stand before God incomplete, but if He has started a good work in us, we can have the confidence and sweet assurance that He will bring it to completion when He returns. Philippians 1:6 says, "being confident in this, that he who began a good work in you will carry it on to completion until the day of Christ Jesus." (NIV)

MY SPIRITUAL JOURNEY

Am I confident that a good work has been started in me?

_____

_____

_____

_____

A GOOD WORK BEGUN

Being confident of this, that He who began a good work in you will carry it on to completion until the day of Christ Jesus. -Philippians 1:6

Not believing that God has begun a good work in us is unconverted behavior. While in Cleveland teaching spiritual development and church growth, a lady came over after the session and said to me, "Dr. McCalep, many years ago you came to John Hay High school to sell investments. I came up and told you I didn't have any money, but you compelled me to just start with $10.00 a pay period. I retired a few years ago and that investment was all the money I had." She reached up and gave me a huge hug. She was thankful that I had enough confidence in that product to compel and persuade her to buy it.

How many non-believers have we persuaded to try Jesus? How many are in heaven now waiting to give us a hug because we had enough confidence and sweet assurance to persuade them that Jesus is the way, the truth, and the light?

MY SPIRITUAL JOURNEY

How many non-believers have I persuaded to try Jesus?

_____

_____

_____

_____

_____

_____

CROWN OF LIFE

Be thou faithful until death and I will give you a crown of life.-Revelation 2:10

No matter what kind of life a person is living, when God converts the new believer, He creates a new life that will eventually be made perfect. In this new life, a good work is started.

We may be delayed in starting the new work if we are not in communion with God. We can listen to tapes or go to symposiums and seminars, but if we don't get in touch with the God that dwells in us, we will always have insecurity, fear and doubt. We must know that we are fearfully and wonderfully made in the image of God, which means that we are capable of doing our assignment if we trust in Him.

He started a good work in us, and He will not give up on us. When life looks like it is turning against us, He still expects us to do the work assigned. Remember, it does not yet appear that we are all that we shall be, but when Jesus Christ shall appear, we shall be like Him and see Him as He is (1 John 3:2).

MY SPIRITUAL JOURNEY

Does my life show that I truly have confidence in God?

_____

_____

_____

A TIME FOR SPIRITUAL REFRESHING

Repent ye therefore, and be converted, that your sins may be blotted out, when the times of refreshing shall come from the presence of the Lord. -Acts 3:19

I get excited about my new found computer skills, and when I mess up and can't get things back in order, I call the help line, which usually instructs me to look up at the top of my computer screen to find the word "refresh." Once I find and click on it, my computer goes right back in order. Some of us need to click on our spiritual refresher, Jesus Christ, to get our lives back in order. If we repent, He will refresh.

Many Christians are now stale. We have allowed life's troubles and hardships to make us stale. We have forgotten what it was like when we first gave our lives to Christ. When we were fresh, we told others about Christ, we studied God's Word, we prayed to God daily, and others sensed our aroma, like freshly baked bread. The time is now for spiritual refreshing. So, get up early praying and meditating. Stop doing those ungodly things and start praising God.

MY SPIRITUAL JOURNEY

Do I need a spiritual refreshing?

233

REVIVAL TIME

Then Peter said to them, Repent and let every one of you be baptized in the name of Jesus Christ for the remission of sins. -Acts 2:38

After King Solomon completed the building of the temple, he got down on his knees, lifted up his hands toward heaven, and prayed for a refreshing and a revival for him and his people (2 Chronicles 6). He prayed that God would always hear their prayers in the temple. After his prayer, fire came down from heaven and consumed the sacrifices. The glory of the Lord filled the temple, and all the people watching fell flat on their faces and worshipped God.

After the dust had settled and the night had fallen God appeared to Solomon. God declared a season of refreshing as long as his people humbled themselves, sought His face, and turned from their sins. Then, He promised He would hear their prayers, forgive their sins, and heal their land (2 Chronicles 7:14). Repentance is the formula for revival. Our season of refreshing comes when we repent.

MY SPIRITUAL JOURNEY

Of what do I need to repent?

_____

_____

_____

_____

_____

August 22

TURN FROM WICKED WAYS AND SEEK HIS FACE

When the heaven is shut up, and there is no rain, because they have sinned against Thee, yet if they pray toward this place, and confess Thy name, and turn from their sin, when Thou does afflict them: Then hear thou from heaven, and forgive the sin...
-2 Chronicles 6:26-27a

God wants to hear our prayers, but iniquity prohibits us from getting through to Him. We need to learn to confess and repent of our sins. It's not corporate but individual confession that we need. We have all sinned and fallen short of the glory of God. If we want breakthroughs, we need to ask God for forgiveness of our sins. Confession of our sin leads to revival of the soul.

It's all about seeking the face of God with bowed down heads and a child-like spirit. How can I come before the Lord? How can I seek His face? Too often we are too concerned about what we can get from God. Rather than seeking His face, we want to seek His hand. When we seek His face, we will find His hand. We need to turn from whatever is displeasing to God and begin to seek his presence.

MY SPIRITUAL JOURNEY

Can I get a prayer off the ceiling?

THE CALL OF RIZPAH

And Rizpah the daughter of Aiah took sackcloth, and spread it for her upon the rock,
from the beginning of harvest until water dropped upon them out of heaven, and suffered
neither the birds of the air to rest on them by day, nor the beasts of the field by night.
-2 Samuel 21:10

During David's reign as king, a famine arose in the land. When David inquired of the Lord why the famine, God told him it was because Saul had killed the Gibeonites. So David called in the Gibeonites and asked them to make amends. They asked for seven men of the household of Saul who had done this to them to be killed. So King David gave seven men over to the Gibeonites, two whose mother was Rizpah and five whose adopted mother was Michal. David gave them over to the Gibeonites and they hung them in the city of Saul.

After the hangings, Rizpah watched over them for five months until the barley season was over. Rizpah was on assignment. Many of us leave our assignment before our season is over. Like Rizpah, we should remain faithful to the assignment put before us until God releases us.

MY SPIRITUAL JOURNEY

What is my assignment? Am I on it or have I left it?

_____

_____

_____

_____

_____

Watch therefore, and pray always that you may be counted worthy to escape all these things that will come to pass, and to stand before the Son of Man. -Luke 21:36 (NKJV)

From the beginning of time when the dead bones of Jacob were brought out of Egypt, to today's funeral services, giving one a decent burial has always been sacred. Everyone wants to give their loved one a respectable burial. Rizpah is known for her actions of love, watching over her two sons' and five grandsons' dead bodies. She took sack cloth and spread it upon a rock and stayed through the entire harvest season to prevent vultures and wild animals from tearing at the flesh of the dead bodies.

We, too, have a responsibility to watch over those who are dead in sin, tradition, and bondage. We have a responsibility to not only look over the dead but to also raise them up. God has given the church a mighty responsibility to watch over, protect, and offer freedom to a lost and dying world. As we look at Rizpah, we see that it's a call for responsive action. We have to do something.

MY SPIRITUAL JOURNEY
What am I doing to raise up those who are dead in sin?

_____

_____

_____

_____

_____

RESPOND AS SAINTS

To the church of God which is at Corinth, to those who are sanctified in Christ Jesus, called to be saints, with all who in every place call on the name of Jesus Christ our Lord, both theirs and ours.-1 Corinthians 1:2 (NKJV)

W e are called to be saints. Our first duty is to demonstrate responsive action to our un-saintly condition. We have to acknowledge that some of us are still in bondage with sin, credit cards, materialism, greed, tradition, and guilt.

The second is the call to a responsive action that will endure, "as long as it takes." We need to take an "as long as it takes" approach to save a dying world attitude, and to work with churches bound up in "tradition attitude."

The third is the call to a responsive action that reflects equality. Rizpah not only watched over her two sons, but she also watched over Michal's five adopted sons. Sometimes we just want to watch over our own but we should work hard to get all unsaved people saved. We cannot limit salvation to our family members. We have been given the Great Commission to go ye into all the world.

MY SPIRITUAL JOURNEY
I have responded as a saint in what areas?

_____

_____

_____

_____

PROMISES AND VOWS BROKEN

If a man vows a vow to the LORD, or swears an oath to bind himself some agreement, he shall not break his word... -Numbers 30:2

One thing God doesn't like is promises and vows broken in His name. To break promises and vows in God's name is to take His name in vain. Our country has made a lot of promises under the constitution that are supposed to be sealed by God. Promises were made to the Native Americans and to African-Americans that were broken. What if we had gotten our forty acres and a mule? There is power in land, but they can keep the mule!! America broke its promise to Native Americans and African-Americans, but kept their promise to sixty thousand Japanese. Where is equality? God does not want us to leave anybody behind. Martin Luther King, Jr. said that none of us would be free until we all were free.

Men and women marry with beautiful and expensive weddings making a vow to be together "'till death do us part," but we find divorce rates at an all time high. Life would be better for all of us if we kept the promises we make to God. God himself is a promise keeper.

MY SPIRITUAL JOURNEY

Have I kept promises that I made in God's name?

WHAT'S OUR MOTIVE?

And again the anger of the LORD was kindled against Israel, and he moved David against them to say, Go, number Israel and Judah -2 Samuel 24:1

We find in 2 Samuel 24 that after David had taken a census of the people, his conscious began to bother him. He confesses his sin to God knowing he had done a terrible thing in numbering the people of Israel. The sin was not in numbering the people, but the motive behind numbering them. David numbered the people to brag on the size of his great army. A word of caution: Everything we do should be done not for ourselves but to the glory of God.

Pride is a deadly sin and we have to be very cautious that we don't become proud in our numbering. David's mistake was bragging rights. He wanted to see how many fighting men were in Israel and Judah. Sometimes Christians want large numbers for bragging rights. How many are in our church, our choirs, and our Sunday school? Boasting on oneself is a deadly sin. David's sin was numbering the people for the wrong reasons and because of it; God sent a plaque upon the land.

MY SPIRITUAL JOURNEY

What is my motive for the things I do for God?

_____

_____

_____

_____

JUST PUNISHMENT

For whom the LORD loveth he correcteth; even as a father the son in whom he delighteth.
-Proverbs 3:12

Many of us praise God for being in the blessing business, but He is also in the correcting business. David confessed and repented of his sin, and like a good father giving an option in punishments to his son, God gave David a choice in how he wanted to be punished. His choice was three years of plague in the land. David knew that punishment from God is just and merciful, but punishment from man is unjust and cruel.

The plague begs a parallel in our lives because there are many evil plagues in our land even now. Murder, selfishness, greed, lust, and domestic problems plague our land today. Plagues today are products of demonic forces and people tend to not fear the punishment. We can easily be part of these plagues if we don't stay in fellowship with God and fear His wrath.

MY SPIRITUAL JOURNEY

At what times have God had to correct me?

_____

_____

_____

_____

_____

_____

_____

EMPTY HANDED

And the king said unto Araunah, Nay: but I will surely buy it of thee at a price: neither will I offer burnt offerings unto the LORD my God of that which doth cost me nothing.
-2 Samuel 24:24

When Araunah met with David, he fell on his face and asked him what he wanted. David told him that he needed a threshing floor to build an altar to the Lord. Araunah told him that he didn't even have to buy it, but that he would give it to him along with an ox to burn, fat for the lighter fluid, and a cart for wood. David's response to Araunah was that he would not worship God with that that cost him nothing. So, David bought the threshing floor, prayed, and the plague was lifted from the land.

David refused to go before God empty handed. Too many of us are going before God empty handed or with praises that cost us nothing. We need to start offering God undignified claps, dances like David, and shouts of "hallelujah." To go before God with praise that costs us something is to praise Him until our praise turns to worship.

MY SPIRITUAL JOURNEY

Do I praise God with that which cost me something?

_____

_____

_____

_____

WORSHIPPING WHILE TROUBLED

And so, falling down on His face, He will worship God and report that God is truly among you. - 1 Corinthians 14:25

God wants us to worship Him even in the midst of trouble. When David built the altar and worshipped, he did it in the midst of trouble. A pastor friend's oldest son was murdered. The son was found several days later. Our pastor friend broke out with praise and worship to God in spite of the hurt and emptiness left from the tragedy.

God invites us to worship Him even though He is not pleased with our behavior. God may not be pleased with our thoughts and actions on Friday and Saturday, but He still wants us to repent and come to worship Him on Sunday.

In the midst of worship God will answer prayer. While David was still on the threshing floor worshipping, God stopped the plague. While my wife was praying and worshiping God in the first church built in Sidney, Australia, God healed her hip.

MY SPIRITUAL JOURNEY

Has God ever answered your prayer in the midst of worship?

_____

_____

_____

_____

_____

WELFARE WORSHIP

Ye are cursed with a curse: for ye have robbed me, even this whole nation. -Malachi 3:9

When we attempt to worship God with that that costs us nothing it is welfare worship. Many feel that the church's purpose is to fulfill their needs instead of fulfilling the purposes of God. When we understand that it is not about us but about God, we can get off Welfare. Some in the church are premier welfare recipients, looking for a free church. They want to park on somebody else's tithe, worship, praise, and gift. Even during praise and worship they are conserving energy that belongs to God.

Giving God that which costs us something is an outgrowth of our desire to worship Him as He intended for us to do. Our outlook will determine our outcome, and if our outcome is to give what we can afford in order to support the ministry we are serving God with that which costs us nothing. Welfare giving leads to welfare living. When our outlook means we are giving to worship God, then He will bless us.

MY SPIRITUAL JOURNEY

Do I give God that that costs me something?

_____

_____

_____

_____

_____

HOLD ON AND STAY IN LINE
... I will not let thee go, except thou bless me. -Genesis 32:26

Genesis 32:24-29, tells the story of how Jacob wrestled with God, refusing to let Him go until He blessed him. Jacob had been a trickster and a liar all of his life. God told him that no longer would his name be Jacob but Israel, which means "prince who has power with God", and because he had prevailed with God, he would prevail with man.

We can find favor with God by persevering and holding on to our blessings. Perseverance is a key factor to finding favor with God. It encourages us to hold on until our change comes, but we have to stay in line. We can't afford to get out of line, because we never know when we are next. I was in a very long line at a Bank one day. I was in a hurry and needed to get back to church, but I decided to be patient and wait. Others, however, became restless and started dropping out of line. About five people in front of me impatiently dropped out of line, and before I knew it, I was next in line.

MY SPIRITUAL JOURNEY
When did I stop "holding on" and get out of the line too soon?

BLESSED THROUGH HARKENING TO HIS VOICE

And all these blessings shall come on thee, and overtake thee, if thou shalt hearken unto the voice of the LORD thy God. -Deuteronomy 28:2

God has promised that if we hearken diligently, He will bless us in powerful ways. He wants us to hear Him and do His will. Hearing must be followed by doing. The word "hear" in the Bible means "do." Hearing means doing. Hearkening to the voice of God is keeping His commandments. If we hearken to His voice, we will be blessed.

We are cautioned to read the fine print in the promise keeper's contract list of promises. Usually the fine print is followed by a little subjunctive clause that begins with "if." God has promised that if we hearken to (do) His will, He will make us the head and not the tail, and everywhere we go, blessings will overtake us. In other words, if we hearken diligently to His voice, we will be so blessed that we will bump into blessings as we journey through life.

MY SPIRITUAL JOURNEY

Can I recall having bumped into blessings?

BLESSED THROUGH FAITH

...And I will make of thee a great nation, and I will bless thee, and make thy name great; and thou shalt be a blessing. -Genesis 12:1-2

God called Abraham, the father of faith, to go to a foreign country. He was called to go, not knowing where he was going or who he would meet there. God promised Abraham multiple blessings, including the promise that he would bless his seed. We are all seeds of Abraham. Therefore, all the blessings that were promised to Abraham are available to us.

God continues to ask us to have faith in Him. In our personal lives, we have to step out on faith and be blessed. Too many of us are holding on to the trunk of the tree. Faith is out on the limb. We have to learn to release the trunk and go out on the limb.

There is a definite relationship between faith and blessings. There are at least three things concerning faith that relate to blessings: 1) faith blesses us with righteousness, 2) faith blesses us with grace, and 3) faith guarantees the promises of God.

MY SPIRITUAL JOURNEY

How has having faith in God blessed me?

_____

_____

_____

_____

_____

September 4
BLESSED THROUGH BLESSING OTHERS

And I will bless them that bless thee, and curse him that curseth thee: and in thee shall all families of the earth be blessed. -Genesis 12:3

God has spiritual laws. When blessings go up, blessings come down, and when blessings go out, blessings come in. In Genesis 12:1-3, God promises Abram a sevenfold blessing. What a wonderful promise that God made available to us that He will bless our name, our seed, and our entire family. He will even bless those that bless us. And He has promised that He will curse those that come up against us. This promise is sure, and we have the availability of all these promises.

The key to receiving these blessings is to bless God and others. When we get up in the morning, we should look for an opportunity to bless God through somebody in need. My wife has "A Ministry of Hope", and our church adopted an elementary school in a very low income area. At Christmas time, each child in the school receives gifts. Each fifth grade student gets a brand new bike. Dr. Sadie McCalep is a blessing to the students, but God has poured out so many blessings to us that we don't have room to receive them. He is a promise-keeper.

MY SPIRITUAL JOURNEY
Am I in the habit of blessing others?

_____

_____

_____

248

STINKING THINKING

Finally, brethren, whatsoever things are true, whatsoever things are honest, whatsoever things are just, whatsoever things are pure, whatsoever things are lovely, whatsoever things are of good report; if there be any virtue, and if there be any praise, think on these things.
-Philippians 4:8

Obedient thoughts produce a blessed life. Think blessed, and be blessed. God has given us the power to govern our thoughts; therefore, we should bring our imagination and thoughts into obedience with God (2 Corinthians 10:5).

Many Christians suffer from what has been labeled "stinking thinking." Stinking thinking is negative thinking, and for the believer, negative thinking is embracing and being intimate with the dead. The Bible tells us very clearly that we were dead in our trespasses, but God has made us alive in Christ. (Romans 6:11). "For to be carnally minded is death; but to be spiritually minded is life and peace" (Romans 8:6). Our sins died when Christ was crucified. He cast them into the sea of forgetfulness never to rise again (Hebrews 10:17), but we keep searching, diving, and washing them up to shore. Get rid of the corpse. Put dead thinking on the cross. Put Jesus on the throne, and be blessed.

MY SPIRITUAL JOURNEY

Am I carrying any 'stinking thinking' that needs to be left on the cross?

BLESSED THROUGH AFFLICTION

It is good for me that I have been afflicted; that I might learn thy statutes.
-Psalm 119:71.

When Daniel was in the lions' den, he wasn't looking at the lions, he was looking towards heaven. When we're in the lion's den, our focus is on our problem, but God's Word instructs us not to focus on our problem, but on Him. How can we be blessed through affliction? Affliction can bring us closer to God and can be used to bring glory to Him.

Affliction can be a problem we can't solve or a sickness that lingers. Affliction comes in many bags, packaged in many ways. God's Word should be a comfort to us in the time of affliction. God uses affliction to correct us and humble us. Like a loving parent, God often has to punish us to make us obey. He sometimes allows us to go through affliction for growth and maturity. He is preparing us to be used by Him.

MY SPIRITUAL JOURNEY

During what afflictions have I allowed (or am I allowing) myself to focus on the problem instead of God?

_____

_____

_____

_____

_____

BLESSED THROUGH PAYING THE PRICE

But unto Cain and his offering, he had not respect. And Cain was very wroth and his countenance fell. -Genesis 4:5

To truly be blessed, we have to pay dues. There are dues of rejection, criticism, envy, jealousy, and isolation. It is lonely at the top. If we are blessed, people are sometimes envious and become jealous of our blessings.

Cain and Abel were brothers (Genesis 4). God blessed Abel's sacrifice. Abel had a more acceptable sacrifice, and Cain didn't like it. So Cain rose up against Abel and killed him. The spirit of Cain still exists today. Cain's children believe that the blessings we have belong to them. Cain's children do not want to pay the price for being blessed. They're set on pulling us back with them. They try to isolate us and stop talking to us. They want us to be part of their unblessed group. Eventually, some of us, rather than finding favor with God, will go back and find favor with the children of Cain.

MY SPIRITUAL JOURNEY

What were the price tags of my blessings? Have I found favor with the children of Cain?

BLESSED THROUGH HUMILITY

Blessed are the poor in spirit: for theirs is the kingdom of heaven.
-Matthew 5:3

The Be-attitudes are attitudes of humility demonstrated. Each of the nine Be-attitudes is characterized by humility. Happy and blessed are they that demonstrate these characteristics of humility. However, Jesus teaches us a great lesson in humility when He washes the disciples' feet. He concluded this action by saying, Happy are you if you do this (John 13:17). In other words, blessed are those who practice humility.

Humility means getting down off our high horse of pride and self-righteousness, achievements, and degrees. We lose humility the moment we think we have it because humility is demonstrated, not spoken.

In fact, Jesus told us that when we are offered the high seat to take the low one. Then, when we take the low seat, men will give us the high seat. That's a demonstration of humility.

MY SPIRITUAL JOURNEY

How do I demonstrate humility?

_____

_____

_____

_____

_____

BLESSED THROUGH TRIALS AND
TRIBULATIONS (Count It All Joy)

Blessed is the man who perseveres under trial, because when he has stood the test, he will receive the crown of life that God has promised to those who love him.

-James 1:12 (NIV)

A re you going through anything? You're probably in one of three categories: you're about to go through it, you're going through it; or praise God, you just came out of it.

The explicit suggestion from James, the half brother of our Savior, Jesus Christ, is that we will have trials and tribulations. They will come in divergent forms and various ways: sickness, disease, accidents, disappointments, sorrow, suffering, and even death. Blessed is the man or woman who makes it through, for there is a blessing on the other side of through.

How do we get through? First, we ask God for wisdom. Secondly, we count it all joy (James 1:2). Rejoice in your present status. In sickness, count it all joy. In suffering and disappointments, count it all joy. In sorrow, count it all joy. In trouble, count it all joy. To be blessed as we make it through, we must change our attitude from negative to positive thinking.

MY SPIRITUAL JOURNEY

Do I believe I can make it through?

253

BLESSED THROUGH BLESSING GOD'S LEADERS

But Moses' hands were heavy; and they took a stone, and put it under him, and he sat thereon; and Aaron and Hur stayed up his hands, the one on the one side, and the other on the other side; and his hands were steady until the going down of the sun. -Exodus 17: 12

Exodus 17:12 tells how the people of God supported Pastor Moses by lifting up his tired, weary, heavy arms in battle. Because the people supported the arms of the leader, God gave them the victory. There is a blessing in supporting God's leaders.

Sometimes the leader gets weak. The leader may not always be able to lead us in praise or dance, or running a victory lap. Someone may have to run a victory lap for the leader. Notice that the people propped Moses up as he sat on a stone or a rock. When we live up to our responsibility of supporting God's leaders, God blesses us. This cannot be done in the flesh, but it can be accomplished in the Spirit. The victory is not ours, but belongs to the Lord, who is our rock and salvation.

MY SPIRITUAL JOURNEY

Do I support God's leaders? How do I disagree with them?

_____

_____

_____

_____

_____

September 11
BLESSED THROUGH BLUNDERS

And we know that all things work together for good to them that love God, to them who are the called according to his purpose. -Romans 8:28

G od has promised in His Word that He can bless us through our blunders. Romans 8:28 assures us of this promise. God will turn our blunders into blessings in due season, if we hold on through the winter. God promised that "all things work together for good to those who love Him and are called according to His purpose." However, there are some provisions that are our responsibility.

These responsibilities are (1) do not grow weary in doing good, especially when bad things happen; (2) trust in the reliability of God's promise; (3) be called according to His purpose; and (4) love Him. God wants to and is able to bless us through our blunders.

MY SPIRITUAL JOURNEY
Have I had blunders that I can now testify have turned into blessings?

_____

_____

_____

_____

_____

_____

_____

_____

September 12

BLESSED THROUGH HIS POORNESS

For ye know the grace of our Lord Jesus Christ, that, though he was rich, yet for your sakes he became poor, that ye through his poverty might be rich. -2 Corinthians 8:9

How rich was Jesus Christ? According to Jude 1:24-25, He dwelt in the glory of the majesty and the dominion that God had. According to 1 Timothy 6:16, He dwelt in a light that no man could approach in all the splendor and brilliance of the Godhead. According to James 1:17, He possessed every good and perfect thing that could be possessed.

Jesus could have stayed on the heavenly throne but volunteered to become a poor and humble man. The perfect one took on flesh and blood and became the rejected sacrifice for sin (Philippians 2:5-8).

He left His throne of riches to be born poor, a child of a carpenter and peasant girl. Though He died poor, He arose rich. How are we blessed through His poorness? Those who receive Him become joint heirs to His throne. Our Father is rich. The earth and the fullness thereof belong to Him.

MY SPIRITUAL JOURNEY

Is this a blessing I usually embrace or tend to forget?

_____

_____

_____

_____

September 13
BLESSED THROUGH THE FEAR OF THE LORD

PRAISE ye the Lord. Blessed is the man that feareth the Lord, that delighteth greatly in his commandments -Psalm 112:1.

Wisdom did not begin in kindergarten. Neither did it begin learning the "three r's"—reading, (w)riting, and (a)rithmetic. Nor did it begin with philosophy. Wisdom, according to God's word, begins with the fear of the Lord. We are even commanded to fear God. "And now, Israel, what doth the Lord thy God require of thee, but to fear the Lord thy God" (Deuteronomy 10:12).

To fear God means to reverence Him enough to be afraid of His wrath. We ought to revere God, who is able to destroy both body and soul (Matthew 10:28). We should fear God because those who fear Him shall be blessed in that: (1) their children shall be blessed, (2) they will be able to overcome crises, (3) they will be remembered for a long time, (4) they will be given exalted power, and (5) they will not be afraid or worry about the future (Psalm 112:2-9).

Our family fears the wrath of God that would result from our not being true tithers. There are many in the church who lie about their tithe. We quiver in fear for them. We remember what happened to Ananias and Sapphira when they lied to the Holy Ghost about their giving (Acts 5:1-11).

MY SPIRITUAL JOURNEY
Am I keeping God's commandments? Do I fear Him?

September 14

BLESSED THROUGH RIGHT GIVING

But this I say, He which soweth sparingly shall reap also sparingly; and he which soweth bountifully shall reap also bountifully. -2 Corinthians 9:6

When we plant a corn seed, a corn stalk comes up and bears many ears of corn. Just like a productive stalk of corn, God has enabled us to plant a garden of blessings. By sowing and reaping bountifully, we don't plant a blessing seed and get just one blessing.

There is a relationship between sowing and reaping just as there is a relationship between planting and harvesting. Planting and harvesting is a natural law that applies to the spiritual law of sowing and reaping sparingly, and sowing and reaping bountifully. I am often asked, "Should I tithe from my gross or on my net?" The humorous answer to that is a question, "Do you want to be blessed on the net or on the gross?" The real answer comes from the natural law that if we sow sparingly, we will reap sparingly; if we sow bountifully, we will reap bountifully.

MY SPIRITUAL JOURNEY

How is my giving? Are my blessings evident of my giving?

_____

_____

_____

_____

_____

258

BLESSED THROUGH THE WORD OF GOD

BLESSED are the undefiled in the way, who walk in the law of the LORD. Blessed are they that keep his testimonies, and that seek him with the whole heart. -Psalm 119:1-2

Blessed are those who keep God's word. Keeping His word is to store up His word. Those who keep His word embrace it with affection and adoration, as we would a precious diamond or jewel that we put in a treasury box. Our treasure box is our heart. We treasure God's word by keeping it in our heart. David said in Psalm 119:11, "Thy word have I hid in mine heart, that I might not sin against thee."

Blessed are those who not only walk in and keep God's word but also seek God's word. Seeking God's word means to study and have a desire to commune with Him more closely. It means to enter into a more perfect communion with Him. To seek His word means to seek His presence. Keeping, seeking, and walking in God's word represent the threefold blessing God has given us.

MY SPIRITUAL JOURNEY

Am I walking, keeping and seeking God's word?

259

BLESSED THROUGH BEING DRESSED RIGHT

No one sews a patch of unshrunk cloth on an old garment. If he does, the new piece will pull away from the old, making the tear worse. Mark 2:21 (NIV)

God wants to bless us with a new Spirit, but we need a new vessel for our new spirit. We need to take off our old garments and put on the garment of righteousness.

Jesus said that no man could place a new piece of cloth on an old garment to repair it. If he does, the new piece will be pulled away from the old, making the tear even worse. He also said that if we put new wine in old wineskins, the fermentation of the new will bubble, the old wineskin will tear apart, and all the wine will run out and be wasted.

It's the same when God gets ready to do a new thing in us. He starts fermentation in our soul. Something starts bubbling up, and the Holy Ghost begins working in our lives. We must be new because the old man cannot hold Holy Ghost bubbling. In old skin, that bubbling will go to waste and all the newness that God wants to bless us with will be wasted.

MY SPIRITUAL JOURNEY

What is the old God wants me to put off?

_____

_____

_____

_____

BLESSED THROUGH THE GOSPEL OF FORGIVENESS

BLESSED is he whose transgression is forgiven, whose sin is covered. Blessed is the man unto whom the LORD imputeth not iniquity, and in whose spirit there is no guile.
-Psalm 32:1-2

We are blessed through a gospel that has a provision for forgiveness of our sin no matter how great our sins may be.

Sin can be viewed in five stages: first, sin committed; second, sin concealed; third, sin's heavy burden; fourth, sin confessed; and fifth, sin forgiven. The biblical concept of sin is revealed from three perspectives: (1) transgression, which means to stray away from; (2) sin, which means to miss the mark; and (3) iniquity, which carries with it the burden of guilt and rebellion. We are blessed because the strength of forgiveness is greater than any sin.

God stands ready to bless us through forgiveness if we repent and confess our sins.

MY SPIRITUAL JOURNEY

Are there sins in my life I feel too ashamed to take to God? Am I ready to take the step of confession and be forgiven?

261

BE BLESSED-BLESS THE POOR

BLESSED is he that considereth the poor: the LORD will deliver him in time of trouble. The LORD will preserve him, and keep him alive; and he shall be blessed upon the earth: and thou wilt not deliver him unto the will of his enemies. The LORD will strengthen him upon the bed of languishing: thou wilt make all his bed in his sickness. -Psalm 41:1-3

God promises that we will be especially blessed if we give to the poor. He also warns us that if we fail to help the poor, the poor may testify against us before Him. "...and thou givest him nought; and he cry unto the LORD against thee, and it be sin unto thee" (Deuteronomy 15:9b). Who are the poor? The poor are those who need help to survive.

Poor people are not poor because God does not love them. The Psalmist says that if we bless the poor, God will deliver us in times of trouble, keep us alive long enough to bless us on earth, not deliver us into the hands of our enemy, and strengthen us on our sickbed (Psalm 41:1-3).

Acts 20:35 states, "It is more blessed to give than to receive." On which end of the equation would we rather be? Would we rather be on the giving end, or on the receiving end?

MY SPIRITUAL JOURNEY

How often do I give to or help the poor?

_____

_____

_____

_____

BLESSED THROUGH FASTING AND PRAYING

Moreover when ye fast, be not, as the hypocrites, of a sad countenance: for they disfigure their faces, that they may appear unto men to fast. Verily I say unto you, They have their reward. But thou, when thou fastest, anoint thine head, and wash thy face; That thou appear not unto men to fast, but unto thy Father which is in secret: and thy Father, which seeth in secret, shall reward thee openly. -Matthew 6:16-18

Fasting as it relates to praying, for the most part, is an undiscovered spiritual phenomenon. It is a potential blessing bombshell ready to explode. God has promised that if we pray right and fast right, he will reward us. Praying and fasting involve not seeking the approval of men for our religious acts, rather, seeking only to glorify God.

Fasting allows us to get closer to God, which in itself is a blessing. Praying and fasting are not optional to the believer. It is a Christian duty. God says, "when" you pray and fast, not "if" you pray and fast. The assumption is that it is something we must do. God is not with us in the flesh. This is a reason for fasting. Although God does not tell us when or how often we should fast, there are some good, best, and most helpful times to fast.

MY SPIRITUAL JOURNEY

When and why did I last fast?

_____

_____

_____

_____

TIME FOR FASTING AND PRAYING

As they ministered to the Lord, and fasted, the Holy Ghost said, Separate me Barnabas and Saul for the work whereunto I have called them. And when they had fasted and prayed, and laid their hands on them, they sent them away. - Acts 13: 2-3

When is a good time to fast and pray? A good time to fast and pray is when we need special power. God has promised such power if the believer prays and fasts. "And he said unto them, This kind can come forth by nothing, but by prayer and fasting" (Mark 9:29).

1. When we need special power. God has promised such power if the believer prays and fasts. *And he said unto them, This kind can come forth by nothing, but by prayer and fasting* (Mark 9:29).

2. When we need to humble ourselves before God and become totally dependent upon Him. *I humbled my soul with fasting; and my prayer returned into mine own bosom* (Psalm 35:13).

3. When a special need arises, such as a need for a healing blessing (Matthew 6:16-18).

4. When we need deliverance (2 Chronicles 7:14).

MY SPIRITUAL JOURNEY

Do I have a need for God's special power at the present time?

_____

_____

_____

BENEFITS OF FASTING AND PRAYING

*Cornelius answered; Four days ago I was fasting until this hour; and at the ninth hour
I prayed in my house, and behold, a man stood before me in bright clothing and said,
Cornelius thy prayer is heard and thine alms are held in remembrance in the sight of God.*
- *Acts 10:30-31*

We are blessed in many ways through fasting and praying. However, there are other benefits that can be counted as blessings.

1. Fasting keeps us in the presence of God.

2. Fasting helps us stay physically fit.

3. Fasting keeps us from being in bondage to bad habits.

4. Fasting keeps us disciplined and in control of our actions.

5. Fasting helps us demonstrate our love and seriousness to God.

6. Fasting humbles us and teaches us to be dependent on God.

7. Fasting helps us to be obedient. Obedience is the key to receiving all the promised blessings of God.

MY SPIRITUAL JOURNEY

How have I been blessed through fasting and praying?

_____

_____

_____

September 22

BLESSED AND NOT CURSED

If ye will not hear, and if ye will not lay it to heart, to give glory unto my name, saith the LORD of hosts, I will even send a curse upon you, and I will curse your blessings: yea, I have cursed them already, because ye do not lay it to heart. -Malachi 2:2

A blessing is only a blessing when it brings peace and joy. Many believe their unaffordable homes are blessings until they end up in foreclosure. Debt is not a blessing: it is a curse (Romans 13:8). Things sometimes look like blessings when we see them, but they just might be curses. The good news is that when we operate in the will of God, He can turn our curses into blessings.

We learn that when we use our blessings in a way that is inconsistent with God's way and purpose, our blessings turn into curses. Our hearts, minds, and bodies have to be prepared for blessings. We prepare for blessings by being obedient to God and by giving Him glory.

MY SPIRITUAL JOURNEY

What are the things I count as blessings? Do they bring me peace? Why or why not?

_____

_____

_____

_____

_____

September 23
WHERE IS THE TEMPLE NOW?

Know ye not that ye are the temple of God, and that the Spirit of God dwelleth in you?
-1 Corinthians 3:16

The temples in the Old and New Testament were made under the divine direction of God to express His nature, thoughts, and purpose. From time to time, the glory of God would appear in these man-made temples.

One day Jesus said to the Jewish leaders, Destroy this temple, and in three days I will raise it up. Jesus was referring to himself as the temple that would one day be crucified and resurrected. In the Old Testament, the Holy Spirit would come upon men. After Pentecost, we, the body of Christ became the temple of God. We are the temples where the Holy Spirit now dwells. It is in us that God, the creator of all mankind, has chosen to live. What a privilege and an honor to be chosen as a temple of God.

MY SPIRITUAL JOURNEY

How can I describe the privilege of being a temple of God?

_____

_____

_____

_____

_____

_____

_____

PREPARING THE TEMPLE FOR REVIVAL

If any man defile the temple of God, him shall God destroy; for the temple of God is holy,
which temple ye are. -1 Corinthians. 3:17

In 2 Chronicles 7:1-20, God teaches us how to prepare a temple for revival. First, there must be a prayer of repentance and forgiveness. Second, there must be a sacrificial offering. The true measure of a thankful heart is to be willing to give up something of value for something of more value. Third, when we prepare the temple for revival, celebration, singing, and joy making are the order of worship.

There are two temples God expects us to honor, the building and the body. If we bless the temple, God will bless us, but if we destroy the temple, God will destroy us. To defile the temple is to destroy it. We defile the building by not keeping it clean and allowing children to spill food, to draw on pews, to deposit their gum, and more. We defile the body by overeating, drinking strong drinks, doing drugs, having unsanctified sex, watching rated "R" movies, and more. God expects us to sanctify the building and the body. Without sanctification of the temple, there can be no revival.

MY SPIRITUAL JOURNEY

How can I sanctify His temple?

_____

_____

_____

THE PROBLEM WITH DOUBLE-MINDEDNESS

But when he asks, he must believe and not doubt, because he who doubts is like a wave of the sea, blown and tossed by the wind. That man [or that woman] should not think he will receive anything from the Lord; he is a double-minded man, unstable in all he does.
-James 1:6-8 NIV

A woman went to a bakery to purchase a chocolate cake. She asked for a slice of the chocolate cake but then asked for the coconut cake. Before the baker could cut it, she asked for the caramel cake. She then noticed the freshly made chocolate chip cookies and wanted them. She wasn't satisfied with her choice. She became disgusted because she couldn't decide what she wanted; she lost her appetite and left with nothing.

Double-minded people can never make up their minds. James 1:8 says, "A double minded man is unstable in all his ways." Every decision a double-minded person makes is without certainty. A double-minded person is always beginning something, stopping something, and starting all over again. They have faith that's shaky, flaky, and raggedy. A double-minded person has difficulty pleasing God because he never trusts Him.

MY SPIRITUAL JOURNEY

How is my faith? Am I a double-minded person?

_____

_____

_____

_____

_____

IF I PERISH, I PERISH

And so will I go in unto the king, which is not according to the law: and if I perish, I perish. -Esther 4:16e

---

Esther had no idea that she would be the one to plead on behalf of the Jewish people. Mordecai had no idea what God was about to accomplish through their lives. However, Mordecai had an idea that the evil Prime Minister, Haman, would destroy his people. So one day Mordecai said a most impacting thing to Esther, "…who knoweth whether thou art come to the kingdom for such a time as this?" (Esther 4:14)

She then told Mordecai to tell the people to fast day and night, and at such a time, she would go to see the king. She asked them to pray that the king would hold out the golden scepter to her for it was dangerous to go to the King without asking. One could be put to death. Esther was ready to face the king for a worthy cause. She declared, "If I perish, I perish." Eventually, Esther went to the king and was victorious.

God's providential hand made Esther's purpose very clear and blessed her actions. God's providential hand is on us for such a time as this.

MY SPIRITUAL JOURNEY

What is His plan for me?

Esther had not shewed her people nor her kindred: for Mordecai had charged her that she should not shew it. -Esther 2:10

I t's time for us to get real. The king didn't know that Esther was Jewish. She was what we call today, "passing." Some people pass for other races to avoid discrimination, maybe even death. Some of us are passing like Esther, wearing Holy Ghost masks when we are not holy. Some of us are wearing unemotional masks when we really want to cry. Some of us are wearing dignified masks when we really need to shout.

Preachers and pastors, musicians and choir members, deacons and trustees, ushers and church members, get real. Holier than thou folk, get real. Esther had to get real to save her people. Getting real is about accepting the fact that we are nothing without God, and everything we have belongs to God. Get Real.

MY SPIRITUAL JOURNEY
In what areas of my life have I failed to be real with God?

HOW TO GET REAL

And ye are complete in him, which is the head of all principality and power.
-Colossians 2:10

God knows each of us by name. He knows everything we've ever done or thought. Some folks think that when they cut the lights off and close the door, God does not see them, but God is the maker of darkness and light and sees all.

In getting real, we need to pull off our masks and stop pretending. We can't save ourselves. We are saved only by God's grace and made complete by His righteousness. We must be real from the inside out if we are to minister to others. No matter what psychologists or New Age religion tells us, we are not okay in ourselves. We are only okay in Christ Jesus. He is all our righteousness, and it is in Him we stand complete.

If we get real with God and ourselves, we can wake up every morning and face the world with a joyful heart. We will be able to reach out and hug anyone in the love of Jesus.

MY SPIRITUAL JOURNEY

How real am I about who I am? How much do others influence who I am?

September 29
WHAT HAPPENS WHEN WE GET REAL?

And all the rulers of the provinces, and the lieutenants, and the deputies, and officers of the king, helped the Jews; because the fear of Mordecai fell upon them. -Esther 9:3

When we get real, we will trust God, and He will make our enemies our footstools. Mordecai trusted God for deliverance. In indirect words, Mordecai told Esther that if she didn't get real and pull off her mask, God would find another way to help them. Because Mordecai and Esther got real and trusted God, Haman was hung on the same rope he had built for Mordecai. Additionally, Esther received Haman's house and Mordecai received his job.

When we get real, our faith increases, and we are willing to sacrifice everything. When we get real with God, we humble ourselves before Him, making ourselves available for His purposes, and He will bless us and use us in mighty ways.

MY SPIRITUAL JOURNEY
Am I available for the purposes of God?

_____

_____

_____

_____

_____

_____

_____

_____

THE OVERLOAD PRINCIPLE

To him that overcometh will I grant to sit with me in my throne, even as I also overcame, and am set down with my Father in his throne. -Revelation 3:21

Many of us today are exercising for health; we're jogging to overload our heart. It's called the overload principle. If we increase our heart rate, depending upon our age, for about twenty minutes, it will help our heart get stronger. If we lift weights, the muscle, when it is overloaded, gets stronger. We overload our physical bodies to become stronger.

God is the originator of the overload principle. God is the author of what we see people now do for their physical bodies and their mental bodies. Similarly, God sometimes permits overload to make us stronger. Through trials, tribulations, temptations, sickness, suffering, disappointment, oppression, depression, and even death, He permits it so that we might overcome and become stronger.

MY SPIRITUAL JOURNEY

At what times have I had to use the overload principle? Did I overcome?

October 1

TESTING AND TEMPTING

Let no man say when he is tempted, I am tempted of God: for God cannot be tempted with evil, neither tempteth he any man. -James 1:13

When Jane met tall, dark, handsome, unsaved Jerry, everyone knew he was bad for her, except Jane. When she finally realized what everyone else already knew, she commented, "God had to tempt me so I wouldn't make the same mistake again, but I've learned my lesson." Yes, God allows testing. Yet we must not mistake God's allowing us to be tested with God tempting us. God does not tempt us to do evil. That would be against His nature. Evil results from our own lusts. The word "temptation" used in the KJV has two meanings. One is "testing for righteousness." The other is "enticement to sin."

Testing, or being tried, results in patience, and patience means perseverance. Perseverance brings us into perfection. God allows us to be tried and tested because it results in perseverance. Just as a child must persevere to come into maturity, so must the believer.

MY SPIRITUAL JOURNEY

At what times have I followed my own lust and claimed it to be God testing me?

_____

_____

_____

_____

_____

GOD IS A PROMISE-KEEPER

... there hath not failed one word of all His good promise, which he promised by the hand of Moses his servant. 1 Kings 8:56

Making promises to God is a serious matter. Many people make promises to God but fail to keep them. God is a promise-keeper, so we ought to be promise-keepers. Every promise God has made has come to pass except the promise of Jesus Christ's return. God is not a liar, so it, too, shall come to pass. We ought to keep our promises to God because He kept His to us. We don't have to wait until He performs His promise; we can shout in advance.

In Judges 11:30-31, Jephthah made a promise to God that he regretted. He promised God that if He would give him victory over the Ammonites, he would offer as a burnt offering to God the first thing that came out of his house to greet him. God gave Jephthah the victory, and when he came home, the first to greet him was his daughter. We need to be careful in making promises to God. We should make promises that our hearts will allow us to keep.

MY SPIRITUAL JOURNEY

Am I a promise-keeper? What promises to God have I not kept?

_____

_____

_____

_____

YOUR PROMISE SHOULD BE HOLY

I will go into thy house with burnt offerings: I will pay thee my vows, Which my lips have uttered, and my mouth hath spoken, when I was in trouble. -Psalm 66:13-14

We usually make promises to God in times of trouble. However, when He delivers us, we break our promises by not giving Him credit for the breakthrough. God heals us from sickness and diseases, and we give praise and credit to our doctors.

We try to negotiate promises with God. For instance, we tell God, we will tithe if He gives us a car or if He pays our house note. We can't cut a deal with the Holy One. God is the deal cutter. He is the one who told us to prove Him by bringing all the tithe into the storehouse, and He would pour us out a blessing.

Promises should be holy and made out of appreciation, not manipulation. God is pleased when we keep our promises. When we don't, it displeases Him. According to Acts 5:1-10, Ananias and Sapphira promised to sell some land and to give the proceeds of the sale to the church. He and his wife lied to God, and because of it, they both fell dead.

MY SPIRITUAL JOURNEY

Have I ever manipulated any promises to God?

_____

_____

_____

LOVE YOUR ENEMIES

But I say unto you which hear, Love your enemies, do good to them which hate you, Bless them that curse you, and pray for them which despitefully use you. -Luke 6:27

W ho is our enemy? Our enemy is that person on our job who is trying to get us fired. Our enemy is that person who steps over us or will not speak to us. Our enemy is that person who talks about us and stabs us in the back. We are to do good to them. One reason we are to do good to our enemies is because God requires it of us. God is a good parent who shares and explains the reason for what He tells us to do. He said that crucifying our fleshly nature is our greatest victory over self. Our flesh does not want to pray for, bless, or love those who do us wrong.

Another reason we are to do good to our enemies is that it is the greatest victory over evil. We can love, pray, and bless the hell out of somebody. We can love the hate out of the world.

MY SPIRITUAL JOURNEY

How has loving my enemy given me victory over evil?

_____

_____

_____

_____

_____

_____

_____

October 5
PRACTICE LOVING EVERYONE
And the Lord make you to increase and abound in love one toward another...
-1 Thessalonians 3:12

The greatest practice strategies for love were given to us by Jesus Christ. Jesus loved us so much that He gave up His life. He showed love to thieves, prostitutes, and to loving and kind people as well. He even showed love for those who murdered Him by asking the Father to forgive them. Practice means to put principles into action. Jesus has given us some principles we need to put into action by His example.

Jesus taught us in the sermon on the mountain to love our enemies. Here is where most of us fail in the practice of the principle. We close our ears, not wanting to hear, because we don't want to believe that loving our enemies is possible. Jesus didn't command us to fall in love with our enemies, but He simply said to show love towards them. He told us to do it by doing good to those who hate us, blessing those who curse us, praying for those who despitefully use us, not judging, and forgiving those who hurt us. We must willfully practice these things.

MY SPIRITUAL JOURNEY
How do I show love towards my enemies?

_____
_____
_____
_____

THE NEXT LEVEL IS LOVING

But love ye your enemies, and do good, and lend hoping to gain nothing; and your reward shall be great... -Luke 6:35

Learning to love our enemies can be obtained through four levels of gradation as we move from devilish to divine.

The first level is in hating those who love us. This level can be seen in a parent-child relationship when the child is rebellious. There is no question in the rebellious child's mind that the parent loves him. Yet he still rebels. It causes the parent to feel a sense of hate for the child, yet, still loving the child. The second level is in hating those who hate us. This is the level the world teaches, an eye for an eye and a tooth for a tooth. The third level is to love those who love us. We love those who love us. We pray for those who pray for us and bless those who bless us. But Jesus says even sinners can do that. Jesus wants to take us to the next level of loving those who hate us, our enemies.

MY SPIRITUAL JOURNEY

Do I pray for my enemies and for those who have hurt me?

BEING BLESSED THROUGH GIVING

Give, and it shall be given unto you; good measure, pressed down, and shaken together, and running over, shall men give into your bosom... -Luke 6:38

Jesus taught us on the sermon on the plain to give. In Luke 6:38, Jesus uses a mixing illustration to teach us how to give, and it's actually the same principle that declares, if we sow sparingly, we will reap sparingly, and if we sow bountifully, we will reap bountifully. God has promised that whatever we measure out, more will come back to us.

As a child, when I visited my grandparents in Lawrence, Kansas, I looked forward to Sunday evening when we would get in their old Chrysler and drive downtown to get hand-packed ice cream. I delighted in knowing that when the container was filled with ice cream, it had to be pressed down so that more could be added. God declares that whatever we measure out, He is going to pack it down and run it over. If we practice loving and giving, God will personally hand-pack blessings on our behalf.

MY SPIRITUAL JOURNEY

Do I give to others like God gives to me?

_____

_____

_____

_____

_____

MEDITATION IMPROVES OUR THINKING

This book of the law shall not depart out of thy mouth; but thou shalt meditate therein day and night, that thou mayest observe to do according to all that is written therein: for then thou shalt make thy way prosperous, and then thou shalt have good success. - Joshua 1:8

God encouraged Joshua to be strong, courageous, and meditate on His word day and night. Notice that God lets Joshua know that meditating on His word would bring good success. God emphasizes good success because there is also bad success. Examples of bad success are people laundering drug money and people moving up the corporate ladder by compromising their principles and others. Because of Joshua's obedience, God pushed back the Jordan River and gave him many other victories. Joshua had good success because he included meditation.

Meditation is a private, devotional, deliberate act of reflecting on God's truths joined by prayer that will determine resolution on future conduct. Meditation builds character that leads to prosperity and success. Meditation is an individual, deliberate act that we simply must practice.

MY SPIRITUAL JOURNEY

How has meditation helped me to be successful?

_____

_____

_____

_____

MEDITATION IMPROVES OUR PROSPERITY

Meditate upon these things; give thyself wholly to them; that thy profiting may appear to all.
-1 Timothy 4:15

If we meditate day and night, we will prosper and have good success. Our lack of success may be contributed to the fact that we don't make time to meditate and be with God. I thought I would never have to speak to my congregation about cell phones in the church, but I did. People are so busy they don't have time to remember to turn off their cell phones.

There are those who believe in order to be holy we must be poor. But God said in 3 John 1:2, "Beloved, I wish above all things that thou mayest prosper and be in health, even as thy soul prospereth." God wants us to prosper so that we can be generous to the less fortunate and build His kingdom. In order to meditate, we must deliberately schedule private time with God. Meditation is thinking. Take time to meditate on God's word.

MY SPIRITUAL JOURNEY

How can I better schedule private and meditation time with God? What frivolous things can I take from my schedule to be replaced with time with God?

283

MEDITATION PURIFIES AND CLEANSES

Create in me a clean heart, O God and renew a steadfast spirit within me.
- Psalm 51:10

Meditation helps to build and determine future conduct. It helps to purify and cleanse the heart and soul and adds freshness to the taste of life (Psalm 19:14, Psalm 104:34). When I was coaching football years ago, while on the bus to the game, my players were required to sit quietly and focus on the game, unlike other teams that laughed, talked, and played while riding. I believe meditation helped to determine our future conduct, causing us to win three championships.

Meditation helps to prepare us for the future. In the Old Testament, the word "meditate" indicates something done before-hand. Joshua was to meditate before he crossed Jordan River. This Old Testament example of meditation ought to be a New Testament example for us. We ought to meditate before we get married, take a new job, ask for a raise, and make other major decisions that will affect us and our family.

MY SPIRITUAL JOURNEY

What decision did I make that I now wish I had meditated on before making it?

_____

_____

_____

DEATHBED STATEMENTS

Knowing that shortly I must put off this my tabernacle, even as our Lord Jesus Christ hath shewed me. -2 Peter 1:14

A young man felt like giving up on life. Within a year, he was laid off his job of several years, was experiencing marital problems, and now his grandmother, the one who raised him, was dying. However, she left him with encouraging words that changed his life. She said, "Son, don't give up. You use to talk about your hopes and dreams, well now is the time to dream bigger. This time, dream with your wife at your side."

Deathbed statements aren't new to us. Joshua in his last days challenged the people regarding their loyalty to God, saying, "And if it seem evil unto you to serve the Lord, choose you this day whom ye will serve; …but as for me and my house, we will serve the Lord." According to 2 Peter 1:14, Jesus had revealed to Peter that He would soon be leaving His earthy life. Later Peter decided to leave us with some words of wisdom. He challenged us to stir up our remembrance of who we are in Christ Jesus.

MY SPIRITUAL JOURNEY

If I knew that I was leaving this earth today, to whom would I want to leave a deathbed statement?

285

STIR UP THE HOLY SPIRIT

Will you not revive us again, that your people may rejoice in you.
-Psalm 85:6 NIV

In 2 Peter 1:13, Peter didn't say he wanted to "bring to our remembrance", but that he wanted to "stir up our remembrance." Stirring reminds me of a fire needing to be tended. Fire is used as a symbol for revival. But stirring is not the only way to get a fire going. Sometimes a fire needs to be fanned. Imagine a fireplace with the coals turning cold. To stir it up is to bring it to a flame. This is the purpose of revival. Sometimes the believer gets cold and needs to be stirred or fanned to a flame. Thankful praise and honoring the goodness of God can serve as a fan to bring the Holy Spirit to a flame.

Blessed are they that fan the Spirit and cursed are they that put it out. Let's fan the flame because we don't want to grieve the Holy Spirit.

MY SPIRITUAL JOURNEY
Do I fan the Holy Spirit's fire or do I put it out?

_____

_____

_____

_____

_____

_____

286

WAYS TO STAY REVIVED

Finally, brethren, whatsoever things are true, whatsoever things are honest, whatsoever things are pure, whatsoever things are lovely, whatsoever things are of good report; if there be any virtue and if there be any praise, think on these things. -Philippians 4:8

How do we keep the flame of revival burning? The first way is to continue to grow in the knowledge and likeness of God. Peter encouraged us to grow in grace and in the knowledge of our Lord and Savior Jesus Christ. Peter declares that as long as he had breath in his life, he would find it fitting to stir up in his heart the knowledge, goodness, loving-kindness, and mercy of God. When we know Him, we act more like Him.

The second way is to make sure we don't grieve the Holy Spirit by continuing and purposely sinning. The Holy Spirit is a person and can be grieved (Ephesians 4:30).

The third way is by not quenching the Holy Spirit's fire. Negative thinking and negative talking will put out our fire as well as the fires of others. Think on whatsoever things are honest, true, pure, lovely, and of good report and keep the fire burning.

MY SPIRITUAL JOURNEY

When and how often are your thoughts cold? Hot?

_____

_____

_____

_____

HELP THE POOR

Blessed is he that considereth the poor: the Lord will deliver him in time of trouble.
- Psalm 41:1

God blessed me with a nightmare as a testimony. I remember when I refused a poor, peg-legged man in downtown Atlanta when I was teaching at Georgia State University. This person asked me for some money to buy some food, and I refused him. I said in my mind that he only wanted to get a drink of whiskey. Then after I walked away I heard the Word of God speak to me: "When you have done unto the least of these you have done it also unto me."

I literally turned around to try to find the peg-legged man. He was running faster on his peg-leg it seemed, than I could run on my good legs. He got on the bus, and I was trying to give him something when the bus pulled off. I ran behind the bus for approximately a half block before I was exhausted. Once in a while, I still wake up in the middle of the night in a cold sweat running behind a bus with the Word of God resounding in my soul. I never want to refuse to help anyone again, no matter what their motive is or what I think it is.

MY SPIRITUAL JOURNEY

How sensitive am I to the needs of others?

FOLLOW HIS STEPS

For even hereunto were ye called: because Christ also suffered for us, leaving us an example, that ye should follow his steps. -I Peter 2:21

To follow his steps means to suffer for God and to do His will, not our will. In following in His steps, we need to ask God for directions before every decision we make and every action we take. Recently a person, who is a member of a very prominent church, came to our church asking for help. I called on God and was led to help the person without any explanation. My will was to send him back to the prominent church where he was a member, but I asked God what would He do? God said "help". So I helped.

Sometimes when we help someone several times, we become frustrated and feel we are being used. Our feelings don't count. How Jesus feels is what counts. What would He do if He were on earth?

Imagine only doing what Christ would do for one year. The results of following in His steps may not always have the happy ending that we want, but the results will always work out for the common good of the entire body of Christ.

MY SPIRITUAL JOURNEY

What have I done to suffer for God?

_____

_____

RESULTS OF FOLLOWING HIS STEPS

The steps of a good man are ordered by the Lord: and he delighteth in his way. Though he falls, he will not be utterly cast down: for the Lord upholdeth him with His hand.

-Psalm 37:23

The psalmist tell us that if our steps are ordered by the Lord, and we step according to His orders, we will not be cast down. Although we may fall, He will protect us.

When I was in Alaska, I observed a deer-like animal called a hind. The hind has the capacity to stand on a slippery surface and defy gravity due to how God made its feet. God says that if we follow in His steps, we will have feet like hinds' feet. Also, the psalmist says it is a joy to follow in His steps "and he delighteth in His way" (Psalm 37:23b).

MY SPIRITUAL JOURNEY

What if I were challenged to make a commitment to walk in Jesus' steps in everything I did in life and then to suffer the consequences? What do I believe would be the results?

October 17
OBEDIENT CHILDREN OF GOD

As obedient children not conforming yourselves to the former lusts, as your ignorance.
-1 Peter 1:14

How do we step in Jesus' steps? Every band has a drum major. The drum major directs or instructs what to do next. Our problem is that we can't decide which drumbeat we want to march to. We march to one drumbeat on Sunday and another on Monday. Monday through Saturday is the beat of the world; however, Christians should march to the beat of Sunday drums everyday.

Our drum major is Jesus Christ. He is the head of the Christian band. He is the one up front leading the band. It is important to know and obey our drum major. When another drummer leads off without permission, it throws off the entire band routine, such is with the Christian Life. When we listen to Satan or our flesh and not God, we step out of God's will and what He has planned for us, causing the body of Christ, our families, and our entire lives to be thrown out of order.

MY SPIRITUAL JOURNEY
Am I walking in the steps of my drum major, Jesus Christ or a different drummer?

_____

_____

_____

_____

FROM PITY TO PRAISE

Lord, how are they increased that trouble me! Many are they that rise up against me. Many there be which say of my soul, there is no help for Him in God. Selah But thou, O Lord art a shield for me; my glory, and the lifter up of mine head.
-Psalm 3:1-3

David was in a season of trouble. Biblical scholars think it was during the time Absalom, his son, was trying to kill him. We don't expect kings to have trouble, but it doesn't matter who we are, trouble will come our way. Even Jesus told us that in this world, we would have trials and tribulations. The problem is that we are too short on cheer and too heavy on pity. Pity should never dominate praise. We ought to be like David: stop the pity party and let the praise begin.

There are two ways to turn from a pity party to a praise party. First, we need to have a 'Selah' moment. The word 'Selah' is a musical word not to be read nor noted. It means to rest and then get louder. As problems increase, 'Selah'. Rest, take a pause, and make sure your praise is louder than your pity. Secondly, we ought to have a personal resurrection day. All Christians need to rise up during their season of pain and trouble and praise God.

MY SPIRITUAL JOURNEY

Am I in a time of trouble or coming out of a time of trouble? Is (or was) it piti-full or praise-full?

TRIPLE PROTECTION

I will not be afraid of ten thousands of people that have set themselves against me round about. -Psalms 3:6

According to Psalm 3:3-4, God not only protects us, but He gives us triple protection. He first of all is our shield from our enemies. Before the enemy can get to us, he has to go through God. God is also our glory. We may be embarrassed by our situation but because God is our glory, we don't have to walk around in shame. Lastly, even in our shame, He is the lifter of our head. Only because of who He is, can we lift up our head.

To resolve our personal problems, we need to have a personal relationship with God. Problems aren't problems until they come to our house. When someone else's spouse leaves them, it's their problem. When someone has a wayward child, it is their problem. But when we experience problems, it becomes personal. That's why David said that the Lord was his shield, his personal shepherd and his salvation. He further stated that God's rod and staff comforted him.

MY SPIRITUAL JOURNEY

Is God personal to my problems?

_____

_____

_____

_____

_____

GOD IS GREATER THAN STRESS

Hear me when I call, O God of my righteousness: thou hast enlarged me when I was in distress; have mercy upon me, and hear my prayer. -Psalm 4:1

It's so easy to become a candidate for stress. It only takes one thing to put us in a stressful situation. One missed paycheck, one lay-off, or even a power outage can cause stress. Stress is something external going through something internal. Our problem is not realizing that greater is He that is in us than the stress that is going through us. Whatever is going through us is going to meet up with that which is inside of us and the greater will have victory. If the Holy Spirit in us is not being fed and operating greatly in our lives, the stress will be greater.

God is greater than our stress. He is greater than our financial and health problems. God has the power to make us bigger than our problems. Most people decrease in their time of distress, but King David praised God for enlarging him in his time of distress. David knew God would make him stronger than whatever he was going through.

MY SPIRITUAL JOURNEY

When have I allowed God to be greater than my stress?

_____

_____

_____

_____

_____

KEEP YOUR JOY TANK FULL

Thou hast put gladness in my heart, more times in the time that their corn and wine increased. -Psalm 4:7

I f someone is lost in a storm, the first thing they usually do is send out distress signals so that help will find them. We need to send out flares of praise, mercy, and joy before a storm. Praise gets God's attention, so pack praise flares!

David asked God to have mercy on him and to hear his prayer. David probably had a flashback about the lion, bear, giant, his sin with Bathsheba, and his fleeing from Saul. The past mercy God has given us is for our current favor. Because God has had mercy on us before, we ought to know and be assured that He will have mercy on us again. God did not bring us this far to leave us; therefore, we should not entertain stress one moment.

We need to make sure our joy tanks are full (Psalm 4:7). When Satan comes to us and finds an empty tank, he fills it with sadness and despair. However when our joy tank or our spiritual tank is full and the distressed enemy is passing through, he can't hurt us because we have no room for stress.

MY SPIRITUAL JOURNEY

How have I stored flares of praise, mercy, and joy

EVIL IS REAL, GOD IS BIGGER

My voice shalt thou hear in the morning, O Lord; in the morning will I direct my prayer unto thee, and will look up. Lead me, O Lord, in thy righteousness because of mine enemies; make thy way straight before my face. -Psalm 5:3,8

Evil is not abstract, it is real. Ephesians 6:12 reads, "For we wrestle not against flesh and blood, but against principalities, against powers, against the rulers of the darkness of this world, against spiritual wickedness in high places." David prayed every morning with a high expectation of answered prayer for protection and vengeance against his enemy. Many people praise God hoping He will answer their prayer, but David praised God because of the assurance he had in knowing that God would answer his prayer.

Each new morning calls for a renewed dedication and fresh feeding from God. To combat evil, we should pray in the morning, and then shout throughout the evening, knowing that God will keep us from evil.

Morning is a good time to lift our head to God. Even as evil pursued David, he looked up. He didn't place his focus on the evil, but on God.

MY SPIRITUAL JOURNEY

How has praying helped to keep evil away from me?

_____

_____

_____

HOW TO DEAL WITH EVIL

And he spake a parable unto them to this end, that men ought always to pray, and not to faint. - Luke 18:1

How do we deal with evil? We either pray or faint. Jesus tells us to pray and faint not. If we don't pray, we will faint. God hates wickedness and is not pleased with those who do such. When evil pursues us, we should give it over to God, because evil will flee from the presence of God.

We need to understand that joy abounds in the sure hope of deliverance and vengeance. In other words, we should walk in the hope that God will deliver and avenge us. Our problem is what I call, too seldom, too late, and no expectation of prayer. Too seldom is when we don't pray often enough. Too late is when we pray in the evening after the devil has whipped us. "No expectation of answered prayer" is when we don't expect God to answer. If we pray in the morning and look for God throughout the day, by the time the evening comes, the only thing left to do is praise and worship Him.

MY SPIRITUAL JOURNEY

How have I dealt with evil in the past? How will I deal with evil in the future?

_____

_____

_____

_____

HOW TO MEET GOD'S APPROVAL

Study to shew thyself approved unto God, a workman that needeth not to be ashamed, rightly dividing the word of truth. -2 Timothy 2:15

Paul gives us several things that God wants us to do in order to meet His approval. First, he tells us to study. The word "study" in this text means diligence. Paul is encouraging us to put forth effort to get to know God. Paul also tells us that a workman should not be ashamed of his work. We were created to do good work for God. Paul also tells us to rightly divide the word of God to cut it straight, like a workman with a saw.

The problem with the church at Ephesus, as it still is with the church today, is gangrene teaching. The problem with gangrene teaching is that it spreads quickly, leaving no circulation-no circulation of diligence, good work, or dividing the word of truth among Christians. When gangrene gets into our limbs, we have no choice but to cut it off. The next time we hear false teaching, we should cut off the TV and/or shut down the communication. We should look to God, not others, and ask, "Approved or disapproved?"

MY SPIRITUAL JOURNEY

How concerned am I about the approval of others?

_____

_____

_____

_____

_____

October 25
PREPARING FOR A STORM

But the ship was now in the midst of the sea, tossed with waves: for the wind was contrary.
-Matthew 14:24

Sometimes in life there is one storm after another, and when it looks like things are getting better, here comes something else. As soon as we get comfortable with our jobs, we get a pink slip. As soon as we bury one loved one, another one dies. As soon as we get our children out of the house, our spouse announces that he or she doesn't want to be married anymore. When it rains, it pours.

Dr. Beecher Hicks' book, **Preaching Through the Storm,** makes this assertion, everybody's in one or three positions, either in a storm, coming out of a storm or going into a storm. I remember first hearing that and thinking, "I'm not in a storm, and I haven't just come out of one. Therefore, I must be getting ready to go through one." So I began to do what we do when we know a storm is coming. When a storm is coming, we prepare ourselves by boarding up the windows and doors. Christians prepare for a storm by boarding up with prayer, devotion, and the word of God.

MY SPIRITUAL JOURNEY
How do I prepare for a storm?

_____

_____

_____

_____

HOW TO MAKE IT THROUGH A STORM

And immediately Jesus stretched forth his hand, and caught him, and said unto him, O thou of little faith, wherefore didst thou doubt? -Matthew 14:31

We must know that Jesus will come to us in the storms of life. Jesus came to Peter and the disciples in the midst of the storm. The other time that the disciples were in the storm, Jesus was in the boat with them. They only had to wake Him up, and He calmed the sea. Jesus was not in the boat this time but was walking on the sea. The disciples were fearful when they saw Jesus walking on the water. They thought Jesus was a ghost, but Jesus spoke to their fears.

Jesus beckoned Peter to come, and Peter began to walk on the water. It was when Peter took his eyes off of Jesus and began to watch the waves and the wind that he began to sink. Peter cried out, "Lord save me." Jesus stretched out His hands and saved him. Once Jesus and Peter were in the boat, the wind ceased and those who were in the boat began to worship Jesus. Not only will Jesus come to us in the storm, but he will also walk with us through the storm.

MY SPIRITUAL JOURNEY

During the last storm in my life, did God calm me or did He calm the storm?

SHIP/BOAT PEOPLE

And straightway Jesus constrained his disciples to get into a ship, and to go before him unto the other side... -Matthew 14:22

We will never do great things for God unless we leave some people behind. All the disciples were in the SHIP, but only Peter got out. Peter left some behind. I call them boat people. There are boat people in the church. They say things like, "Peter, you are crazy. You'd better stay in the boat." That's boat talk. "Pastor we are moving too fast. The vision sounds good, but I just don't see it." That's boat talk.

Don't let a boat-talking friend plan your itinerary. If we are going to do some great things for God, we have to leave boat people in the boat. I remember when we had outgrown our old church and were discussing building or buying a new facility. The few boat-talking people voted against the plan, but once we entered the new facility, they became very active workers. When God does something great, even boat people will serve Him.

MY SPIRITUAL JOURNEY
Who are the boat people I believe God wants me to leave behind?

_____

_____

_____

_____

HOW TO PREPARE FOR REVIVAL

And they gathered their brethren, and sanctified themselves and came, according to the commandment of the king, by the words of the LORD, to cleanse the house of the LORD.

-2 Chronicles 29:15

King Hezekiah tore down the idol gods and cleaned up the temple. He then orchestrated a great praise celebration. The singers were gathered, the trumpets, and cymbals sounded, and then worship began. They worshipped Him with the giving of offerings, sin offerings, burnt offerings, wave, and thanks offerings.

In preparation for revival, we ought to follow a similar orchestrated activity. We ought to ask people to come and literally clean the church, washing windows and painting walls. In addition, we should ask them to clean up their lives by turning from sin. We ought to ask people to fast and pray and bring a thanks offering. Then we should pump up the praise before entering into worship with Him.

Praise Leaders can pump up a congregation's praise but not their worship. Praise can be a one way connection, but worship is always a two way communication. We can give God some praise, but we must enter into worship with Him.

MY SPIRITUAL JOURNEY

How frequently do I praise? When was the last time my praise led to worship?

_____

_____

WHAT HAPPENS WHEN REVIVAL TARRIES

And all the congregation worshipped, and the singers sang, and the trumpeters sounded: and all this continued until the burnt offering was finished. -2 Chronicles 29:28

The word "tarry" means not to leave right now and to wait awhile. What we sometimes experience in revival makes us want to tarry in the sanctuary. When revival tarries, the house stays clean. No longer do we have to clean up when guests come because the house, the temple of the believer, is already clean. When revival tarries, the results are demonstrated with evidence. Fasting, prayer, obedience, and thanks offerings become a part of our routine.

When revival tarries and the house stays clean, something ought to be cooking in the kitchen. It's good to have a clean house, but something ought to be stirring in the kitchen. We ought to stir up our gifts, obedience, love, forgiveness, and power.

When revival tarries, success is measured by increased Bible study, Sunday school, love, kindness, reconciliation, volunteerism, and membership.

MY SPIRITUAL JOURNEY

What evidence do I have that revival is tarrying in me?

_____

_____

_____

_____

KEEPING A REVIVED HOUSE CLEAN

Know ye not that ye are the temple of God, and that the Spirit of God dwelleth in you?
-1 Corinthians 3:16

Our body, the temple of God, is the house we ought to keep clean. Hezekiah was brought up in a dirty house, but he set an example of not staying in one. Just because our parents were mean, cursing, sex addicts or drunken wife-beaters, doesn't mean that we have to go the same route.

On occasion, I have visited juvenile detention centers. The majority of juveniles return after having been released because they fail to report to their probation officer. I once said to a young man, "You would rather be here than at home, wouldn't you?" Tears welled up in his eyes as he answered, "Yes." He had more family in the jail than at home. He needed some Christian love and training.

Just because we were brought up in a dysfunctional church doesn't mean that all churches are dysfunctional. We need to find a clean church home, get to work, and help keep it clean through prayer and service.

MY SPIRITUAL JOURNEY
The blood of Jesus is what makes my house clean. How am I keeping it clean? Is it still dirty?

_____

_____

_____

SERVING GOD PAYS OFF

And behold, I come quickly; and my reward is with me, to give every man according as his work shall be. -Revelation 22:12

Our service is the proof of our love for God and the evidence of His grace. God works in us to produce fruit and then gives us credit for the fruit we produce. Not serving God is evidence that we don't love Him and have refused His gift of grace. If we are not serving God, that makes us a suspect as one who has gained the whole world but will lose his soul.

Every man's service will be judged and rewarded according to His work. Our purpose in life is found in our service to God. It pays to serve God. Oftentimes, people come to my office for counseling, and in the midst of the session, I recommend that they participate in a service like feeding the hungry. Out of obedience they do it and usually return with a testimony concerning how they were helped. It is known that you can't help someone else without receiving a blessing from God. The songwriter was right when he penned, "It Pays to Serve Jesus."

MY SPIRITUAL JOURNEY

How has serving God paid off for me?

_____

_____

_____

_____

A FREEWILL OFFERING

Accept, I beseech thee, the freewill offerings of my mouth,
O LORD, and teach me thy judgments. -Psalm 119:108

A freewill offering is an act of lavish giving to God. When Moses and the Israelites built the Tabernacle, they did it lavishly. Nothing is too good for God. When God blesses us, He blesses us lavishly. God did not just come so that we may have life but have life more abundantly. We ought to shower Him with our blessings because He has showered us.

The freewill offering is also an act of willingness. Those who are not willing should not give; neither should we expect unbelievers to give to the church. We love the unbelievers, but we shouldn't expect them to give or praise until Jesus comes into their hearts. Those of us who have grown in the grace of giving and can think of all that God has done ought to willingly and joyfully grow in our giving.

MY SPIRITUAL JOURNEY

What is the freewill offering that I bring to God?

_____

_____

_____

_____

_____

_____

_____

REALIZING THE PRESENCE OF GOD

And Jacob awaked out of his sleep, and he said, Surely the LORD is in this place; and I knew it not. -Genesis 28:16

Genesis 27 tells the story of a boy named Jacob who tricked his brother Esau out of his birthright. Out of fear of what Esau might do to him, Jacob had to leave home. One night while sleeping on stones, he had a dream. He dreamed of a staircase going up to heaven where angels were ascending and descending. Many refer to his dream as "Jacob's Ladder." It was in this dream that God spoke blessings into Jacob's life.

When we realize the presence of God in our lives, we will pay our tithes. Once Jacob realized the presence of God in His life, he vowed to give a tenth of everything God gave to him back to God (Genesis 28:22). Recognizing the presence of God in our lives will motivate us to give freely, and we will worship Him. When Jacob woke up, he took a pillow, poured oil on it, and worshipped God. On a personal note, the authors of this book love the Lord and can't give back enough to Him. At this point we are **15% above the tithe,** and our prayer is to be able to continue to grow in our giving until we give all that we earn back to God.

MY SPIRITUAL JOURNEY

Do I recognize the presence of God in my life?

_____

_____

_____

GOD'S ACCEPTANCE

LORD, I cry unto thee: make haste unto me; give ear unto my voice, when I cry unto thee.
-Psalm 141:1

We live in a world where acceptance from others is of the utmost importance. Children desire to be accepted by their parents. Teenagers desire to be accepted by their peers. Failure to be accepted by others can end in tragedy, even in suicide. We should desire God's acceptance more than the acceptance of others.

David knew the importance of being accepted by God. It was God he desired to hear from, not man. That's why he asked that his prayer and his sacrifice be acceptable to God (Psalm 141:2). It is God who receives our prayer as a sweet fragrance and our uplifted hands as a sacrifice. When we look to man for acceptance, we never know what we will get in return, but when we look to God, we receive answered prayer. David knew where to keep his focus. In Psalm 141:8 he said, "But mine eyes are unto thee, O God."

MY SPIRITUAL JOURNEY

How important is it for others to accept me?

_____

_____

_____

_____

_____

November 4
LET THE RIGHTEOUS SMITE ME

Let the righteous smite me; it shall be a kindness: and let him reprove me; it shall be excellent oil, which shall not break my head: for yet my prayer also shall be in their calamities. -Psalm 141:5

---

avid desired to be told of his faults from the people of God. When he was wrong, he wanted someone to tell him, even if it pierced him like a blow or cut to the head. Too many of us don't want to be cut, but being cut with the truth is good for the soul. Proverbs 1:5 reads, "A wise man will hear, and will increase learning; and a man of understanding shall attain unto wise counsels." Furthermore, Proverbs 1:7 reads, "The fear of the LORD is the beginning of knowledge: but fools despise wisdom and instruction."

Many of us don't like receiving instructions from others. That's why we don't attend classes offered at our church or won't go back to school. Our problem is in not wanting to feel hurt. It hurts when we are told we are wrong about something. We fail to realize that the victory is in correcting. If we never acknowledge the wrong and correct it, we can never move into the right that is our calling.

MY SPIRITUAL JOURNEY
Do I mind being smitten by the righteous?

_____

_____

_____

November 5
GOOD GRAPES

I am the true vine, and my Father is the husbandman. Every branch in me that beareth not fruit he taketh away: and every branch that beareth fruit, he purgeth it, that it may bring forth more fruit. -John 15: 1-2

We have given in to buying seedless grapes. Little do most of us know that most of the grape's nutrients are found in the seed. According to natural law, there must be a seed in order to produce another seed, but in the society where we are so driven by convenience, this law is being overshadowed.

Jesus is the vine, and we are the branches. We know that we are good branches by the good fruit we produce. Isaiah 65:8 lets us know that when a branch is worn and appears as though it is no longer productive, it is cut off from the vine, but if it is found to produce even a few grapes, it will be spared. The same is true with the believer. We remain connected to the vine as long as we are producing even a few good grapes.

MY SPIRITUAL JOURNEY

What am I producing?

_____

_____

_____

_____

_____

_____

_____

THE CHURCH – A BACKSLIDING HEIFER

For Israel slideth back as a backsliding heifer: now the LORD will feed them as a lamb in a large place. -Hosea 4:16

Backsliding refers to being stubborn, unwilling to move or change. The church is in a backslidden posture. The New Testament church is the New Israel, and the position is the same, a backsliding heifer.

What makes us backsliding heifers? We are still doing church the same as it was done years ago and not willing to change. Failure to change because we like church a certain way is sin. It is time to clean the house of sin, making way for The Holy Spirit.

When Jesus comes back, He is not coming back to clean the house. He is coming back for the clean house. It is time for the church to make a deliberate decision to come into obedience with the word of God and release the growth potential of the kingdom of God. For this to happen, change is necessary.

MY SPIRITUAL JOURNEY

Am I bothered by change in my church?

_____

_____

_____

_____

_____

_____

CURSED GIVING

Will a man rob God? Yet ye have robbed me. But ye say, Wherein have we robbed thee? In tithes and offerings. -Malachi 3:8

We hear little about how God's people have abused the church by withholding the tithe. We need an "Act of Church Reform" to conform to what the Bible tells us about tithing. God said, "Bring ye all the tithes into the storehouse (the church), so that there may be meat in mine house" (Malachi 3:10).

___

In most churches, the percentages of tithers range from ten to twenty percent of the total congregation. Approximately eighty percent of the total congregation is left out of the will of God. The meat, or tithes, in the house is needed to feed the hungry and shelter and clothe the homeless.

Those who refuse to give according to how God instructed us to give will never be fully blessed and are not in a perfect relationship with God. Jeremiah 17:5 says, "Thus saith the LORD; cursed be the man that trusteth in man, and maketh flesh his arm, and whose heart departeth from the LORD."

MY SPIRITUAL JOURNEY

Am I walking in obedience by tithing and showing love?

LEANING ON OUR OWN UNDERSTANDING

Trust in the LORD with all thine heart; and lean not unto thine own understanding. In all thy ways acknowledge him, and he shall direct thy paths.
-Proverbs 3:5-6

Leaning on our own understanding is carnal and secular thinking. When we move away from scripture, we move ever so closely to the garbage heap of carnal thinking. Too often, the Church permits secular thinking to determine methods of operation. We have adopted secular procedures for our church environment.

The ways of the world are contrary to Biblical principles. For example, the world values rugged individualism. Yet, God calls us to be an army. The world esteems independence. Yet God calls us to be dependent on Him and each other. The world values competition and aggressiveness, but God calls us to be compassionate and humble. Our society values self. God calls us to deny self. If we don't overcome secular thinking, we will always walk in the flesh and not in the Spirit. We will forfeit the power of the Holy Spirit working in our lives and in the life of the church.

MY SPIRITUAL JOURNEY

How have I allowed secular thinking to overrule God's will?

_____

_____

_____

_____

CREATED TO SERVE HIM

For we are his workmanship, created in Christ Jesus unto good works, which God hath before ordained that we should walk in them. -Ephesians 2:8-10

God created us and ordained us to serve Him. Yet, we have missed the mark of service. It is a sin when we fail to do our part as a co-laborer with Him. Stored salvation is not the will of God. We have been saved for the glory of life everlasting and also for the task of building God's kingdom by growing His church until the day of His return.

The word "stuck" implies that something is preventing us from moving. Being stuck on salvation is refusing to grow in Christ after the point of conversion. Jesus came and died on the cross for the purpose of giving us the gift of salvation.

If we don't get beyond being stuck on salvation, we will not become what we were created to be. The army of God will be continually weakened due to a lack of soldiers, and the Church will not be an army in the world due to a lack of Christian disciples.

MY SPIRITUAL JOURNEY

Am I a true disciple of God or am I stuck on salvation?

_____

_____

_____

_____

_____

ACCEPT SPIRITUAL THINGS

For they that are after the flesh do mind the things of the flesh; but they that are after the Spirit the things of the Spirit. -Romans 8:4

Selfishness is the result of our fleshly nature. We must understand that we are dealing with flesh, and flesh by nature, is sinful. Small children are selfish and do not want to share their toys with anyone. Adults are selfish. They hoard what they deem to be theirs. Refusal to change the order of worship or the tempo of church music to become more reachable to a younger generation or to another culture is an example of our selfishness.

Our problem is in wanting to be happy before being holy. God has called us to holiness before happiness. Yet, he has promised us that if we are holy, we will be happy. However, due to our fleshly nature, we prefer our happiness over God's holiness. The best cure for selfishness is to give ourselves away.

MY SPIRITUAL JOURNEY

Am I selfish? In what areas in my life have I given myself away?

_____

_____

_____

_____

_____

_____

_____

THE HOLY GHOST

And they were all filled with the Holy Ghost, and began to speak with other tongues, as the Spirit gave them utterance. -Acts 2:4

We give lip service to our belief in the Trinity, but our behavior puts less emphasis on the person of the Holy Ghost. We honor the Father, glorify the Son, but theologize and debate over the person of the Holy Ghost. This failure causes Christians to be less than conquerors, leaving the Church in a weaker posture, unable to fulfill all her God-given purposes. This omission grieves the Holy Ghost, and to grieve the Holy Ghost is a sin (Ephesians 4:30).

One of the reasons we underutilize the Spirit of God is because of fear. The word "ghost" itself connotes something frightening. "Spirit" does so to a lesser extent but still implies that it is something that is outside the realm of human control. The good news is that the Holy Ghost will not hurt us but will guide us and pray for us when we can't pray for ourselves. The scripture tells us "to be filled with the Holy Spirit." (Ephesians 5:17)

MY SPIRITUAL JOURNEY

How do I know I am filled with the Holy Ghost?

_____

_____

_____

_____

_____

THREE WISE WORSHIPPERS

Saying, Where is he that is born King of the Jews? For we have seen his star in the east, and are come to worship him. -Matthew 2:2

B etter known as the Three Wise Men, the Magi provide us with an excellent illustration of coming into His presence for no other reason than to worship Him. Like the Wise Men of old, we may have our quest to worship Him interrupted by the Herods of the world, who represent the enemy of God, and the "Great Pretender" of worship, claiming he also wants to worship Him (Matthew 2:8).

Unfortunately, the spirit of Herod has crept into our churches today. He has stolen much of the victory and joy of worship out of the Church. We should rejoice like the wise men with exceeding great joy, if indeed we have seen the star (Matthew 2:10). We have diluted our worship. Let us press on with our gifts of gold, frankincense, and myrrh that represent the best that we have for God, and indeed present our total self to Him, holy and acceptable, which is our reasonable worship.

MY SPIRITUAL JOURNEY

Have I seen the star?

_____

_____

_____

_____

_____

_____

November 13
FALSE SECURITY

And he said unto them, Take heed, and beware of covetousness: for a man's life consisteth not in the abundance of the things which he possesseth. -Luke 12:15

In Revelation 3:16-17, we find that the Laodiceans felt secure because they were rich and had plenty. There was no need for God because they were financially blessed. The church at Laodicea was not burdened with debt, but it was burdened with wealth.

Jesus spoke a parable about another man who felt himself to be secure because of what he had. According to Jesus, there was a man whose crops had been blessed greatly. His barns were full, and there was no room to put the crops that needed to be gathered. The man felt self-sufficient and, therefore, reasoned within himself. The decision was made to tear down the existing barns and build bigger ones. The future looked bright and secure, but because he had put his security in his things, God required his soul that night, leaving all his things behind. This parable should remind us that only what's done for Christ will stand forever.

MY SPIRITUAL JOURNEY

Has acquiring things become more important to me than doing the will of God?

_____

_____

_____

_____

SOLUTION TO THE POLLUTION

Repent ye therefore, be converted, that your sins may be blotted out, when the time of refreshing will come from the presence of the Lord; -Acts 3:19

Pollution is one of the number one problems in society today. We try in various ways to solve our pollution problems. We dig holes and bury it, only for it to show up later in our water, creating more water pollution. We burn it, only for it to show up later in the air, creating more air pollution. It affects and yields concern of global warming and the ozone layer.

We have an even bigger pollution problem as Christians. We are haunted by sin pollution. Our lives are polluted with sin. We are polluted by sins of incest, divorce, adultery, homosexuality, abortion, and more. Sin produces guilt and suppresses joy. These sinful acts have left our stomachs tied up in knots of guilt and suppressed joy because of unforgiveness. Jesus Christ is the only solution to sin pollution. We can't unscramble an egg or unbreak a glass, but through Jesus, we can be forgiven and forgive others.

MY SPIRITUAL JOURNEY

Is there sin in my life that is keeping me bound?

_____

_____

_____

_____

_____

_____

THE PROBLEM WITH SIN POLLUTION

Repent ye therefore, be converted, that your sins may be blotted out, when the time of refreshing will come from the presence of the Lord. -Acts 3:19

We try to be the solution to our pollution by telling ourselves that it is only natural. However, the natural man is a sinful man and tries to trivialize sin. We try to justify our sin by trying to make wrong, right. Unmarried couples live together and justify it by saying they are happy, and God wants them to be happy.

We try to conceal our sin, like Adam and Eve. After they sinned, they took leaves and covered themselves. Proverbs 28:13 reminds us that those who cover their sins will not prosper. We try to escape our sins by using alcohol and other drugs. Some even commit suicide to escape sin.

Moving pollution from one place to another does not get rid of it. Such is with Christians today; instead of ridding our lives of sin, we carry it around from one church to another. Jesus is the solution to our sin pollution.

MY SPIRITUAL JOURNEY

Do I have a problem getting rid of sin pollution in my life?

_____

_____

_____

_____

CONDITIONS TO GOD'S FORGIVENESS

Repent ye therefore, be converted, that your sins may be blotted out, when the time of refreshing will come from the presence of the Lord. -Acts 3:19

There are conditions to God's forgiveness. Repentance is the condition that must take place to be forgiven by God. Repentance is an activity of the mind that leads to a change in behavior. It means to be regretful and truly sorrowful.

In Matthew 21:28-32, Jesus tells a parable of two boys who were told to work in their father's vineyard. One boy initially refused to go but later changed his mind and decided to go. The second boy said he would go but never did.

Jesus told the Pharisees that the prostitute and tax collectors would enter heaven before they would. The Pharisees were like the second boy as are many in the church today. Many say they will go but never do. There are others who say that they will not go, but they later repent and go. When we repent, we must turn to the Savior, the solution to our pollution.

MY SPIRITUAL JOURNEY

When I sin, am I sorry about sinning or just sorry that I got caught?

_____

_____

_____

_____

BE CONVERTED

Repent ye therefore, be converted, that your sins may be blotted out, when the time of refreshing will come from the presence of the Lord; -Acts 3:19

There is completion to God's forgiveness when our sins are blotted out. Don't misunderstand, blotted does not mean covered. Before ink had acid in it, we could use the same paper over and over again after writing on it. We would take a damp cloth to erase and wipe the paper clean. That is how Jesus forgives our sin. He wipes our slate clean.

I once counseled a lady who couldn't forget about her abortion experience. I said to her, "Maybe you can't forget about it, but God has forgotten about it. God won't ever bring it up again. It is Satan who keeps bringing it to your memory so that you can't be effective for God right now." That's how Satan operates. His first effort is to keep us from becoming Christians, and when he fails at that, he uses our memory to keep us from becoming victorious and effective Christians.

MY SPIRITUAL JOURNEY

Is there sin which I have asked for and received forgiveness from God, yet I can't get it out of my mind?

_____

_____

_____

_____

_____

CONSEQUENCES TO GOD'S FORGIVENESS

Repent ye therefore, be converted, that your sins may be blotted out, when the time of refreshing will come from the presence of the Lord. -Acts 3:19

There are benefits to God's forgiveness. The results are spiritual refreshment. God doesn't focus on our failure, we do. Focusing on our failures in the past makes us ineffective for God in the present. Too many of us have had adjustments and not true conversions. In true conversion, we are new, our eyes become clear, our hearts become clean, and our desire to follow Jesus is with fire and Holy Ghost power.

A prostitute once went to the home of some church folks, and there she found Jesus. When she found Him, a change came into her life. With an expensive bottle of perfume, she washed His feet with tears of sorrow, regret, and joy. The church folk mumbled saying he should have known the woman was a prostitute. Though Jesus agreed that her sins were many, He forgave her of them all.

MY SPIRITUAL JOURNEY

Am I effective or ineffective for God's purposes?

323

I BELIEVE I'LL TESTIFY

And they overcame him by the blood of the Lamb, and by the word of their testimony; and they loved not their lives unto the death. -Revelation 12:11

We defeat the devil by the blood of the lamb and the word of our testimony. The only testimony non-believers have is the testifying of their sins. It's time to remove the testimonies of sin from God's face. Repent, sin no more, and testify of His forgiveness, grace and mercy.

When we tell others of God's goodness, it inspires them to trust God. When we fail to share our testimonies, it leaves others hopeless, thinking that God doesn't answer prayers. They, therefore, remain in their hopelessness.

We have been given victory over Satan with our testimony. Our greatest testimony is the blood of the lamb, Jesus Christ. To testify is to tell. When we tell others of the saving grace of the blood of the Lamb, we don't just win a battle, we win the war.

MY SPIRITUAL JOURNEY

Do I have testimonies I believe are worthy of sharing that I have held back?

CLEAN THE HOUSE

But if we walk in the light as He is in the light, we have fellowship with one another and the blood of Jesus His Son cleanses us from all sin. -I John 1:7

When our clothes are dirty, we wash them with products like Tide, Cheer, Gain, and Clorox. These products can clean our clothing, but they cannot clean our sins. There is sin in the house of God that needs to be cleaned up. The only detergent to clean the house of God is the Word of God. God's Word will either drive us away from or draw us to Him. It will clean us up or we will intentionally stop bathing with it.

Refusal to obey and apply God's Word is like refusing to bathe with soap. Refusal to apply God's Word to our lives leaves an awful smell in His nostrils. Those who refuse to bathe with God's Word tend to stop coming to church when the Word of God is preached uncompromised. They will make all kinds of excuses not to come to church, like the youth ministry is not all it should be or the church is too big. Failure to serve God is a sin and leads to a broken relationship with Him. Clean your house.

MY SPIRITUAL JOURNEY

Am I bathing in God's Word or do I smell dirty?

_____

_____

_____

_____

_____

MISSING THE MARK

But they rebelled , and vexed his holy spirit: therefore he was turned to be their enemy, and he fought against them. -Isaiah 63:10

The Bible tells us that our bodies are the temples and residents of the Holy Ghost. We are the house of God. The sad commentary is that there is sin in the house of God. Christians think they need only be concerned with sexual sins and other overt sins like drinking and doing drugs, but there are many other behaviors classified as sin.

In the Hebrew language, sin is missing the mark or moving away from God. One sin can be cursed giving because of not tithing. God has asked us to bring the tithes into His house, but we hold back, treating it as if it is our money. It is sinful to refuse to share the gospel with others. Yet another sin is grieving The Holy Ghost. We don't acknowledge the Holy Ghost in our lives, leaving our lives without direction and guidance. Another sin is secular, carnal thinking. We have been commanded to be transformed from the ways of the world, yet we accept the world's way of thinking. We are simply missing the mark which means there is sin in the House of God.

MY SPIRITUAL JOURNEY

Does the Word of God convict me about the sin in my life?

_____

_____

_____

CHRIST IS OUR PASSOVER

Purge out therefore the old leaven, that ye may be a new lump, as ye are unleavened. For even Christ our Passover is sacrificed for us. -1 Corinthians 5:7

When the people of God celebrated the Passover, they were instructed to clean their homes of leavened bread. The Passover feast was the celebration of the escape from bondage in Egypt when the death angel smote the first born of all who did not have the blood of the lamb on their doorposts. Biblically, leavened symbolizes the power of sin. Eating leavened bread caused a person's soul to be cut off from Israel (Exodus 12:15).

In 1 Corinthians 5:5-8, Paul speaks to the Church at Corinth and to us. He teaches us that Christ is now our Passover. Christ is our unblemished Lamb. His blood was shed for all those who believe. It is the blood of Christ that will allow us to pass over from death into eternal life. Paul was encouraging the people to keep the Passover by keeping a clean house, the temple of God, individually and collectively. When each house (physical body) is kept clean individually, the entire house (body of Christ) will be clean collectively.

MY SPIRITUAL JOURNEY

Let me clean my house! What can I do to clean my house?

_____

_____

_____

PUT AWAY ALL SINS

Every sin that a man does is outside the body, but he who commits sexual immorality sins against his own body. -1 Corinthians 6:18

There was an influential man in the church who was sleeping with his step-mother. This was not gossip, it was the truth. Paul told the church that this sin was not to be ignored and compromised. He was urging the people to deal with the sin in the house because, if left unattended, it would only get worse and others may start doing the same thing. It is the business of the church to judge the sin in the church. Christians are never to judge the world, but God gives the church the privilege and the authority to judge each other.

Because Christ died and shed His blood for us, we need to put away all sin which includes malice, jealousy, and pride and celebrate the feast with the unleavened bread of sincerity and truth. God left us a word. We know better, but we just don't do better.

MY SPIRITUAL JOURNEY

Have I chosen a life of sin over a life with Christ?

_____

_____

_____

_____

_____

_____

_____

SHEPHERD THE CHURCH

Therefore take heed to yourselves and to all the flock, among which the Holy Spirit has made you overseers, to shepherd the church of God which he purchased with His own blood.
-Acts 20:28

A clean church is a powerful church, whereas, a dirty church is a paralyzed church. Many churches are paralyzed in their status quo, not because they don't have resources but because of their refusal to follow the Word of God.

We are guilty of dipping and dabbling in sin until it escalates. We are like nibbling sheep. We nibble on sin. It tastes pretty good, and we nibble a bit more. The next thing we know, we are about to fall off a cliff. Sin begets sin. It will take us farther than we want to go and keep us longer than we want to stay.

Sin left uncorrected in the church will cause other Christians to go astray. That is what Paul meant by a little leaven leavening the whole lump. Sin grows sin. It is its own fertilizer. Paul warned us to purge the house so we can praise God in sincerity and truth and stop playing church. Christ is our Passover. Greater is He that is in us than He that is in the world.

MY SPIRITUAL JOURNEY

Have I dipped and dabbled in sin until it escalated?

_____

_____

_____

November 25

FAINTING OVER SMALL STUFF

Therefore I say unto you, Take no thought for your life, what ye shall eat, or what ye shall drink; nor yet for your body, what ye shall put on. Is not the life more than meat, and the body than raiment? -Matthew 6:25

In Matthew 6:27, Jesus asked, "Which of you by taking thought can add one cubit unto his stature?" Jesus was teaching his disciples that worry was such a meaningless and unproductive waste of time. God will not have us worry or be anxious about anything.

In Jeremiah 12, the Prophet Jeremiah was crying out to God. He was upset because the wicked were prospering while he was suffering. Some of us can identify with Jeremiah. We look at our wicked neighbors and wonder why they seem to be prospering while we are struggling. We wonder why he or she has a bigger home, nicer car and job than we, who love the Lord. God needs us to recognize that He is sovereign and will bless whomever He wants. We need to understand that wickedness may reign for a season, but if we are right, we will reign forever with God.

MY SPIRITUAL JOURNEY

Do I usually worry or turn problems over to God?

_____
_____
_____
_____
_____

GOD IS CALLING US TO HOLINESS

Those things which ye have both learned, and received, and heard, and seen in me, do: and the God of peace shall be with you. -Philippians 4:8

Fainting over small stuff prevents us from seeking God's righteousness. God said to seek first His kingdom... (Matthew 6:33). God is calling us into holiness. He saved us from sin. Now, He wants to sanctify us and prepare us for His glory. It is a process that goes from salvation, to sanctification, to glorification. He is calling us to clean up our acts.

God doesn't want us to faint over small stuff because it is all His stuff. He is Creator and has given us dominion to take care of His creation. The best way not to faint over small stuff is to think on good stuff. Paul tells us in Philippians to think on things of good report. If we take the time to count and thank God for our blessings, we won't have time or concern over the small worldly incidents of life. This will give us more time to concentrate on God's call to Holiness.

MY SPIRITUAL JOURNEY

How is fainting over small stuff keeping me from obeying God's call to Holiness?

_____

_____

_____

_____

_____

IN TIMES LIKE THESE

Be still, and know that I am God: I will be exalted among the heathen. I will be exalted in the earth. -Psalm 46:10

Our country is living in troubled times. The 9/11 terrorist attack brought our nation to its knees. The Twin Towers fell and lives were lost, the Dow Jones dropped, Airlines declared bankruptcy, and loved ones went to war. In times like these, we need a comforter, protector, and refuge. We need a word from the Lord.

The word is to be still and know that God is God. Be still and know that God has not forsaken us. There is a God who rules with a hand of power and a heart of love. He can take wickedness and turn it into good, and He can take a terrorist attack and unite a divided nation.

Evil men crucified Jesus. It could be called a bad Friday but God turned it into a Good Friday. Be still and know that God is God. He is still turning evil into good, and He wants to be lifted up and exalted. When we lift Him up, He will draw all men unto Him. One day, every knee will bow and confess that Jesus is Lord, but it will be too late for those who died without accepting Him.

MY SPIRITUAL JOURNEY

At what times have I failed to know who God is?

OUR PRESENT HELP

God is our help, refuge and strength in the time of trouble. -Psalm 46:1

God is in our midst. He is at His best in troubled times. He is a present helper and strength and will not put us on hold during a 911 call. In spite of terror, we should not fear. Psalm 91:5 tells us not to be afraid of the terror by night or the arrows that fly by day. The word is clear that we shouldn't stop living when terror strikes.

Christians shouldn't live in fear even though we may walk through the valley and shadow of death. To live in fear is bondage. Because Jesus lives, all our fear should be gone. I may not know what tomorrow holds, but I know who holds tomorrow. God is my refuge in that my soul has found a resting place with Him.

The cleft of a rock is where the rock has a hole in it. We can get in it, and when we do, the wind can't get to us. Jesus is the rock we should hide in and behind. The joy of the Lord is my strength and my help. I won't stop praying, worshipping, and exalting His name.

MY SPIRITUAL JOURNEY

What terror have I witnessed that keeps me in fear?

_____

_____

_____

_____

A MOUNTAIN TOP EXPERIENCE

When Moses came down from Mount Sinai with the two tablets of the Testimony in his hands, he was not aware that his face was radiant because he had spoke with the Lord.
-Exodus 34:29 (NIV)

God called Moses to the mountain to be with Him forty days and forty nights as he wrote out the Ten Commandments. During those forty days and nights, Moses didn't eat or drink anything. He didn't need to because he was being fed bread from heaven, and the presence of the Lord was His strength. Sometimes, when God really wants to deal with us, He has to take us high on the mountaintop.

Moses' face was shining after his encounter with God. It shone to the point where Aaron and the people were afraid of him. Sometimes, when we have an experience with God and go places, people act like they are afraid of us, too. Moses shone so greatly, he had to put a veil over his face to speak to the people, but when he spoke to God, he took off the veil. The people couldn't handle his shine, but God could. When we go into the presence of God, there ought to be a shine on us. If we have been converted, saved, and transformed, we ought to shine. We ought to shine with God's love, hope, power, joy, and glory.

MY SPIRITUAL JOURNEY

Have I ever had a mountaintop experience? Am I continuing to shine?

RISE, SHINE AND GIVE GOD THE GLORY

When Aaron and all the Israelites saw Moses, his face was radiant, and they were afraid to come near him. -Exodus 34:30 (NIV)

Many of us have no shine. Many of us are desiring and even yearning for God's shine but have not experienced it because God knows our motive. God gives us His shine to express, not to impress.

When Moses came down from his mountaintop experience, he began to express all that God had given him, and did not brag about his mountaintop experience. Our problem is when we get our shine, we try to out shine each other. We try to see who looks the holiest. God gave us His shine to express His grace, mercy and goodness.

From watching the news, we can clearly see that the world needs to see our shine. The world doesn't need to see churches fighting each other to see which one is the biggest and the best. The world needs to see a solidified and unified Church stand and shine for the true and living God. God wants us to not only give Him glory but also to be His glory.

MY SPIRITUAL JOURNEY

Does the world see my shine? Do I have a shine?

_____

_____

_____

DRESS FOR SUCCESS

Stand therefore, having your loins girt about with truth, and having on the breast plate of righteousness…Above all taking the shield of faith…and take the helmet of salvation, and the sword of the Spirit, which is the word of God.
-Ephesians 6:14-17

God has designer clothing for the believer – God's Designer Wear (GDW). Paul refers to it as the armor of God and tells us to put it on. In this battle between God and Satan, it is important that we dress for success if we expect to win. Any soldier going into the battlefield unprepared for combat will be defeated. If we do not wear GDW, we will not be strong in the Lord and have the power of His might.

What is the designer wear God urges every soldier to put on? Ephesians 6:13-18 list them as the belt of truth, breastplate of righteousness, shield of faith, preparation of the gospel of peace, helmet of salvation, sword of the Spirit, and prayer. Our wardrobe is not complete until we put on all seven pieces of spiritual clothing. Without these seven pieces of armor, we are bound to be fatally wounded in battle.

MY SPIRITUAL JOURNEY

Am I fully dressed?

_____

_____

_____

_____

_____

THE PROBLEM WITH DRESSING DOWN

Finally, my brethren, be strong in the Lord, and in the power of his might.
-Ephesians 6:10

Paul urges us to put on the whole armor of God and not just some of it. The problem with dressing down is that some of us only dress in the "helmet of salvation." In other words, we know we are saved, but we never pick up the sword of the Spirit or the Word of God. Some of us have picked up the sword of the Spirit, but we have never put on the "helmet of salvation." Thinking that something will happen just by carrying a Bible or trying to impress people with the size of a Bible will not defeat Satan when in spiritual battle.

Some of us have put on the "shoes of preparation" and are always ready, but they never do anything with our readiness because we left behind the "shield of faith." Others of us have put on the "belt of truth" but have yet to put on the "breast plate of righteousness." We must put on the whole armor of God in spiritual battle. Don't get caught dressed down. God's armor empowers us to fight Satan and win the battle.

MY SPIRITUAL JOURNEY

Am I fully dressed?

_____

_____

_____

_____

THE BELT OF TRUTH

That we henceforth be no more children, tossed to and fro, and carried about with every wind of doctrine, by the slight of men, and cunning craftiness; whereby they live in wait to deceive.
-Ephesians 4:14

Paul urges all Christians to put on the belt of truth. Christ is the truth or belt that we must wear. The truth is that the Gospel of Jesus Christ, as written by God Himself, is our true doctrine. Knowing the truth of who Christ is keeps us from flapping from one false doctrine to another. The belt of truth (Jesus Christ) gives us strength and support in times of trial and tribulation. Truth helps us tighten up our belt. Think of it as a soldier's belt. A soldier caught with his pants down can get in a lot of trouble.

If the true doctrine of Jesus Christ is not taught, it is not a true Christian Church. If you find yourself in a church where Jesus Christ is not the focus, it is time to exit and run to God's true church. If Jesus Christ is not the focus of our personal lives, it is only a matter of time before our pants fall. Nothing we do will hold without Jesus Christ being the glue that keeps it together.

MY SPIRITUAL JOURNEY

Is the truth belt keeping my pants up or something else?

_____

_____

_____

_____

338

THE BREASTPLATE OF RIGHTEOUSNESS

The way of the wicked is an abomination unto the Lord: but He loveth him that followeth after righteousness. -Proverbs 15:9

Paul urges all Christians to put on the breastplate of righteousness, the accessory needed in battle. The term "accessory" is not used to minimize the role of the armor of God. Just like in our clothing, it's the accessory that makes the difference. We can have on a nice suit, but if the tie, shirt, or shoes are not coordinated, the beauty of the suit is lost. Likewise, the proper spiritual accessories prepare us to do God's work and prepare us for victory when in spiritual warfare.

What is this "breastplate of righteousness" we should be wearing? Why should we be wearing it? We have been made right with God by the blood of Jesus Christ, but still, as Christians, we have the responsibility of living right. We have been called to walk in righteousness; therefore, we must not give in to wrongdoing. The breastplate of righteousness shields our hearts from wrong living. The breastplate of righteousness protects the spiritual heart of a Christian solider in battle by keeping it protected from Satan's fiery darts.

MY SPIRITUAL JOURNEY

Is there anything hindering me from right living?

THE SHOES OF PREPARATION

But as for me, I will walk in mine integrity: redeem me, and be merciful unto me.

-Psalm 26:11

Paul urges all Christians to put on the shoes of preparation. Shoes are a sign of readiness. For example, imagine that you and your family are getting ready to leave the house to go to church. All of a sudden, somebody announces he or she can't find his or her shoes. That means that person isn't ready to go. We are not ready to go anywhere worth going until we put on our shoes. Don't dare go to war without shoes! I am talking about a soldier's shoes with cleats on them.

The Christian's shoes of preparation represent his readiness for spiritual battle. Satan is always ready for battle and always starts the war; therefore, we must also be ready for the attack that we know is coming. Also, we should be dressed in our shoes of preparation at all times because we never know when we will be led by the Holy Spirit to go and share the gospel of peace.

MY SPIRITUAL JOURNEY

Am I ready for spiritual battle?

_____

_____

_____

_____

_____

_____

THE SHIELD OF FAITH

Wherefore take unto you the whole armor of God... -Ephesians 6:13-16

Paul urges all Christians to put on the shield of faith. Doubt can mess us up. A man went to see his pastor just to talk to him and be assured that he wasn't crazy. The man was beginning to doubt his sanity. His motivation for work was to increase the ministry of the church, so he worked hard. He reasoned that the more money he made, the more he could give to the ministry of that church. People were beginning to tell him he was crazy. He wanted the pastor to assure him that he wasn't.

What does the shield of faith do for the believer? Faith is believing God when Satan tries to get us to doubt Him. Faith should be worn every day so that the adversities we confront won't cause doubt in the plans God has for us. The shield of faith is our protection. It provides strength and protects Christians from the fiery darts of doubt that Satan shoots at us. The shield of faith should be worn throughout the day. Growing up in His strength means knowing that the shield of faith is our protection.

MY SPIRITUAL JOURNEY

In times of doubt, does my faith increase or decrease?

_____

_____

_____

_____

_____

THE HELMET OF SALVATION

And take the helmet of salvation, and the sword of the Spirit, which is the word of God.
-Ephesians 6:17

Paul urges all Christians to put on the helmet of salvation. The helmet of salvation covers the head and the mind. Jesus healed a lunatic who was cutting himself in the graveyard (Mark 5:1-15). This man didn't even know his real name but called himself Legion because there were so many demons inside of him. Jesus delivered the man from these demons by casting his demons into some pigs and then drowning the pigs in the water.

When the people from town came, the man was sitting up, clothed in his right mind. The people became frightened and not able to rejoice in this man's salvation because they were bound in materialism. They were concerned about their pigs.

We, too, become frightened, lose our focus, and can't rejoice in the salvation of others. In other words, when we are bound by materialism, we can shout over materialistic things but can't give a word of praise to God when He saves someone. The helmet of salvation reminds us that we are already covered by the blood of Jesus Christ.

MY SPIRITUAL JOURNEY
Am I wearing the helmet of salvation?

_____

_____

_____

THE SWORD OF THE SPIRIT

...But his delight is in the law of the Lord; and in His law doth he meditate day and night.
-Psalm 1:2

Paul urges all Christians to put on the sword of the Spirit, which is the Word of God. A Christian is naked without the Word of God. Being naked is not being dressed for spiritual success.

Psalm 119:11 tells us of the importance of God's Word to us, "Thy Word have I hid in mine heart, that I might not sin against thee." The Word is the only offensive weapon in the collection of spiritual armor that makes up the full armor of God. Everything else is a piece of equipment designed for defense. The Word is a two-edged sword. It cuts to comfort those who need comforting, but it also cuts to disturb those who need disturbing. A Christian soldier on the battlefield without the Word of God is bound to be fatally wounded. We need to know the Word of God so that the Holy Spirit will have something to bring to our remembrance in times of battle.

MY SPIRITUAL JOURNEY

Is my sword dull or sharp?

_____

_____

_____

_____

_____

December 9

PRAYER: GOD'S SHINING ARMOR

Hear me when I call. O God of my righteousness: thou hast enlarged me when I was in distress; have mercy upon me and hear my prayer. -Psalm 4:1

Paul urges all Christians to put on prayer. Prayer is the armor that most Christians overlook because it is not armor that can be limited to one piece. Prayer is the armor that out shines all other. A good soldier keeps his armor shined and cleaned.

When our belt of truth begins to slack, we need to pray for the truth of God to set us free. When our breastplate of righteousness begins to slack, we need to pray that God will lead us back on the path of right living. When our helmet of salvation begins to slack, we need to pray for the peace of God which passes all understanding. When our shield of faith begins to slack, we need to pray for faith the size of a mustard seed that can move mountains. When our sword of the Spirit begins to slack, we need to pray that we will meditate on God's word day and night so that His word is hidden in our hearts and we don't sin against Him. Keep the prayer line opened.

MY SPIRITUAL JOURNEY
What part of my God's Designer Wear needs shining?

_____

_____

_____

December 10

LETTING GO OF THE PAST

And the LORD said unto Samuel, How long wilt thou mourn for Saul, seeing I have rejected him from reigning over Israel? Fill thine horn with oil, and go...

-1 Samuel 16:1

There is a difference in memorializing and hanging on to the past. When we memorialize, we remember for the sake of honoring and celebrating. When we hang on to the past, we are remembering that which God would have us to let go. Hanging on to our past puts us in a state of having a pity party.

King Saul disobeyed God, and God removed him from his kingship. Just as God can lift us up, He can also bring us back down. Samuel mourned for a long time. God asked him, "How long will you mourn for Saul?" God told him to fill his horn with oil and go to Bethlehem. The oil represented God's anointing on the next king. The word 'Bethlehem' means house of bread. God was sending Samuel to Bethlehem where there would be physical and spiritual bread. We can't go to Bethlehem and have a pity party; it is located in a place of praise. Here, we can praise our way out of the past.

MY SPIRITUAL JOURNEY

What in my past do I need to praise my way out of?

_____

_____

_____

_____

345

PRAISE PARTIES

See, I have set before you an open door, and no one can shut it.
-Revelation 3:8

Samuel had a character flaw. He was a prisoner of the past. We should be products of our past but not victims. How long will we cry about the parents we didn't have or the spouse who left us? How long will we cry about not having the chance to go to college or not having a father in our home? How long will we mourn the past? There are some things that will not go away until we move on. We should be having praise parties instead of pity parties.

God had closed the door on Saul and had opened a door for a new king. When God closes one door, He opens another one. We can't become all that God wants us to be by lingering in the mess of the past. We want to resurrect the past so we can kill it again, our way. Those who hang on to the past are really afraid of the future because they don't have active faith in God.

MY SPIRITUAL JOURNEY

Is my past keeping me from being all that God wants me to be?

_____

_____

_____

_____

_____

SURELY GOD IS IN THIS PLACE

And Jacob awaked out of his sleep, and he said, surely the LORD is in this place; and I knew it not. -Genesis 28:16

The natural man does not recognize the presence of God, but the spiritual man does. Therefore, if we walk after the flesh, we will not know that God is with us. If we walk after the Spirit, we will be able to say, "Surely God is in this place."

We have been set free to love, not to sin (Galatians 5:13). To know that we are walking in freedom is to know that God is in us. When we are being led by the flesh, we will produce impure thoughts, eagerness for lustful pleasure, idolatry, demonic activity, hatred, fighting, jealousy, anger, selfishness, complaints, criticism, envy, murder, drunkenness, and other sins of the flesh (Galatians 5:20-21). When we walk in the Spirit, we will manifest love, joy, peace, patience, gentleness, goodness, faith, meekness, and self-control (Galatians 5:22-23). When we walk in the Spirit, we will be able to say, "Surely God is in this place."

MY SPIRITUAL JOURNEY

Can I sincerely say, "Surely God is in this place?"

Throughout life, God has an angelic ministry. God sends angels to us in different seasons. One of those seasons is during our youth. There is an angel of youth that will come and visit us, but he does not stay long. He will come to trouble the water, but if we don't move, He may not come back again. Why do angels visit us while we are young? It is in our youth when we are strong and have great possibilities and potentialities. 1 John 2:14 says, "I have written unto you young men that you might be strong." It is possibility and potentiality. There is nothing like looking into the eyes of possibility.

There is an angel that comes during hard times to help us become stronger in our suffering. Angels also visit us and guide us down the right path during our crossroads or turning point seasons. Some may have been in situations where angels kept us from doing something foolish. Angels can prick our consciousness and stir us up. Angels do come.

MY SPIRITUAL JOURNEY

What season am I in for an angelic visitation?

_____

_____

_____

_____

_____

A BAD ATTITUDE TESTED

But it displeased Jonah exceedingly, and he was very angry. -Jonah 4:1

Jonah had a bad attitude about the people of Nineveh. He refused to give them God's warning of repentance or destruction because he felt they didn't deserve it. He ended up being cast into the sea. Even then, he refused to have the slightest attitude adjustment. God being the God of a second chance sent a whale to swallow him up. After being released from the whale, Jonah obeyed God, warning the people of Nineveh to repent. Even though the people repented, Jonah's attitude towards them did not change. He was angry with God for being merciful to them.

God had to teach Jonah a lesson to adjust his attitude. God sent him a vine for shade, and then God sent a worm to eat the vine. Then God set the record straight with Jonah and reminded him of His sovereignty. He also let Jonah know of his disappointment in him for being more concerned about the shade tree than the people. The message to Jonah and to us is that God loves all people and so should we.

MY SPIRITUAL JOURNEY

Are there certain people I have a problem loving?

_____

_____

_____

_____

CHANGING OUR ATTITUDE

And be not conformed to this world: but be ye transformed by the renewing of your mind, that ye may prove what is that good, and acceptable, and perfect, will of God. -Romans 12:2

O ur attitudes are much more important than we realize. Our attitude toward life determines life's attitude towards us. It is not what happens to us that determines the outcome of our lives but rather what happens in us. Our attitude tells the world what we expect of the world. Our attitude toward people tells people what we expect of them.

A bad attitude can multiply negative experiences in our lives. We will have trials, tribulations and bad experiences. Bad attitudes can even accentuate our negative experiences. A bad attitude promotes self-fulfilling prophecies of doom and gloom, and is like onions on our breath. The whole world can smell it. When we change our attitude to be like Jesus, we also change our lives.

MY SPIRITUAL JOURNEY

What is the fragrance my attitude usually sends out to the world?

_____

_____

_____

_____

_____

_____

_____

ARE YOU DEAD OR ALIVE?

And you hath he quickened, who were dead in trespasses and sins;
- Ephesians 2:1

A re you dead or alive? The answer to this question will explain the mystery of life, erase the mistakes of life, and establish the meaning of life. Yes, it is possible to be physically and biologically alive, yet spiritually dead. We can be dead in our trespasses and sins. Those who are dead in trespasses and sins are characterized in scripture as being those who are directed by the course of the world, dictated by the prince of the air, disobedient to God's will, and dominated by fleshly desires.

There are two categories of spiritually dead people, those who seek to live without God and those who seek to manipulate God. Some fall into the first category, but most fall into the second. We are either dead or alive. God has made us alive in Christ.

Those alive in Christ have accepted Him as Lord and Savior, but that is only part one of being alive. The other part is that those alive in Christ will obey God. They are obedient to His word and His will, leaving them dead to their flesh.

MY SPIRITUAL JOURNEY

Am I dead or alive?

_____

_____

_____

ARE YOU PREJUDICED?

And hath raised us up together, and made us sit together in heavenly places in Christ Jesus.
-Ephesians 2:6

Prejudice is disobedience to the work and the will of God. We can't be made spiritually alive and hang on to our prejudices. Verse 6 tells us that God has raised us together and has made us to sit together in heavenly places in Christ. Verse 14 tells us that God is our peace who has made us one and has broken down the middle wall between us.

When we hang on to prejudices against any race or culture, it goes against what God has done. Our prejudices can run so deeply that we will not want our children to marry outside their own culture. Sometimes we will tell our children, "Whatever you do, don't bring anybody different to this house." Basically we are saying "Smoke all the pot you want, cut classes, drink liquor, etc., just don't bring anybody different home." God raised the Gentiles to the level of Jews but he did it by tearing them both down and raising them up together.

MY SPIRITUAL JOURNEY

Do I have prejudices against the other races?

_____

_____

_____

_____

_____

352

BEING SPIRITUALLY DEAD

The thief cometh not, but to steal and to kill, and to destroy: I am come that they might have life and that they may have it more abundantly. - John 10:10

To be spiritually dead is to forfeit abundant life now and eternal life later. Jesus came so we might have abundant and eternal life. It is appointed once for every person to die and then face the judgment. If we are spiritually dead on this side, we will experience death on the other side.

Luke 15:24 tells of a father who says, "My son was dead and now he is alive again." This was the prodigal son who wanted all of his stuff right then and there. He went off, engaged in fast living, and ended up eating what the pigs ate; slop. Some people today are eating slop in a pig pen when it comes to having abundant life. The prodigal son came to himself and went home where his father ran to him and said, "This is my boy. He was dead, but now he is alive." Coming from death to life means no longer living and smelling like a hog. It means realizing that we are not hogs, but we have been made for the Father's house. We were not made to be directed by the prince of the air or controlled by the desires of our flesh. We need to come to ourselves and be made alive.

MY SPIRITUAL JOURNEY

Am I dead or alive? Have I accepted Jesus Christ as my Savior?

CALLED TO COME ALIVE

Likewise reckon ye also yourselves to be dead indeed unto sin, but alive unto God through Jesus Christ our Lord. -Romans 6:11

God's power to make those who were dead come alive is indisputable, unlimited, and all inclusive. Look at three miracles where God brought someone from death to life. Look at the miracle of Jairus' daughter. He was a ruler of the synagogue, and his young daughter was dead. Jesus spoke to her and said, "My child, get up!" (Luke 8:54 NIV) Another time in a city called Nain, a widower's 20-year-old son was dead and being funeralized. Jesus stopped the procession. He simply touched the coffin and the young man came alive (Luke 7:14). Lazarus was dead a little longer, and he had begun to smell. Jesus called out with a loud voice, "Lazarus, come forth." Lazarus came out and Jesus said, "Loose him." (John 11:43-44)

When God called me to be alive, He loosed me to preach His word, to witness, to praise, to lift my hands in worship, and to tithe. Many are still tied up in the desires of their flesh, but God has loosed us from these desires. His power is unlimited, unchanging, inclusive, and indisputable. God is calling us to come alive.

MY SPIRITUAL JOURNEY

Do I know anyone who is spiritually dead? What will I pray for them?

354

BE STRONG AND OF GOOD COURAGE

Be strong and of a good courage: for unto this people shalt thou divide for an inheritance the land, which I sware unto their fathers to give them. -Joshua 1:6

After the death of Moses, God appointed Joshua as the next leader of the Israelites. He instructed Joshua to lead the Israelites into the Promised Land. Many churches sing about the Promised Land as a reference to the place we call heaven. There is a spiritual Promised Land and a Biblical earthly Promised Land. In Joshua 1:6, God gave the Promised Land to the Israelites. He instructed them to be strong and of good courage when they entered into it. Why did they need to be strong and of good courage? They had to fight for it even though it was theirs.

I'm reminded of how God speaks a promise in our lives, but instead of pressing towards the promise, we sit back and wait for it to happen. In the meantime, the devourer steals it. Just as the Israelites had to fight for what was already theirs, we must similarly fight for the promises of God. Once the Israelites got to the Promised Land, they had to have faith to believe God's promise. God has made many promises to us, but faith needs to be activated in order for us to receive them. It's time for the body of Christ to take back what God has promised us and what Satan has stolen.

MY SPIRITUAL JOURNEY

What has Satan stolen from me?

VISION

...For the vision is yet for an appointed time, but at the end it shall speak, and not lie: though it tarry, wait for it; because it will surely come, it will not tarry.

- Habakkuk 2:3

God has a vision for each of our lives, and He wants us to know it so that we fulfill it. He wants us to write our vision down and run with it so we will know where we are going. Each time God gives us a vision, it is for an appointed time. The vision God gives to us will speak and not lie because if God gives the vision, He will give the provision.

Habakkuk cried out to God for help for his people. God's people were living in a sinful state, and God was sending the Chaldeans to punish them. Habakkuk stood on his watchtower waiting to receive a word, a vision from God (Habakkuk 2:1). The word "Habakkuk" means embracing. Habakkuk embraced the people as God is embracing us today with words of instruction and comfort. He is saying to us to stand high and watch. We may bow our head when we pray, but when we look for our vision, we have to look up to God.

MY SPIRITUAL JOURNEY

Has God given me a vision? Write it here.

_____

_____

_____

_____

WRITE THE VISION

And the LORD answered me, and said, Write the vision and make it plain upon tables, that he may run that readeth it. -Habakkuk 2:2

It is said that reading makes a full man. This may be true, but writing makes an exact man. God said to write the vision and to make it plain so that those who read it can run with it. It should be written so plainly that you and others who read it can implement it and someone passing by will be captured by it. Picture an athlete running through a city: he's running fast, but he looks up, sees the vision, and wants to be a participant in the vision. In other words, when we cast the vision, God will send people to help us fulfill it.

God gives us a vision, but we speak the vision instead of writing it. If we write it and make it plain, others will understand it and run with it, helping the one who wrote it to accomplish it. There ought to be a written vision for our ministries, families, careers, and personal lives.

MY SPIRITUAL JOURNEY

What is the vision God has for my ministry that I need to plainly write out?

_____

_____

_____

_____

_____

Patience is a problem, but another problem is having no vision. Without a vision, people perish. Many are drifting day by day not knowing which road to take. If we have no vision, no aim, no goal, no purpose and no plan, we are doomed for failure. If we don't aim at something specific, we might hit destruction. With no vision, we can go to the wrong school, have the wrong career, marry the wrong person, and live terribly. With no vision of what God wants us to become, we might not represent Christ. Without a vision, we won't wait on the appointed time, but we will move to the beat of our own drum. God's timing is just right. Stay focused, watch and pray, and don't become slothful and lazy.

A vision is for an appointed time in the future, but it will come. It may take a while, but it will come in God's appointed time. We just have to be patient and wait on it. Some of us want to rush it, but we have no control over God's appointed time. The just shall live by faith.

MY SPIRITUAL JOURNEY
What visions has God given me in the past that have come in their appointed time?

_____

_____

SPIRITUAL ELEVATION

For as much as ye are manifestly declared to be the epistle of Christ ministered by us written not with ink, but with the Spirit of the living God; -2 Corinthians. 3:3

When Abraham was given the vision of Jehovah Jireh, he was not in the valley but on Mt. Moriah. When Moses was given the Ten Commandments, he was high on Mt. Sinai. When the disciples saw the vision of Jesus transfigured before them, they were on Mt. Heron. When Habakkuk was given a vision, he was high on his watchtower. The Psalmist tells us to look to the hills from whence cometh our help. God may have us in a low place for another purpose, but if we want to get the vision, we have to come up to the high land.

We must be faithful to expect God to do what He has already shown us. Act like He has already done it. If God has shown us that He will save someone in our family, we need to start treating that person like they are already saved. Wait in faith, shout in advance, and act like He has already done it. Vision plus faith equal victory.

MY SPIRITUAL JOURNEY

Am I receiving the visions God has for me? Do I need to come up a little higher?

_____

_____

_____

_____

A KING IS BORN

Saying, Where is he that is born King of the Jews?
For we have seen his star in the east, and are come to worship him. -Matthew 2:2

Every king has a kingdom. If Jesus was born king, then where is His kingdom? We are it. Those who believe Jesus is the Son of God and have accepted Him as Lord and Savior are part of His kingdom. We are God's royal priesthood, heirs to His throne, princes and princesses, sons and daughters. Just as an ordinary king has new citizens arriving in his kingdom, so it is with God's kingdom. Each time we share the gospel of Jesus Christ with a sinner and that person accepts our invitation to live for Jesus Christ, God's kingdom has been increased. When we share the gospel, we bring citizens out of the wilderness and darkness into God's kingdom of light.

Our problem is treating God's kingdom as though there is no more room in the inn. Unlike a man-made kingdom that can run out of room, God will always find room for citizens in His kingdom. Luke 1:33 says, "And he shall reign over the house of Jacob for ever; and of his kingdom there shall be no end." Share the gospel often. There is room.

MY SPIRITUAL JOURNEY

When is the last time I invited someone into the Kingdom of God?

BE YE TRANSFORMED

Be ye not conformed to this world but be ye transformed by the renewing of your mind which is the pleasing perfect will of God. -Romans 12:2

We can live holy and still not be of the mind and heart of God. We can stop using profanity, drinking, smoking, going off on our family, and still not be of the mind and heart of God. We are still displeasing to Him.

Repentance is required for us to have transformation. Transformation is change. Too many Christians go to church every Sunday and leave the same way we came into the church. We should leave a little better. We receive information and inspiration, but unless we repent, there will be no transformation. Repentance is more than just feeling sorry for what we have done. Many people say they are sorry, but they are only sorry they got caught. Repentance means turning away from sin by the renewing of our mind and heart. It is like an extension of confession. Confessing our sins is not telling God something He doesn't already know, but agreeing with Him, acknowledging that we are wrong.

MY SPIRITUAL JOURNEY

When is the last time I agreed with God that I was wrong?

_____

_____

_____

_____

_____

GOD OF A SECOND CHANCE

If we confess our sins, He is faithful and just to forgive us of our sins and cleanse us from all unrighteousness. -1 John 1:9

God is the God of second chances. He gave the people of Nineveh and Jonah a second chance. A man named Saul spent his life persecuting Christians, but one day he met Jesus. Jesus changed his life that day and gave him a new name, Paul.

We should never fear coming back to God. I'm reminded of a story told of a little boy who called the principal's office after getting in trouble at school and said, "John Doe will not be at school today." The principal asked, "To whom am I speaking?" The little boy replied, "This is my father speaking." We sometimes, like the little boy, will try anything to keep from confessing and repenting of our sins.

We cannot sink so low that God will not welcome us home. There is no sin too big for God. There is nothing we can tell God that He can't handle. He knows every sin that has ever been and ever will be committed.

MY SPIRITUAL JOURNEY

Are there times when I feel unworthy to return back to God?

MATERIAL BLESSINGS

Every good and perfect gift is from above, and cometh down from the Father of lights, with whom is no variableness, neither shadow of turning. -James 1:17

When the Summer Olympic Games came to Atlanta in 1996, we really wanted to be there. We pursued every avenue we could but could not find tickets to any of the games. As we were getting discouraged, a Christian deaf woman, whom we have never met, sent us four tickets to one of the evening track and field games. We used the tickets and we were thrilled to observe history in the making. God blessed us with a desire of our hearts.

God does bless materially, but not all material things are blessings from God. For instance, many Christians purchase homes and cars they cannot afford. They praise God for the items they purchased but get hostile with God when they can't afford to keep up the payments. The truth is that it wasn't from God in the first place; He does not put His people in debt. In fact, He teaches us that if we obey his Word, we will be lenders, just the opposite of being debtors (Deuteronomy 28:1-6, 13). The material blessings of God bring peace, not worry and hardship.

MY SPIRITUAL JOURNEY

Can I recall a time when I wanted something so bad that I went ahead and purchased it then later realized that it was not a gift from God?

TRUE BELIEVERS MUST DIE

Verily, verily, I say unto you, Except a corn of wheat fall into the ground and die, it abideth alone: but if it die, it bringeth forth much fruit. -John 12:24

Every believer needs to die to the flesh because the flesh keeps us from being used for God's kingdom. If a kernel of corn is not planted, it is just a kernel of corn alone, but when it is planted and dies, it can then produce fruit. When we die to our flesh, surrendering ourselves to God, then we will produce much fruit.

Jesus had to die to fulfill the purposes of God. Without the purposes of God being fulfilled through Jesus, there would be no salvation or eternal life. He had to die. Usually, death is spoken of in a negative light, but there is a death that is important to the believer just as it was important to Jesus. Jesus died to his flesh so that others might live eternally.

MY SPIRITUAL JOURNEY

Am I dead yet? Am I producing much fruit?

_____

_____

_____

_____

_____

_____

_____

_____

But those things which proceed out of the mouth come from the heart; and they defile a man.
-Matthew 15:18

Too often, many of us are intimidated by others. They make mockery of our faults as if they were perfect. We allow the mocker of others to cause us to make immediate and inappropriate responses. Sometimes we even "give them a piece of our mind." Have you ever thought about the fact that if you give away part of your mind, your mind will be lacking. We use profanity and "read them up and down." We do not have to respond to negative criticisms or actions from others because God says that vengeance is His.

Proverbs 18:7 declares that a fool's mouth leads him to destruction, and his lips endanger his soul. Proverbs 29:11 declares that one is a fool who says everything that is on his mind. We all fit into the fool category when we allow our opinion to be spoken instead of waiting and listening for God's wisdom.

MY SPIRITUAL JOURNEY

When have I failed at being slow to speak? How did it affect the circumstance?

_____

_____

_____

_____

_____

December 31

THE PLANS GOD HAS FOR ME

For I know the thoughts that I think toward you, saith the LORD, thoughts of peace, and not of evil, to give you an expected end. -Jeremiah 29:11

G od has a plan for every life. His plan is for the unsaved to be saved. His plan for the saved is to live in victory. His thoughts for us are thoughts of peace and not evil. God does not want to harm us. He wants to help, heal, and deliver us. He wants to set us free from the evil that the devourer has placed in our lives. He wants to give us abundant life now and eternal life later.

God's plan is good and perfect. His plan is not to keep us indebted, sick, demon possessed, and living in fear. God is a good God, and His plan is to bless us and not harm us. It is Satan, the evil one, who comes to kill and destroy us. Too many believers give credit to God for the work of the devil. God's plan is to bless, heal, and deliver.

MY SPIRITUAL JOURNEY

Have I been blessed, healed or delivered?

_____

_____

_____

_____

_____

_____

Books and Other Resource Materials
By Drs. George O. and Sadie McCalep

A Good Black Samaritan

Breaking the Huddle

Church Growth Made Simple

Faithful Over A Few Things (Book, Study Guide, Audio Version, Resource Kit)

Faith Raising vs. Money Raising

Fulfillment Hour: A Nontraditional Sunday School Model *by Jackie Henderson & Joan Johnson, Compiled & Edited: George McCalep* (Book, CD- Study Course)

Growing Up to the Head (Book, Leader's Guide, Journey/Journal)

How to be Blessed

"Jabez's Prayer" (Sermonic Audio Series)

Messages of Victory for God's Church in the New Millennium (Sermonic Audio Series)

Stir Up the Gifts (Book, Leader's Guide, Workbook & Study Guide, Sermonic Audio Series)

Praising the Hell Out of Yourself (Book, Workbook, Audio CD)

Sin In the House

When Black Men Stretch Their Hands to God (DVD, 6 AudioVersions)

Tough Enough: Trials on Every Hand *By Sadie McCalep, Ph.D.*